# Business Ethics

## The Path to Certainty

Frank Daly
Carl Oliver

**Business Ethics: The Path to Certainty**
**1st edition, 1st printing**

**Authors**
Frank Daly and Carl Oliver

**Cover designer**
Christopher Besley, Besley Design.

**ISBN**: 978-0-7346-1129-1



Published by:
**Tilde Publishing and Distribution**
**PO Box 72**
**Prahran VIC 3181 Australia**
**www.tup.net.au**

TUP-BusinessEthics-DalyOliver-1e1p

# Contents

# About the authors

**Frank Daly**, MA, University of San Francisco, is a nationally known leader in business ethics and served as chairman of the Ethics and Compliance Officer Association (ECOA). He was the corporate ethics director at a US$30 billion *Fortune* 100 firm for nine years, after having served that company as an ethics officer at various levels for the first ten years of its ethics program.

Frank is currently a Kallman Executive Fellow at the Center for Business Ethics at Bentley University. He has served as a member of the Working Group of the Defense Industry Initiative on Business Ethics and Conduct, a Fellow at the Markkula Center for Applied Ethics at Santa Clara University, and is co-founder of the Southern California Business Ethics Roundtable. Frank has lectured on business ethics and the role of business in society at the College of Business Administration of Loyola Marymount University, and has presented widely on same in business and academia.

**Carl Oliver**, PhD, Fielding Graduate University, has a variety of experience with business ethics and corporate social responsibility. For twenty years, as a US Air Force officer and special agent, he led investigations into serious compliance and ethics allegations.

For ten years he trained managers to turn around broken ethics in a *Fortune* 500 company. For seven years he served as corporate ethics process administrator for a *Fortune* 100 company. Since 2006 he has been teaching business ethics and corporate social responsibility at Loyola Marymount University Los Angeles and at the University of Redlands. Previously he was on faculty teaching leadership and management at Stanford University and served as department chair.

# Foreword

*Good, Better, Best*

*Good: Some people think ethical business.*

*Better: Some think and talk ethical business.*

*Best: Some think, talk, and do ethical business.*

Our goal is to *prevent* business ethics problems if we can, and minimize their impact if we must. We want to emphasize that this can be done effectively at reasonable cost. We describe a business process that should be as sensitive to the imperatives of preserving time and money as any other business process. While large businesses, due to their size, can afford to add a layer of management focused just on business ethics and compliance, a key to successful business ethics in any company, large or small, is to have every leader be an ethical leader and set an ethical example. A condition required to achieve that is a culture of open communication allowing everyone and anyone to speak up about any business concern in good faith and without fear.

As 'business ethics practitioners', by definition our role is to think, talk and do ethical business. Professor William Frederick points to a difference that scholars recognize between two terms – 'business ethics' and 'ethical business'. 'Business ethics', he says, refers to philosophers' concepts and principles of ethics, which may be unfamiliar and uninteresting to our readers. 'Ethical business', he says, refers to a company's system to implement ethics in its operations – and that is exactly our focus: a process that employees and managers can use to spot ethics issues and properly resolve them. However, as practitioners we use the term 'business ethics' to describe what we do (our process) to *practice* 'ethical business' (the outcome). Frederick's considered opinion is that 'the worth of any business ethics book is … its relevance to and impact on the *practice* of business'.[1]

There is bad news and good news – first, the bad news: Rutgers professor Carter A Daniel studied the impact of two 1959 reports on the state of business education in America, one by the Ford Foundation and the other by the Carnegie Corporation. He argued that universities reacted to those reports by changing in the wrong direction: they emphasized theory instead of focusing the business school curriculum and research on the real world. As a result, said Daniel, 'it's commonplace to hear business people scoff that academic research never has any influence on what they actually do in their companies'.[2] Daniels said that it is taking business schools decades, not just years, to rebuild their credibility, but that they are making progress.

Professor Thomas I White, director of the Center for Ethics and Business at Loyola Marymount University, built on Daniel's conclusions, saying that corporations marginalized ethics and compliance programs in the past and still do. 'It is difficult to avoid the conclusion that, from the perspective of ethics' impact on the practice of business, the business ethics movement has been more of a failure than a success.'[3] Expanding on that thesis, White opined that business ethics has hit a 'glass ceiling', and that the series of ethics scandals and disasters in recent years 'is testimony to the fact that rigorous analysis of the ethical dimensions of problems and decisions is noteworthy more for its absence in many C-suites'.[4]

Now the good news: Even if business people scoff at academic research, and even if many businesses marginalize business ethics and suffer ethical failures, we've been inside corporate business ethics and we've seen a sizeable number of companies, both large and small, doing business ethics very well. Indeed, many companies do business ethics so well that you rarely, if ever, hear their names associated with any business ethics failure. Our research has been hands-on in real-world companies. This book reports what those companies do to succeed ethically. We think it is what any company can do to succeed ethically.

With respect to business ethics, a corporation is not like a big ship that changes course very slowly. If it were, then one person could move one rudder and the corporation would change its ethical course. If a company has 125,000 employees at more than 1,200 locations, it is pretty obvious that there is no single 'big ship' rudder that one person can turn. The company must somehow touch every employee — not only touch them, but get them to actively set their personal ethical course in the right direction.

Touching every employee … influencing every employee … that can be done only by a company's leaders, with all of them working together. Recognize, too, that over the course of time every employee performs some kind of leadership role. Therefore, we want this book to reach every business leader — present and future. 'Future' includes traditional undergraduates studying management. 'Present' includes: students with work experience under their belts and now enrolled in coursework leading to the MBA or a Master's degree in management; mid-career adults returning to the classroom to study management; adults enrolled in professional development programs; corporate ethics officers striving to expand their professional expertise while on the job; the managers and executives who recognize that the serious work of implementing effective business ethics is a crucial, hands-on task for them; and the employees everywhere who at times look around, see that others are depending on them, and recognize the reality that they *are* the leader.

We discourage companies from basing company ethics on a whistleblowing strategy. Years of hands-on experience with major corporations' business ethics programs has taught us that it is unwise for a company to rely on 'whistleblowers' to signal corporate ethics problems. That is a reactive strategy. It leads to fire-fighting. Although whistleblowers sometimes are honored as 'saviors' who cause important changes, the truth is that, by the time someone 'blows the whistle', much damage has already occurred. Some companies label reports to company leaders — i.e. internal reporting — as whistleblowing. Our practice is to identify only reports to authorities *outside* the company – i.e. external reporting – as whistleblowing, probably the more general understanding of the term but obviously not universal. Either way, internal or external, reliance on a whistleblower ethics problem detection system has proven itself to be unreliable and messy, and nobody emerges from the turmoil looking like a winner.

Highly-publicized business ethics scandals harm the company, the whistleblowing employee and society. No question about that. Trouble has not only started, but usually has developed into a massive wildfire before any whistleblower speaks up. Commercial books designed to help, counsel, coach, train and guide potential whistleblowers recount scandal after scandal, along with the harms suffered by whistleblowers who revealed them, and they stand as evidence that whistleblower-based systems produce no winners. But keep in mind that those stories are not a 'scientific sample'. They are biased and skewed by a focus on scandalous events known to the public. In their handbook coaching employees on how to blow the whistle, Tom Devine and Tarek Maassarani say that everything they've written about strategy, advocacy and legal rights for whistleblowers becomes irrelevant if company leaders listen and act constructively and in good faith.[5]

We favor the strategy of prevention. Provide a process that recognizes people's values and gives them the training, resources and experience to act on those values, to speak up in a timely fashion, to be heard, and to involve other people appropriately so that the company and everyone involved emerges as a true winner. Set a company's ethical direction on the right course by creating a corporate culture that teaches and encourages everyone to ask questions early, to point out possible issues, and to show courage in confronting practices that are - or might be - unethical or illegal, even if they only *suspect* something may be amiss. The earliest questions are the best questions because they enable the organization to solve a concern while it is small – well before it escalates into a large problem, well before much damage occurs, and well before anyone is likely to find the 'hard evidence' society wants 'whistleblowers' to deliver.

From experience, we know that a very large number of non-scandalous business ethics events exist, events in which employees reported trouble inside their company, leaders listened to those reports, and changes ended the trouble. In short, the problems were corrected while they were new and small, before they grew to scandal proportions. Counting such non-scandal events is hard, but we can illustrate from our own experience: over a ten-year period we have handled approximately 30,000 questions about ethics from employees, and none of them have become the ethics scandals described in the media or in commercial books.

What can an organization do to encourage early questions and thereby eliminate the need for whistleblowing? This book describes practical process, already proven in multiple companies, that any large or small company can adapt to its situation. The appendices then contain sample scenarios to illustrate how a company can build effective business ethics training using just its own staff members, without the need to hire outside consultants or buy expensive commercial training packages. Each chapter ends with a Challenge puzzle designed to expand experience, awareness and competence.

October 1, 2012

Frank Daly
Duxbury, MA

Carl Oliver
Thousand Oaks, CA

---

[1] Frederick, WC 2009, 'Review of Business Ethics and Ethical Business, by R. Audi', *Journal of Business Ethics Education* 6: 201-202.

[2] Daniel, CA 2009, 'How Two National Reports Ruined Business Schools', *Chronicle of Higher Education*, November 8, 2009.

[3] White, TI 2012, 'Extending Carter Daniels: Substantive and Methodological Reflections on Business Ethics' Ongoing Slide Into Irrelevance', College of Business Administration, Loyola Marymount University, January 17, 2012.

[4] White, TI 2012, 'Jan 31 Research Seminar', College of Business Administration, Loyola Marymount University, January 27, 2012.

[5] Devine, T & Maasarani, TF 2011, *Whistleblower's Survival Guide,* Berrett-Koehler, San Franscisco: xi-xv.

# Chapter 1

# Nine important fallacies of business ethics

## LEARNING OBJECTIVES

By the end of this chapter you should:

- □ know that people want to be ethical in the workplace.
- □ know that people are uncertain how to make a workplace ethical.
- □ be familiar with nine fallacies that contribute to uncertainty.
- □ be familiar with nine low-cost responsive initiatives.

### A TRUTH: UNCERTAINTY ABOUT HOW TO CREATE AN AFFORDABLE ETHICS PROCESS KEEPS TOO MANY COMPANIES FROM PROGRESSING PAST ENTRY-LEVEL BUSINESS ETHICS — WHICH THEY DISCOVER DO NOT WORK WELL

Jennifer [pseudonym] said:

> *My father worked for one of the big accounting firms. His manager divided employees into two teams: the 'dumb team' and the 'smart team'. He gave the dumb team all of the work until they screwed it up so badly that the smart team had to go in and fix everything. Because of the way the manager coordinated these audit teams, each auditing job required more time and therefore each client was billed more than they should have been. My father described this manager as the most unethical person he ever worked for.*[1]

## People want to be ethical

Rationally, good business ethics should be an easy sell. Three reasons why people want to practice high business ethics coincide with three reasons why companies want employees to do so:

- We all want to maximize our success on the job. We want to avoid mistakes, especially ethics mistakes that could derail our careers and put us out of work. Likewise, companies want every employee to work with maximum success. It's a wrap-up principle. If every employee achieves maximum success ... then every department does ... and theoretically the company should as well.
- We all want to work for a company we can be proud of. Companies for their part want to enjoy a good reputation, to be publicly known as 'a good place to work'. We try to identify and join ethical companies. We try to identify and avoid unethical companies.
- By and large, we all want our work to promote values we hold dear. We want our work to be meaningful and productive. We want it to contribute good to the world. We do not want to think of our work as a waste of time, a waste of effort, or useless. Companies also want their employees to serve a great purpose and contribute to society.

Business ethics, as 'a social change issue', gets very serious analysis from a lot of people these days, and special attention from those in academic fields like philosophy, sociology, psychology, history, and management. This is a positive development, but whoever you are — executive, manager, or touch-labor employee — academic fundamentals, important as they may be, do not drive your concern that your company be an ethical one. You want your company's ethics to be successful. You want practical results now. You want methods and systems in place. You want data and confidence that you and your company are not only doing things right but doing all the right things, everything needed to create both a corporate climate and a corporate culture that help all employees live up to 'the better angels of our nature'. Business and other organizational history over the past few decades has shown that this is not easy to do.

After Enron's public collapse, marked by its disclosure of a $1.2 billion reduction in shareholder equity, *Forbes* magazine began to list online an 'avalanche' of corporate scandals, starting with Enron in October 2001 and including twenty more over the next nine months.[2] The question then was: When will the scandals stop? The answer today: They have not stopped yet. People are joking about the situation, acting as if bad ethics are normal. It's all over the internet: today CEO means 'chief embezzlement officer', CFO means 'corporate fraud officer', and EPS no longer means 'earnings per share' but 'eventual prison sentence'. In the words of Wesley Cragg, Canadian ethics professor emeritus:

> *[I]t is unlikely that there is any other period in business history when unethical business conduct has had so damaging an impact on so many economies and the people whose well-being is dependent on them in so many parts of the world.*[3]

Professor Cragg is not alone in feeling that way. From a global perspective, Pope Benedict XVI lamented that the belief that economic process 'must be shielded from 'influences' of a moral character' has led people to thoroughly and destructively abuse our economic process.[4] And from a single-company perspective, Robert Lutz lamented that when he answered the call to lead Exide, then the world's largest maker of lead-acid batteries, he found 'mismanagement, dishonest accounting, excessive debt, questionable business practices, and a leadership team that ultimately was sent to prison'.[5]

What people bring with them to the workplace is a variety of lifetime experiences and values and vast differences in ability. Their education levels differ. Their stages and styles of learning are different. They read at different levels and some don't read at all, either by choice or because they never learned to. Some are newcomers, literate in their home countries but struggling in our society while they work to learn English as their second, third, or fourth language. People's moral sensitivities and sensibilities differ. Some come from environments that were freewheeling and some are more conservative.

Almost universally however, people bring to the workplace a belief that they personally have high ethics. Just ask them! They'll say, 'Of course I'm an ethical person and I want to do the right thing'. We bring good ethics from home to work with us. We come to work as angels. A company's business ethics strategy really isn't to teach people how to be ethical. Its strategy ought to help people who are already ethical to make good decisions.

## People are uncertain how to make a company ethical

The seemingly endless string of news stories reporting discovery of ethics scandals today can be misleading. They are true. They are reprehensible. But they are misleading because many companies — we count them in the thousands — are working hard to prevent scandals and have learned, or are learning, how to do that pretty well. They get no publicity because they are doing things right, and being right and ethical is not newsworthy! We need to 'stand on their shoulders', to take what they learned and apply it to our own workplace.

Misleading or not, the chain of scandals in today's news makes it clear we do face a significant and severe business ethics problem. We know that only one mistake by one person, or by a few people, especially if they work in a sensitive or critical area, can destroy the reputation and the business of a company, large or small. We want to avoid that. And more important, we want *ourselves* to be ethical. We want *our company* to be ethical.

There is a community of interest between the company, its employees and management, and a convergence between this sensitivity to ethics and newer styles of management that encourage employee participation and collaboration in contrast to 'the old autocratic style'. We want a good manager to keep commitments (an ethical concept — commitments, after all, are promises) to customers, employees, managers, and so forth. In a study done when she was a doctoral student at the University of Southern California, Barbara McGraw, JD, PhD, found employees of a *Fortune* 500 company thought that initiatives to implement a formal corporate ethics and values program and switch from an autocratic 'Theory X and ... kick ass' management style to a participative team management style that values people were both working because they were undertaken virtually simultaneously. One interviewee said:

> *They [the old-style managers] weren't necessarily promoted [so much] for management skills as they were promoted for their ability to get results. And so, if someone was able to achieve, no one really went and walked his ... line to see how he was able to achieve. So, had they done that, they probably would have come out terrified in some camps ... how they actually made it happen. There were sheer reigns of terror. The guy who took the high road and tried to do it right had a much more difficult journey. It was easier for the guy that just was a brutal tyrant and threatened everybody.*[6]

Many companies and managers remain uncertain how to make a workplace ethical — it is the problem we need to solve. 'Uncertain' is the key word. The uncertainty is not generated by ethics but by how to 'do' ethics, how to organize for it in a business setting, and what in fact are its key elements.

Today, people face uncertainty in their lives in multiple ways: they are uncertain about their jobs, their mortgage, their children's future, and so forth. The one place they expect or at least hope to find the refuge of certainty is in principles, beliefs, love, and ethics. The cover of this book features an *inukshuk*. In the language of the Inuit people, *inukshuk* means 'in the likeness of a human'. The *inukshuk* is a raw stone monument found throughout the Arctic wilderness. Each is a signal from ancestors who marked 'the right path' for generations to come. Inuit culture forbids destruction of an *inukshuk*.

People in business seek signals like the *inukshuk*. Its notion of 'on the right path' suggests both the right path ethically and the right path organizationally with respect to the relationship of business, ethics, and compliance. They may use different words but, at national conferences held by organizations like the Ethics and Compliance Officer Association, or at local meetings and gatherings of groups like the Southern California Business Ethics Roundtable, leaders new to business ethics often ask the same basic question: 'I am uncertain … what am I supposed to do?'

At a national business ethics conference held in Washington, DC, a *Fortune* 100 company's new business ethics officer explained 'best practices' he or she had learned during her or his first six months in the ethics job. What he or she said resonated with another manager in the audience, a fairly senior manager in a *Fortune* 500 company, also newly appointed to the ethics role, who said, 'Thanks, now I know what I'm supposed to do.'

Part of the joy in that feedback, 'now I know what I'm supposed to do', is realizing that even sophisticated companies put people in charge who are new to the profession of business ethics.

This is a scholar-practitioner book. 'Practitioner' because it describes business ethics best practices. It shares the practical, hands-on experience of front-line corporate ethics officers, people who can explain what needs to be done and ways to do it. 'Scholar' because it provides underlying social psychology and organization development theory and research explaining why the best practices work — reflective learning tying together scholarly knowledge, practical experience, and observations that inform the practices business ethics has adopted as useful.

In this book we strive to present a positive approach. It includes lessons that ethically successful companies have learned, garnered from hands-on experience the authors had at a *Fortune* 100 corporation, where they led successful business ethics for years (Frank led at various levels for 18 years and Carl's involvement adds up to about 17 years), and from the firsthand experience of dozens of other companies and colleagues.

What happens in the workplace is that all comers — and what they bring — blend into an organizational culture. That 'culture' is the pattern of fundamental beliefs and assumptions that organization members share as they learn to cope with problems in the workplace, a pattern they consider successful and worthwhile for new organization members to learn.[7] The blend can be shaped by multiple influences. Indeed, it inevitably is. Of major importance are society's ethical norms, which are familiar to everyone and enable companies to capitalize on good values employees bring with them to the workplace. Other influences include the company's 'system', deliberate interventions, mission statements, promotion practices, public expectations, education, and a philosophy of positive organizational development.

### Ethical 'climate' and ethical 'culture'

What a company can structure is its ethical climate. 'Climate' is policies, procedures, rules, processes, communications — all the things a company does to evoke the best possible response from employees. 'Culture' is that employee response — what employees actually do. Companies can use feedback to readjust climate until climate and culture are aligned and both meet the company's and the employees' objectives.

That approach applies the principle that in *every* instance, organization members' shared values and beliefs are the foundation of the organization's ethical culture (its employees' behaviors). To make a company ethical, the organization must find out what its people's widely shared values are and which of those values are relevant to the organization's success. Research shows that people's motivation and performance are best governed by goals they set for themselves rather than goals other people might set for them.[8] If employees see creating an ethical company as a goal they have voluntarily undertaken because it is presented as a company value, then virtually nothing will stop them from living up to it. It becomes a goal driving self-respect. Self-respect is a powerful self-motivator. No uncertainty here.

## Nine fallacies contribute to uncertainty

'Uncertainty' about how to do ethics afflicts business today largely because of nine important fallacies, nine ideas people believe that are false or mistaken, nine ideas companies incorporate into their well-intentioned ethics programs that inevitably cause their business ethics to fail. We do not say everyone believes these fallacies, only that each is believed by some of the people some of the time.

- *Fallacy 1.* To stop ethics failures we need only to have rules, teach people the rules, and punish anyone who violates those rules.
- *Fallacy 2.* Ethical decision-making is complicated and requires expertise.
- *Fallacy 3.* Bad people cause all business ethics failures.
- *Fallacy 4.* Company ethics programs are expensive, time-wasting, and of little practical value.
- *Fallacy 5.* One ethics program is as good as another — no uniform standard exists.
- *Fallacy 6.* Raising ethics issues is career suicide.
- *Fallacy 7.* No one can really know how ethical companies and their people are.
- *Fallacy 8.* 'Whiners and complainers' should be ignored.
- *Fallacy 9.* A company's charitable contributions make it socially responsible.

If even one of these nine fallacies creeps into a company's well-intentioned ethics program, business ethics are at risk of failure.

## Nine low-cost initiatives

We emphasize low cost. It's important. If an ethics effort is going to have credibility in a business setting, it has to be careful and resourceful about the things everyone else in business has to be careful of, namely: time and money.

*Re Fallacy 1, 'we need only to have rules ...'*

We all need to know the laws and rules that affect our job. For private and public sector managers, an important part of their job is to ensure we are trained and competent on those laws and rules. We see that theme expressed frequently in news stories:

- We will require mandatory ethics training that will ensure all members and staff understand and follow procedures.[9]
- My company requires all employees to complete a self-directed training course on the *Foreign Corrupt Practices Act*.[10]
- More than 2,200 administrative employees, nearly 500 working at the forest preserves, and about 6,700 working in the public health system will have to take the training to make them familiar with all county ethics rules.[11]

So here's the riddle: if there's more to business ethics than laws and rules, what is it? While indeed there is an ethical sense that can be highly developed in people with either a little education or a lot, that doesn't let us off the hook in recognizing that ethics also has complexities and is an area of study warranting rigorous advanced academic degrees and expertise. Chapter 2 provides a visual answer to the riddle, a practical answer for business ethics, by explaining the Ethics Dynamic. It's a zero-cost initiative to prevent Fallacy 1 from taking hold in any company.

Much of 'what's more' is the difference between compliance and ethics. 'Compliance' focuses on rules a court can enforce; 'ethics' focuses on values and trust – standards we choose to live up to that are basically unenforceable. In the words of President George W Bush, 'Washington passes laws, but it doesn't pass values legislation. Values exist in the hearts and souls of our citizens.'[12] Dawn-Marie Driscoll, executive fellow at the Center for Business Ethics, Bentley University, echoed the same theme. She feels 'underwhelmed' by the *Sarbanes-Oxley Act* of 2002 because 'you can't legislate an ethical corporate culture, a diligent board of directors, or senior executives with integrity'.[13] Her main point: recent high profile ethics scandals were caused by 'inattention to ethics and values'.

Leaders and managers have the responsibility to create and foster high ethics in their workplace. What people, especially those at the top of the organization, decide, say, and do influences the ethics displayed by all other members of the organization. Leaders and managers need to mentor each other and all employees to achieve the success and high ethics they already aspire to.

*Re Fallacy 2, 'ethical decision-making is complicated ...'*

When people talk ethics they often refer to complexities they think must be sorted out by the courts:

- Can an employee be fired for writing bad comments about a supervisor on Facebook?
- When a company hires a new employee, should it tell that employee insider information – not publicly known – that the company is about to be bought by another company?
- Is a company responsible for a letter of recommendation about a former employee written on its letterhead?

Actually, most ethics issues can be sorted out by employees if the company's climate and culture are based on values, build trust, and encourage open communication without fear of retaliation. What employees face are choices, not just any old choices but ones that could have ethical implications. They are not unlike choices people have to make in any other area of life. Do you check your children's computer surreptitiously, for example, or do you deal with it openly to assure yourself they are not doing something that violates family values, could subject them to embarrassment, or will lead to trouble with the law? What you really want to achieve is that all employees, no matter what their education and knowledge of the particulars of the law, know from the climate and culture 'that's not the way we do things around here' and get help if needed. Chapter 3 points to the responsive initiative, and later chapters show how to make it a low-cost or zero-cost initiative.

*Re Fallacy 3, 'bad people ...'*

The news 'proves' that bad guys cause business ethics failures. Culprits get fined and jailed. When Stephen M Cutler announced his plan to end service as director of the Securities and Exchange Commission's Division of Enforcement, that agency praised him for being what every prosecutor should be: tough but fair. The SEC identified him as a key leader of investigations into financial failures at (*inter alia*) Enron, WorldCom, Adelphia, Quest, Tyco, and HealthSouth that caused 'enforcement actions' against (*inter alia*) Kenneth Lay, Jeffrey Skilling, Andrew Fastow, Scott Sullivan, John Rigas, Joseph Nacchio, Dennis Kozlowski and Richard Scrushy.

But the news media is biased toward publicizing 'bad guys'. Sometimes another perspective is possible: a 'culprit' may not be a 'bad person' so much as a 'good person' trying too hard to achieve the results the company expects. Through that lens, we can see Jennifer's father's manager focused on being a good employee, meeting or exceeding the expectations of his company and his supervisor by maximizing how much each customer could be billed, maximizing how much revenue his department could generate and maximizing how much profit his company could earn.

Barbara McGraw observed that a company could inadvertently institutionalize that wrong approach by creating 'fiefdoms'.

> *[Each function] felt they could win or lose by themselves. They didn't have to worry about the other functions succeeding. As a matter of fact, they seemed to take delight if the other functions were having a tough time. It made them look superior.*[14]

Chapter 4 explains how to use policies, training, guidelines – anything employees can see, touch, or hear[15] – and values to build trust that will prevent good people from causing business ethics failures. The initiative mostly requires thought, not any special expenditure of time or money. It's another low-cost or no-cost initiative.

*Re Fallacy 4, 'ethics programs are expensive' ...*

Consulting on business ethics has become big business: three large and expensive membership organizations exist in the US alone, with others in Europe and Asia. These numbers grow: at one count there were 29 ethics centers, 23 professional associations, and uncountable private consultants. Once companies know what to do, the process of business ethics actually is within their grasp unaided.

However, ethics efforts have more punch if they are part of an industry-wide effort. Beginning at least as early as 1986,[16] the US government has encouraged companies to commit to 'collective and highly constructive action', to meet together and freely share their ethics best practices, and to 'level the playing field' with respect to business ethics. In this realm, collaboration is preferred to competition so all companies perform at a high level of ethics. Moreover, leaders in the industry talk and, without engaging the news media, word gets out that participant companies have credible ethics. It's good news, and the news media is more interested in bad news anyway. Industries collaborating to improve ethics include defense contractors (the Defense Industry Initiative), health care purchasing (the Healthcare Group Purchasing Industry Initiative), and the construction industry (Construction Industry Ethics & Compliance Initiative).

Some large companies spend millions each year, hire expensive consultants, and license rights to use famous characters like Dilbert, Fred Flintstone, and Homer Simpson to make ethics training 'fun'. Nevertheless, some of these companies still experience ethics disasters. This approach is fundamentally flawed. 'Throwing money' at ethics tends to create a silo organization around business ethics, a set of 'experts' quickly overwhelmed by work because the company funnels all ethics issues to them. At the same time, managers and employees wrongly think ethics is only in the ethics experts' job description.

Chapter 5 explores fundamentals of building business ethics programs to create decentralized ethical decision-making and shows the roles of campaign-model training, an effective code of ethics, and annual conflict of interest certificates. It's possible to spend big money for training materials, but low-cost teaching materials can be as good or better. An ethics program needs a budget, but it can definitely be a small one, a high-priority but low-cost effort.

'Convergence' applies here. Though not often stated, some of the more positive management trends are moving in the same direction as business ethics, creating a synergy that could bring more power to both of them.

*Re Fallacy 5, 'no uniform standard …'*

To see ethics programs as independent, one as good as another, is to perceive a feudal culture, each company reigning as lord over its corporate castle and the peasants who do the castle's bidding throughout the corporate land surrounding the castle. Companies do have personalities with different legends, customs, and historic personalities. But beginning in the mid-1980s, public policy in the United States clearly began to end whatever feudal ethics society existed. Government policy first brought defense companies into a voluntary ethics confederation supporting common principles. A few years later, government policy extended similar principles to all US organizations for their voluntary adoption through an incentive program called the US Sentencing Guidelines for Organizations. With respect to business ethics, the differences between companies are not so much in the elements of good ethics approaches but in how they are implemented and who becomes a leader.

Chapter 6 reviews the development of public policy in the US, the uniform standard it has created, and how that standard reflects and affects business ethics standards elsewhere in the world.

*Re Fallacy 6, 'career suicide …'*

Raising ethics issues is dangerous only if other people react with fear or anger. For her doctoral dissertation, Ariane Spade interviewed in depth five women who identified themselves as people who spoke up at work and suffered negative repercussions.[17]

- Karen provided senior management with evidence of fraud and embezzlement by several managers. The response was denial and retaliation.
- Veronica provided factual information to a federal agent investigating an employee's sexual harassment complaint against a manager. Veronica's manager chastised her for speaking to the investigator and placed her on a 'reduction of force' list.
- Essie, a registered nurse, spoke up in a hospital's community meetings about declines in patient care and wrote a letter to the business manager informing him of the chief administrative officer's effort to create a rift between licensed vocational nurses and registered nurses. She was sued for libel.
- Akaya showed the data she had gathered for her dissertation to her mentor, who said it was shallow and unscientific, then published it

under his own name in a major journal. When she notified the department head and the dean she was told the university would take no action – silently accept what happened, or leave.

- Denise, an exotic dancer, joined other dancers in a lawsuit against club management's policy of treating dancers like employees for work but like independent contractors for pay – no employee protections or benefits. She was fired by the club and blacklisted at most other clubs.

Joyce Rothschild and Terance Miethe studied 147 people (96 women, 51 men) who reported misconduct to officials inside their company and 247 (111 women, 136 men) who reported misconduct to authorities outside their company. They reported that about two thirds lost their job or were forced to retire, received negative job performance evaluations, were more closely monitored by supervisors, were criticized or avoided by co-workers, and were 'blacklisted' from getting another job in their field.[18]

No company should allow bad consequences for raising issues in good faith. Government regulators have articulated a dim view of retaliation for years, various laws include specific whistleblower protections, and official discovery of retaliation allowed or encouraged within any company would likely draw a very negative reaction. The way to prevent such consequences is to deliberately open ethics communication channels. Managers should be trained, coached, and mentored to create trust and listen to employees. Alternative communication channels need to be easily and safely available. Employees should be coached on when to support (take responsibility for decisions that have been made) and when to challenge (if you believe something is illegal, unethical, or inconsistent with company values). Chapter 7 explains how to do both at low cost or no cost.

'The chief ethics officer has to be the CEO', says Ben Heineman, former General Electric executive. 'If it doesn't start at the top and it's not driven down by the CEO, then it won't happen.'[19] More than that, primary responsibility for company ethics always belongs to managers; they are the ones who make ethics happen, not some silo ethics organization. Read this as emphasis on the importance of modeling ethical behavior, something the CEO and every other company leader must do 24/7. It is easy to spot leaders who behave ethically, and even easier to spot those who don't.

The CEO or owner of a small business has to be the chief ethics officer and has to serve as a catalyst enabling all employees to make sound decisions about ethics situations that inevitably arise during the normal course of work. To do so, they must create a climate fostering safe, open communication so employees act as the eyes and ears of management and so that questions, concerns, and issues surface at the earliest moment and can be properly addressed using the full resources available to the business.

### *Re Fallacy 7, 'no one can really know …'*

It is vital for companies to know how ethical the company and its people are and to watch for trends – for better or for worse – so the company can figure out what ethics initiatives pay off and what the company should stop doing because it degrades the ethics culture. Companies that are signatories to the Defense Industry Initiative systematically evaluate themselves each year and submit self-evaluations to an independent overseer. The US Sentencing Guidelines for Organizations call for companies to voluntarily evaluate their own ethics periodically.

Program reviews and risk analyses are the responsive initiative. Ultimately, companies must do their own, although they may choose to hire consultants or contractors to perform supporting assessments in order to get an objective outside perspective and ensure the company is up to 'industry standards'. We want to advocate that companies perform beyond industry standards, that they perform to 'best practices'. Some industries today might have minimal or even inadequate standards.

Chapter 8 includes generic models for reviews and risk assessments. While consultants and contractors can be pricey, reviews and analyses done by the company can be low cost or no cost.

*Re Fallacy 8, 'whiners and complainers ...'*

Information yields opportunity in product development, in marketing, and in strategic planning. It should be no surprise that information yields opportunity in business ethics. One mistake we see in company after company is that managers are too busy, unwilling or not wise enough to listen to information that employees (and others) try to give them. Bob Lutz pointed out that even when the suggestion is made in a counterproductive way, it is the manager's job to hear what is said, to recognize validity even if the information is presented in a way the manager perceives as annoying or obnoxious, and to responsibly act on the information.[20] Another mistake is failure to listen to information that the ethics process can provide at no extra cost. Indeed, managers sometimes hire consultants to conduct expensive surveys and interviews in an effort to collect essentially the same information that the ethics process already has in hand.

Chapter 9 shows how to use ethics information to positively support mentoring, performance appraisal, and inspirational storytelling. It also explains what vital ethics records every company should have, and how to document ethics history. These take some time and thought, but they are no-cost initiatives that have potential to generate high trust, morale and productivity.

*Re Fallacy 9, 'charitable contributions ...'*

One product of corporate social responsibility should be a good name for the company: a perception that the company is generous and practices good citizenship. Business ethics is a component of that initiative, perhaps even the bedrock foundation for corporate social responsibility.

A business as an institution in society can demonstrate corporate social responsibility by making a good product or providing a good service, by standing behind that product or service and its value, by treating employees well, by being responsive to customers, and by respecting the local community.

But historically, some companies have sought to go beyond that.

In some cases, companies have used 'philanthropy' to mask problems that would be characterized as unethical if fully exposed. Professor Marianne Jennings points to some prominent companies and nonprofit organizations that have tried to use philanthropy as a balancing scale: if they were good to the environment and the community, promoted diversity and gave generously to charities, then it was all right for them to pursue schemes and frauds in their work.[21]

In other cases, companies have genuinely contributed to improvement of the world. Chapter 10 uses a pillars model and explains its four components – legal, financial, social, and ethical – to analyze corporate social responsibility opportunities. It describes a classroom exercise that opens college students' eyes to differences between charity, stewardship, and citizenship approaches to philanthropy.

It's hard to determine if this is low cost or no cost. Many companies have found that a wise plan can multiply the impact of corporate money. That is, if a company plans to spend $10 million on philanthropy this year, a wise plan can give that $10 million the impact of $18 million, $20 million or more – without spending an extra dime.

A thesis of this book is that overwhelming evidence shows that business ethics is not generally failing. Most people aspire to be ethical and leaders can choose to create bad conditions that influence good people to do bad things or to create good conditions that help good people achieve the good ethics they already aspire to. Basically, people already know the root problem and the root solution although we may not articulate them. Life experience tells us that many companies and many employees meet today's ethics norms every day. Appreciate the reality that employees, managers and leaders are already promoting ethics, whether they recognize that or not, and whether or not they are as successful at it as they and the company would like them to be.

This book shows how process can help people do even better, eliminate uncertainty, and bring out the better angels of most everyone's nature.

## Challenge puzzle

It's widely known as the 'Goldman dilemma' and reveals a situation affecting world-class sports and perhaps other businesses. While writing his first book, physician Bob Goldman felt 'stunned' by the answers more than 100 elite runners gave to a question posed by another physician, Gabe Mirkin: 'If I could give you a pill that would make you an Olympic champion – and also kill you in a year – would you take it?' More than half the runners said 'yes'.[22]

Goldman followed up for a number of years. He started in the early 1980s by asking 198 elite athletes – 'mostly weight lifters and field competitors [such as] discus throwers, shot-putters, jumpers' — a similar question. Fifty-two percent said 'yes'. Goldman asked athletes similar questions repeatedly over the years and always about half said 'yes'.[23] It was not a scientific survey. It was not a random sample of elite athletes. We do not know the athletes' demographics: gender, age or sports. The way the question was asked might have influenced results. It was posed as a hypothetical, and what people say may differ from what they actually do in real life. On the other hand, reports indicate that at least some elite athletes do use drugs that they believe will enhance their performance even without any guarantee that they will win and in the face of the risk they will get caught or even die.[24]

In 2008, to more scientifically test the Goldman dilemma, two professors in Australia telephoned 250 people randomly selected from the population living in Sydney, collected their demographic characteristics, and asked if they would 'take an illegal performance enhancing drug that was undetectable' on guarantee that they would win an Olympic gold medal but die in five years. Only two said 'yes'.[25]

It's a puzzle. Why would elite athletes answer so differently? Can or should leaders manage the Olympics and other world-class sports events differently? Would elite performers in fields other than athletics answer like the athletes? Can or should business leaders generally pay attention to the Goldman dilemma and manage differently?

---

[1] Jennifer (psued.) [Redacted], 'Ethics Essay', unpublished manuscript, November 11, 2008.

[2] Patsuris, P 2002, 'Accounting: The Corporate Scandal Sheet', *Forbes,* last modified August 26, 2002, accessed January 20, 2012, www.forbes.com/2002/07/25/accountingtracker _print.html.

[3] Cragg, W 2010, 'The State and Future Directions of Business Ethics Research and Practice', *Business Ethics Quarterly* 20(4): 720-721.

[4] Benedict XVI, 'Encyclical letter 2009: Caritas In Veritate', accessed January 20, 2012, www.lifeissues .net/writers/doc/civ/civ_caritas.in.veritate5.html.

[5] Lutz, RA 2003, *Guts: 8 Laws of Business from One of the Most Innovative Business Leaders of Our Time* (rev. edn), Wiley, Hoboken NJ.

[6] McGraw, BA 1998, 'Business Ethics Fellowship Study', unpublished manuscript.

[7] Schein, EH 1992, *Organizational Culture and Leadership* (2nd edn), Jossey-Bass, San Francisco: 12.

[8] Bandura, A 1997, *Self-Efficacy: The Exercise of Control,* W. H. Freeman, New York.

[9] 'Members of New York State Senate Will Get Ethics Training', Fox23 News, January 11, 2011.

[10] Cohen, R, 'Doing What the Company Wants', *New York Times,* January 9, 2011.

[11] Dardick, H, 'Cook County Employees to Get Online Ethics Training', *Chicago Tribune,* December 20, 2010.

[12] Bush, GW 2001, 'President Speaks at Pittsburgh Steelworkers Picnic', accessed January 20, 2012, http://georgewbush-whitehouse.archives.gov/news/releases/2001/08/20010826.html.

[13] Driscoll, D-M 2003, 'Sarbanes-Oxley: Pardon Me If I'm Underwhelmed', *Ethics Matter Magazine,* February 2003.

[14] McGraw, 'Business Ethics Fellowship Study'.

[15] Organizational culture scholars group such items under the term 'artifacts', which include visible products of a group such as architecture, language, technology and products, artistic creations, clothing, manners of address, emotional displays, myths and stories, rituals and ceremonies, visible behaviors of people, and organizational process in which behaviors are routine. See Schein, *Organizational Culture and Leadership.*

[16] President's Blue Ribbon Commission on Defense Management, *Conduct and Accountability: A Report to the President,* Author, Washington, DC: June 1986.

[17] Spade, AC 2001, 'The Beginning of a Journey: Posttraumatic Change in Women Who Take a Stand', PhD diss., Fielding Graduate University.

[18] Rothschild, J & Miethe, TD 1999, 'Whistle-Blower Disclosures and Management Retaliation: The Battle to Control Information about Organization Corruption', *Work and Occupations* 26(1): 107-128.

[19] Light On Productions (producer) 2009, 'In Search of the Good Corporate Citizen: Hitting the Numbers' (transcript), accessed January 20, 2012, www.lightonpro.com /transcripts/InSearch_Hitting.pdf.

[20] Lutz, *Guts: 8 Laws of Business.*

[21] Jennings, MM 2006, *The Seven Signs of Ethical Collapse: How to Spot Moral Meltdowns In Companies . . . Before It's Too Late,* St. Martin's Press, New York.

[22] Goldman, B, Bush, P & Klatz, R 1984, *Death In the Locker Room: Steroids and Sports,* Icarus Press, South Bend, IN.

[23] Goldman, RM, email to authors, September 19, 2011. Goldman, Bush, and Klatz, *Death In the Locker Room.* Reidbord, S 2010, 'Would You Trade Years of Life For Happiness?' *Psychology Today,* www.psychologytoday.com/node/37681, accessed January 20, 2012.

[24] Bamberger, M & Yaeger, D 1997, 'Over the Edge', *Sports Illustrated* 86(15) April 14.

[25] Connor, JM & Mazanov, J 2009, 'Would You Dope? A General Population Test of the Goldman Dilemma', *British Journal of Sports Medicine* 43(11): 871-872.

# Chapter 2

# The true driver

## The ethics dynamic

### LEARNING OBJECTIVES

By the end of this chapter you should:

- be able to apply the ethics dynamic model to business ethics issues.
- understand strengths and weaknesses of Stage 1 compliance.
- understand strengths and weaknesses of Stage 2 values.
- understand strengths and weaknesses of Stage 3 trust.
- be familiar with the HERO concept and situational leadership.

## FALLACY 1: TO STOP ETHICS FAILURES WE NEED ONLY TO HAVE RULES, TEACH PEOPLE THE RULES, AND PUNISH ANYONE WHO VIOLATES THOSE RULES

Alpha Corporation [a pseudonym] faced a crisis, of violations of US export laws. This was no minor problem. The company's survival was at stake. As part of its legal defense, Alpha deliberately created a corporate ethics program, hired a new, full-time corporate ethics director and expected the director to focus on compliance with laws and regulations.

The devil must cheer when a company, like Alpha, innocently, unwittingly and mistakenly focuses its business ethics narrowly on compliance with laws, regulations and rules, and then appoints an ethics 'czar' to take charge, perhaps aided by a few people in a silo organization. That sets the stage for business ethics to fail because those conditions free most leaders throughout the company from feeling responsible for ethics. They frame ethics as someone else's job. They allow and perhaps even encourage employees to see business ethics as just an administrative square-filler. They ignore two fundamental truths: (a) that ethics is in everyone's job description and (b) that leaders must feel personal and professional responsibility for the ethics of their company.

'Framing' contributes to business ethics uncertainty. A frame offers perspective on an issue. It can help us consider, overlook, or organize thoughts about aspects of an issue. With respect to business ethics, people often use too narrow a frame. They often expect to focus just on compliance with the law. That frame creates Fallacy 1, the idea that ethics requires only making rules, teaching rules, and punishing anyone who violates those rules. We need to adopt a broader, more long-term perspective. It is necessary to have rules, teach people the rules, and have consequences for those who violate the rules. However, in the words of notable business ethics advisor Jeff Kaplan, that is 'necessary but not sufficient'.

Luckily for Alpha, the new ethics director realized the company was using too narrow a frame. The director sent an email to colleagues in the business ethics community: 'I have defined my role as covering governance, compliance, and ethics. As a lawyer, I am much more comfortable in the first two realms since I can generally identify the source of the rules. In the realm of ethics, I could use some definition and navigational advice'.

Let's be clear early on, so no one misunderstands: nothing in this book impugns lawyers or plays to the lawyer jokes crowd. For reasons we will explain later, we see placement of ethics within a company's legal department as a problem and we recommend against it. Nevertheless, whoever a company appoints to lead ethics must establish and nurture a close, open relationship with the company's lawyers. They are vital members of a corporate ethics team.

Anne Takher stands as an example of a lawyer who has undertaken to foster close relations between lawyers and ethics officers. Her focus is 'preventive law'. She has become an anti-bribery expert and will tell you 'preventive law' plays such an important role in corporate compliance that she has built her career around it. Her objective aligns exactly with the ethics officer's goal: keep companies and their employees out of trouble in the first place. We focus this book on ways to do that while appealing to what Abraham Lincoln called 'the better angels of our nature'.[1]

Thus, it is not only lawyers who play important roles. Leaders in the professional business ethics community encourage a team effort, where:

- the law department helps to identify compliance rules and to design training so that employees know the rules and how to meet them;
- the accounting and finance department helps to design and test financial controls;
- the internal audit department helps to evaluate and test procedures and policies; and
- the training department helps to educate employees so they are able to meet compliance requirements and understand how all these efforts relate to the company's stated values.

We recommend a team effort encompassing the entire company and extending to other companies, including competitors, so all are ethical equals, playing on a level field and performing at the highest possible level of ethics. We're thinking of membership in business ethics groups like the Defense Industry Initiative on Business Ethics and Conduct (DII) or the Ethics and Compliance Officer Association (ECOA). Such membership delivers important advantages in terms of learning, networking and getting your company's name out as one that is serious about ethics. While the news media may express some interest in a company's ethics effort as an initial novelty or when the company gets in trouble, the best way to communicate to others about your company's ethics is through multi-company ethics group meetings attended by peers, vendors and regulators.

More about that later. First, let's help ethics officers – and business owners, and managers and supervisors, and business leaders in general – by answering the question about definition and navigational advice in the realm of business ethics.

## The ethics dynamic

The ethics dynamic model provides a broad frame that supplies both definition and navigational aids. A Venn diagram (Figure 2.1) shows the three stages of the ethics dynamic model, dramatizes why laws, regulations, and rules deserve to be recognized as a necessary but small part of business ethics, and clarifies why the frame of reference should expand to include values and trust as the dominant traits and drivers of effective business ethics.

Stage 1, compliance, is all of laws, rules, and regulations. Stage 2, values, encompasses all of Stage 1 and adds decision guidelines based on values. Stage 3, trust, encompasses all of Stages 1 and 2 and adds strategic decision guidelines based on building trust.

**Figure 2.1** Venn diagram of the ethics dynamic

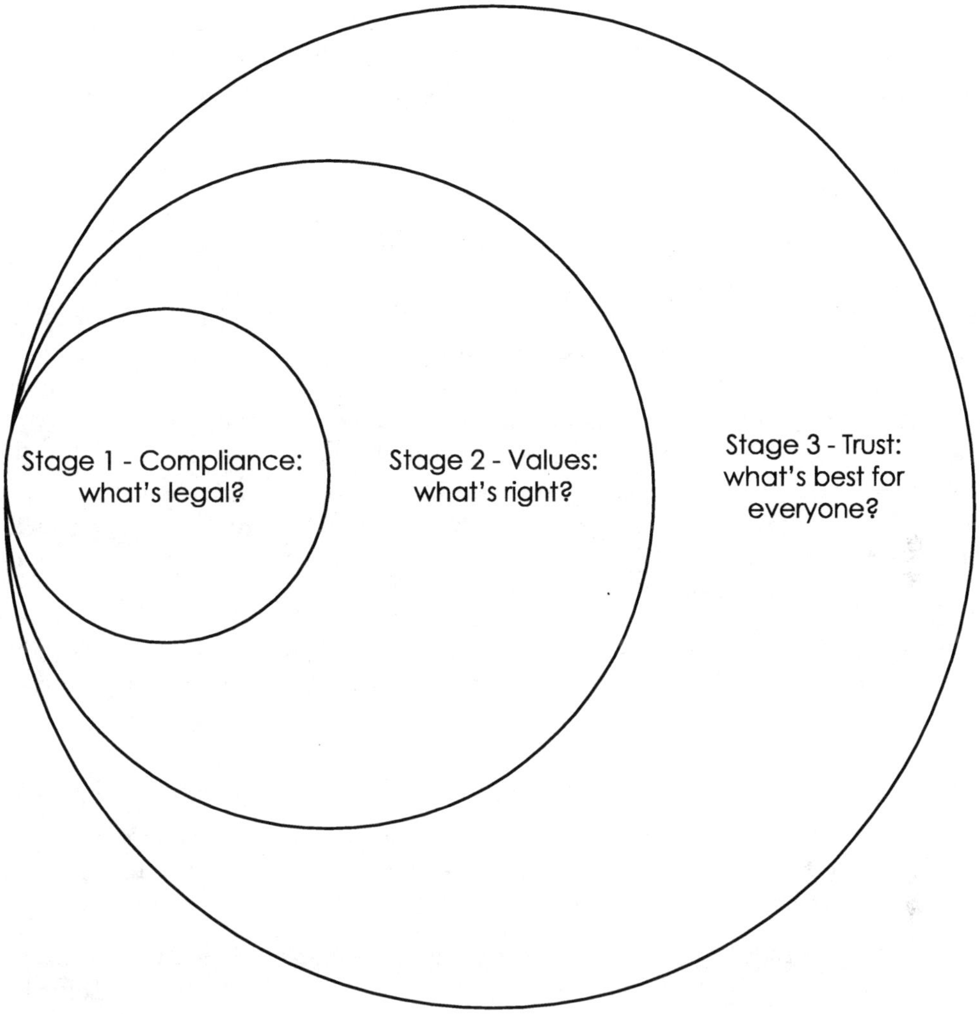

## Stage 1 is compliance

Many companies start here because they are in crisis mode, responding to allegations that they have violated the law. Sometimes they start here because they want to respond to new laws and regulations, like the US Sentencing Guidelines for Organizations or the *Sarbanes-Oxley Act* of 2002. They want to teach employees the law so that they can avoid new allegations. The primary question at Stage 1, the *compliance* question, is: what is legal or illegal? What are the rules? Teach employees the rules so they will not commit new violations.

Nothing is inherently wrong with that! Employees who know and abide by laws and rules protect the company and themselves from bad consequences like investigations, fines, trials, and jail. Moreover, following the law does send a supportive message honoring the larger community, a message that benefits society in general. People who know and follow the rules respect community social values that contribute to order and civility in both the workplace and broader society. In fact, a narrow focus on the law robs it of these larger communitarian values.

This is a strength of Stage 1. It is important that rules and laws exist as clear guidelines for those who might need them. Company climate and culture always must send the message that compliance, respect for the law, and responsibility and accountability to society are valued in the organization.

Yet Stage 1 alone does not work. Stage 1 characteristically focuses on rules, more rules, and still more rules. Infinitely more rules? That is not practical for long. Scholars find themselves formally stating an obvious truth: 'there is simply no way to create enough rules to cover even the most ethically important occurrences, even if they could be identified before they occurred'.[2] A code of ethics overloaded with rules becomes ineffective; even if some people are willing to wade through reading it, few are likely to remember much of what they've read. To illustrate, we ask our students how many have drivers licenses – it's everyone – and then how many have read the state motor vehicle code (not the driver handbook summary of laws, which has now grown to 108 pages, but the full vehicle code that is now nearly 1,000 pages long). Everyone drives, but none of our students has ever tried to read all of the rules.

Many companies, however, don't advance beyond Stage 1 because of 'tone-at-the-top', the attitude and perspective of the company's most senior leaders. Our analysis suggests a number of reasons why:

- Small company or large, the leaders look outside the company for vendors who can supply ethics expertise. Especially since Congress enacted the *Sarbanes-Oxley Act* of 2002, law and accounting organizations that focus on their compliance expertise aggressively market such services.
- For perspective, the leaders seek guidance from academics, some of whom teach the intellectual issues of business ethics but misperceive the business ethics practitioners' role as limited to compliance. Some academics appear to think ethics and profit are not compatible and that the evaluation and guidance business ethics practitioners bring to companies are not really ethics. That's a strange position because it suggests that work – an activity millions engage in for at least one-third of their waking hours – is not worthy of any ethical evaluation except condemnation when errors become apparent.
- Culturally, the leaders allow themselves to be influenced by news media reports that highlight initiatives by government ethics committees almost universally focused on compliance with rules and laws and on punishing offenders.
- Organizationally, the leaders choose to assign ethics responsibility to their general counsel's office or law department because it is chartered to protect the company from harm – a compliance with laws approach.

We observe, unfortunately, that many if not most programs are almost exclusively compliance oriented and report to the organization's law department. We do not deny the necessity of compliance. Jeff Kaplan, who is an attorney in addition to being a bright star in the field of business ethics, identifies the greatest fallacy in designing business ethics programs as the belief that because promoting compliance with laws and regulations is necessary it is also sufficient, and that a company therefore need not also address the need for ethical analysis and conduct.[3] People must know the rules – key rules even when it is impossible to remember all the rules – but they also must be motivated, supported, and rewarded for making good decisions when there might not be a rule or the rules aren't clear. That's when the organization's values, customs, and culture guide them.

Observers usually see companies move progressively from Stage 1 to Stage 2 to Stage 3 as they gain experience, as their ethics program matures, as it evolves with time.[4] However, companies and subcultures within companies can operate at any of the three stages at any time – sometimes changing stage with little or no warning. Sometimes companies start their ethics program at Stage 2. Sometimes companies regress, as could happen if a new CEO overlooked a company's traditional values (Stage 2) and ordered mere compliance with the law (Stage 1).

## Stage 2 is values-based ethics

As companies have developed business ethics programs in recent years, something of a tug-of-war has emerged: compliance versus values – rules versus values.

Given the influence of the Sarbanes-Oxley Act of 2002, compliance seems to be winning. For example, the Ethics Officer Association (EOA) was known by that name from its founding in 1992 until an act by the board in 2005 reframed the organization's purpose by renaming it the Ethics and Compliance Officer Association (ECOA). This renaming probably was a response to 'competition' by another business ethics group, the Society of Corporate Compliance and Ethics (SCCE), a decidedly more compliance-oriented organization. While the renaming might be a wise move with respect to attracting a broader membership, a side effect is to strengthen focus on compliance. In contrast, the ethics dynamic provides good reason for values to be ascendant instead.

Some companies advance to Stage 2 whether they want to or not. Employees pull their company into Stage 2 when they recognize that rules resolve only some of their issues and concerns. Employees ask for guidance about gray areas the rules do not adequately address. Stage 2 is 'developmental' – it grows people's ability to make ethically wise decisions in a variety of circumstances that are hard to foresee. Compliance remains important, but the primary question becomes one of *values*: what is the right thing to do?

Stage 2, values, encompasses all of compliance and adds so much more that it reaches the 'next level'. This is the domain of values-based ethics, of attention to the organization's values, customs and culture, and thus it is the logical focus for managers dedicated to making their company's contribution to customers and society meaningful. The community surrounding a company provides both broad and specific influences. The broad influences include customs and norms of society, diversity, and globalization. Specific influences include laws and regulations that warrant protective controls within a company.

Of the two, broad influences probably are more powerful than specific ones. *The Kite Runner* is a novel by Khaled Hosseini, a physician in northern California who is a native of Kabul. He tells a story of boyhood, growing up in Kabul, and describes an old winter tradition in Afghanistan, a kite-fighting tournament. Contestants compete to cut each other's line, and the winner is the last kite flying. There are no rules, but custom is that whoever ends up with a fallen kite keeps it no matter what. 'Afghans cherish customs', said Hosseini, 'but abhor rules'.[5]

In US culture the relationship is not quite the other way around. 'Cherish' might be too emotional a word for our relationship to rules. 'Abhor' certainly does not describe our relationship to custom. But we think it is safe to say that, over the past 20 years, compliance with laws and rules has been at the top of the dance card for most business ethics programs in companies and organizations.

It is fascinating to see that we are not the only society to face the challenge of balancing the relationship between compliance (read rules) and values (read customs – the Latin root for 'customs' is 'mores', the semantic root of morals, which is related to values).

Customs are among the building blocks of culture, a reality that has acquired added significance and scrutiny in the ethics, compliance, and corporate governance world over the past few years. In fact, 'customary beliefs' are included as an element of culture in one definition that you will find in *Webster's Third New International Dictionary*.[6]

Customs characterize organizations and groups. This distinctiveness can contribute to the signature of a company or organization much more than simple adherence to laws that apply in the same way to every entity. At a US Senate hearing on February 13, 1900, in widely-quoted testimony about women's suffrage, Carrie Chapman Catt made the memorable observation that 'No written law has ever been more binding than unwritten custom supported by popular opinion'.

We find that to be true in an everyday practice or custom that we all participate in, namely use of the automated teller machine. When someone is at the ATM, virtually no one in the US has to be reminded to stand back, behind an invisible line. People do it automatically and, in fact, frown on those who don't respect that space. Why? Almost anyone will respond, 'privacy'. Privacy is such an overriding value in US society that it dictates a custom or behavior without law, regulation, or even a visible line. Frankly, customs go beyond laws and rules and give a fuller picture of what an organization really values. We ignore their important role in building and maintaining an ethical culture at our peril.

In practice, Stage 2 companies base ethics on values, a few principles that guide employees to make intelligent decisions. They are confronting head-on this central question: is an ethics program a tactic to protect a company and prepare it to defend against possible prosecution, or is it something more? Is ethics just law abidance? Or is it also leadership and employee development, systems analysis, attention to culture, mindfulness, and tacit wisdom?

Extending ethics beyond Stage 1 compliance requires a leap of faith that a respected, successful organization will emerge from a corporate culture that encourages and values observance of law, civility, respect for others, and a sense of personal responsibility for others and the organization. To some degree, a Stage 1 compliance program is like having 100,000 employees walk atop a narrow wall — sooner or later, someone will slip off. A company that really wants to be ethical must do more: it must create a values-based, high-ethics organizational culture. It's protective, like putting handrails along both sides of the path atop that wall.

A substantial body of systems theory research explains why companies' practical experience is that Stage 1 compliance *does not* work and Stage 2 values-based ethics *does*. We'll talk more about this later, but for now simply point out that business ethics is a system influenced by inputs from many sources outside the company's control. Because everything happens for a reason, the inputs do determine what outputs will happen, but the complexity of the inputs means they can never be fully known and so the system's outputs are not completely predictable — uncertainty exists. Research shows such systems are governed best by a few simple rules (Stage 2 values), not by extensive and detailed rule sets (characteristic of Stage 1).[7]

The strength of Stage 2 is that companies build effective ethics by developing a few values and striving to create an open climate that allows people to use those few values to make good decisions and behave ethically. Scenario-based training gives everyone practice in recognizing ethics issues in the workplace and using values to wisely resolve them.

The role of example is also important. Francis of Assisi's comment is germane here: 'Preach the Gospel always. If necessary, use words.' The message must be sent so employees, regardless of their level of education, feel encouragement to always do right; to not proceed — to stop! — when they sense 'that's not the way we do things around here'; to seek help to properly resolve an uncertain situation.

A weakness of Stage 2 would be focusing on values while ignoring Stage 1 laws, rules, and regulations. In many companies, uncertainty and confusion reign now due to a misleading diversion that happened because some people defined business ethics as 'compliance' on one hand or as 'values and virtues' on the other. Often the difference is described as law versus ethics or as rules versus values. Discussion of the relationship between these two elements has focused largely on their differences and the suggestion that they are alternatives to choose between. But defining 'rules' and 'values' as alternative approaches rather than a pair of essential components means that embracing one may necessarily exclude the other. The ethics dynamic makes clear that that would be wrong.

Nevertheless, four factors have reinforced the debate: (a) companies often create ethics programs because they already face costly law violations and want to comply with the law to prevent more; (b) the original 1991 version of the US Sentencing Guidelines for Organizations spoke in terms of compliance programs;[8] (c) so do stock exchange requirements; and (d) so does the *Sarbanes-Oxley Act* of 2002.

Well … not exactly. The New York Stock Exchange (NYSE) implemented a requirement that listed companies must 'adopt and disclose' a code of business conduct and ethics, then explained that the code can focus management on areas of ethical risk and help foster a culture of honesty and accountability and contain compliance standards and procedures. It required effort 'to deal fairly' with customers, suppliers, competitors, and employees, then specified no manipulation, concealment, abuse of privileged information, misrepresentation of material facts, or other 'unfair-dealing practice'.[9]

Overall, the NYSE requirement emphasizes compliance. It could have been different. In response to an NYSE request for input, the [then] EOA recommended flexible requirements, suggesting that member companies should:

(a) create an 'effective' ethics and compliance program consistent with the US Sentencing Guidelines for Organizations (which *promotes an organizational culture* that encourages ethical conduct and a commitment to compliance with the law);

(b) designate a board committee to oversee that program; and

(c) provide periodic ethics and compliance 'orientation' to all board members.[10]

This would have emphasized fostering ethics in corporate culture without neglecting compliance.

With respect to the *Sarbanes-Oxley Act* of 2002, companies have given overwhelming emphasis and resources to implementation of Section 404, which required 'establishing and maintaining an adequate internal control structure' and assessing/testing the effectiveness of those controls — all compliance. The Act also contains Section 406, which required a code of ethics 'for senior financial officers' — standards reasonably necessary to promote (a) 'honest and ethical conduct' — integrity; (b) full disclosure of violations; and (c) compliance with rules and regulations. If legislative documents, like Vatican documents, should be read carefully to discern messages contained in style, placement and so forth, then that section arguably seems to give priority to an ethical culture (as well as compliance), at least among senior financial officers, but we observe that measures to implement Section 404 compliance controls have been so overwhelming that most people do not even know Section 406 exists.

In addition, people have several times explored creating an ISO standard for business ethics. ISO is the short, all-purpose name adopted by the International Organization for Standardization. Because the acronym for that organization would differ depending on language (IOS in English, OIN, in French), the founders of this nonprofit organization chose to use ISO as the short name in every language. 'ISO' comes from the Greek *isos*, meaning 'equal'. There is nothing wrong with industry-wide or world-wide standards, which ISO promotes. But ISO standards, by definition, are compliance-driven.

Beginning in 2008, a newly created US government standard affected companies doing business with the federal government. That standard requires such companies to promptly tell on themselves if they find fraud, conflict of interest, bribery, gratuities or false claims at their firm.[11] That clearly demonstrates a focus on compliance.

*Ethics and values or rules and laws?*

Emphasizing either without stressing the necessity of the other would be too simplistic and leave employees and the company vulnerable. Judge Richard P. Conaboy, the first chairman of the Federal Sentencing Commission, called business leaders' attention to this on September 7, 1995: 'You must take on the obligation to lead this effort, to be in the forefront, not only by working to ensure that your company's employees follow the law but by embracing and placing at the very top of your company's priorities the basic good citizenship values that make law abidance possible'.[12]

So, as part of governance, corporations need to establish policies and procedures that recognize and apply the ethics dynamic. Companies, managers, and individuals must go beyond the rules and establish a corporate culture that sees rules and values as ethical allies.

## Stage 3 is trust

This next evolution of the ethics dynamic includes all of the values and compliance domains and keeps both important, but the primary question becomes one of 'trust'. Stage three is a natural focus for leaders. It is a strategic stage: are each decision's outcomes right for everyone? Is ethics a ground rule when big decisions are made? Has the company achieved a climate and culture allowing each employee to comfortably follow her or his own personal moral compass?

> *For we will hear, note, and believe in heart, that what you speak is in your conscience wash'd as pure as sin with baptism.*
>
> – *William Shakespeare: Henry V, Act 1, Scene 2*

Research indicates that companies and government show progress toward Stage 3. A study using hierarchical complexity theory found three public policy documents the US government published since the mid-1980s to shape US corporations' ethics scored at progressively 'higher' moral reasoning stages. By 'higher' stage, we mean not just doing more compliance, like attending to 20 rules instead of just two, but thinking about ethics in a different plane, like changing from linear logic (e.g. if in doubt, tell the truth), to systems thinking (e.g. organize managers of this company to create a climate of open communication that allows everyone to speak what they believe is the truth), to supersystems thinking (e.g.

companies in various industries should share, compare, and evaluate their ethics best practices so we all can become ethically more sophisticated and we all can learn to achieve our ethical best).[13]

Trust is a two-way street: employees and management need to trust each other. The CEO of a *Fortune* 100 company confided that he sometimes lies awake at night worrying that an ethical lapse by just one employee – and there are more than 100,000 employees in that company – will jeopardize the survival of the entire corporation. This is a perverse example of employee empowerment. In such a situation, the power of one employee is enormous.

Indeed, 15 years before, under a previous CEO, that corporation's survival was jeopardized by just five employees. Given what we know about this, not all were motivated by the best intentions. Some were, but other motivations were not so noble. Nevertheless, they tried too hard to be outstanding performers, tried too hard to get the results they thought the company expected, would not admit they could not do the job correctly in the time allotted, and therefore 'bent the rules a little'. Two of the five went to jail. The company survived by paying more than $17 million in fines and remediation (which ate *all* of the profit the company had earned from sales totaling more than $100 million!), by shutting the doors permanently on a 2,000-employee division, and by proving it had a good ethics program in place. A big corporation might have the financial wherewithal to do that; a smaller company likely would be wiped out. Either way, some people's jobs suddenly vaporize.

Companies need to build comprehensive ethics processes around the entire ethics dynamic model. The process should encompass several efforts that companies have thought of separately, such as business ethics, social responsibility, environmentalism, philanthropy and citizenship. This is not to say all of those efforts ought to be in one bucket. Their scope is broad and they may require leaders with differing education, experience, and sensibilities.

Where large corporations can afford to hire experts to handle a compliance or ethics specialty, small businesses cannot. Governance of a small business needs to focus on process that simplifies how business is conducted and prevents compliance or ethics problems from arising. Small business benefits from operating at Stage 2 or Stage 3 of the ethics dynamic. Good values prevent legal issues. Where trust exists, myriad problems simply do not arise.

Companies must comply with thousands of laws and rules today. To protect the company and employees, functional managers must teach each employee the laws and rules that are critical to successful performance of her or his job. Hence, managers must teach compliance. They should be familiar with compliance laws that generally affect the company and especially familiar with compliance laws that affect their area of work. You would expect all managers to be familiar with overtime and break rules for hourly employees, but you would expect procurement managers to be thoroughly familiar with procurement integrity regulations. Laws and rules offer basic and helpful clarity and direction to even the most motivated employees. A value we want to inspire and motivate is a pattern of regard for laws and rules as essential for mutual respect and the success of common process.

But more than that, and even if the department is embedded in a company which lacks formal ethics process, managers can promote Stage 2 values-based ethics and Stage 3 trust. They can motivate employees, inspire them if you will, to levels of integrity and virtue beyond the minimums set out in specific rules or laws. An emphasis here is on modeling behavior.

Individuals always are free to consciously act as 'law-abiding citizens'. In common parlance, describing someone as a 'law-abiding citizen' says more than the narrow meaning of the phrase. Like any expression, 'law-abiding' has a base meaning as well as layers of meaning and nuances that go beyond the base and deepen it. 'Law-abiding citizen' is not a simple statement about one act or even about a person's character. It indicates a pattern that says something about the person's goodness, sense of community responsibility, and ability to be counted upon. This suggests that the law, at its broadest, is not simply an instrument of order and protection in society, preventative and protective, but also a reaffirmation of justice and responsibility as societal values.

Failure to understand and implement the ethics dynamic is an important cause — perhaps the number-one cause — of business ethics failures. Stage 1 programs give too little help to the company, to employees of the company, and to all of us who want to be proud of our nation and its business community.

## High ethics reliability organization (HERO)

At some point in the evolution of a company's business ethics program, the vision is likely to become one of flawless company ethics. Karl Weick and associates studied a similar concept they called high reliability organizations (HROs). They focused on organizations like the US Navy, where aircraft carriers are nuclear powered and potentially armed with nuclear weapons. The reliability of people and equipment must be super high because even a single failure could cause a devastating *physical* catastrophe. HROs must build processes and cultures that effectively address the enormous physical risk and make the organization safe.[14]

Following Weick's lead, what if such a concept could be applied to business ethics? Would a HERO be valid and desirable? On the face of it, a HERO would seek to avoid even one ethics failure. Such an organization would value the integrity of its people and believe even a single failure could cause a devastating *ethics* catastrophe. If that seems far-fetched, look at the Enron and Arthur Andersen companies to see the impact an ethics breach can have on business and society. A trend observed in US public policy approaches HERO standards by expecting major US corporations to avoid ethics disasters because they could be a catastrophe for both the company and the nation.

The HERO concept offers an attractive vision of great business ethics. It's the way people want to live. Ask a group, 'Does anyone here *not* want to be ethical? Does anyone here want to work for an *unethical* company?' We've had only one person raise his hand: a stalwart member of Rotary International, an organization famous for its strong ethical cornerstone called the Rotary 4-Way Test. He quickly admitted he raised his hand in jest, just to see what we would do. Would anyone seriously raise a hand if asked, 'Does anyone here *not* want to work for a HERO — a company committed to having no ethics failures?' ... Yes, actually, some people would object because they see and fear a downside.

A downside of the HERO concept — a risk — is the specter of perfectionism. Taken to an extreme, any mistake would evoke blame and punishment. People don't like that environment and prefer companies that encourage ethics-without-punishment, pursuing excellence, taking moderate risks, learning from mistakes, and avoiding blame or punishment of risk-takers.[15] At issue is this: can a company allow employees to take ethics risks?

The HERO concept emerges as realistic only if it is divorced from perfectionism. While no company can encourage or even allow employees to violate laws, employees face enough gray areas not clearly resolved by law that necessarily they must make judgment calls — and 'judgment' inherently means they are taking a risk. What the HERO concept requires is supportive, protective company processes that (a) help employees make a good decision in the first place and (b) quickly surface problems resulting from those decisions — or from any other cause — so the full resources of the company can correct them while they are still small. The HERO concept must recognize that any company will constantly face a potpourri of small errors and problems and provide processes to detect, investigate, correct, and learn from them. A true HERO is a learning organization, not a tyrant.

This reality is supported by collateral evidence developed by a taskforce appointed by the American Psychological Association (APA) to examine zero-tolerance policies developed in the 1980s to stop drug use and curtail unruly and violent behavior in schools. Those policies required severe punishment of any misbehavior and allowed no mitigation based on the student's intent, so a child caught taking aspirin for a headache was punished as severely as one spiking punch with methamphetamines. The APA recommended keeping the zero-tolerance standard but tailoring response to the specific infraction and developing interventions that will prevent violations in the first place.[16]

## Leadership

A key component of a company's trust system is its leaders. They hold responsibility to build trust in their organization. Pennsylvania State University professors Linda Treviño and Michael Brown point to Arthur Andersen, the founder of the accounting firm that bore his name, as an exemplary builder of that firm's trust system. 'Think straight, talk straight' was a mantra there for years. Every employee was trained in the 'Andersen Way': strong ethics, integrity and high-quality work. Employees learned to speak the same language and share the same values.[17]

Andersen, in years gone by, personally demonstrated that integrity was more important than cash business. To a railway executive who demanded Andersen approve his financial accounts, Andersen said, 'There's not enough money in the city of Chicago to induce me to change that report.' The railway took away its business, but later filed for bankruptcy, and the situation reinforced the Andersen firm's reputation for trustworthiness. (In *Final Accounting: Ambition, Greed, and the Fall of Arthur Andersen,* Barbara Toffler explains how the Andersen company's ethical culture slipped badly in later years.[18])

Attempts to build trust popularized training courses designed to teach 'situational leadership'. Basically, situational leaders diagnose other people by the amount of direction and support they need to successfully complete their current work. Leaders and employees then openly agree on a mix of direction and support using these assumptions:[19]

- people new to a job (or task) want high direction about exactly what their manager expects them to do but bring such enthusiasm for the new work that they need little supportive encouragement from that manager;
- people who have worked a job for a while, but who are still learning it, still want high direction about what the manager expects them to do and by now have encountered surprising, discouraging difficulties so they want supportive encouragement from the manager too;
- people who have worked the job long enough to overcome the difficulties no longer want much direction about what the manager expects them to do but do want supportive encouragement indicating the manager appreciates their work; and
- people who are true masters of the job set their own high standards. They are 'craftsmen'. They thrive on independence. They need and want little or no direction or supportive encouragement from the manager.

While critics complain that no hard evidence proves that situational leadership works, managers in industry intuit that it pretty well describes 'how things work around here'. One explanation of the difference may be that critics are looking for objective evidence that employees perform their jobs better in a situational leadership environment – something very difficult to measure – and managers in industry are subjectively judging the trust that emerges from matching leader-employee expectations and behaviors based on situational leader relationships.

The ethics dynamic describes how people make business ethics work: compliance, plus values, plus trust. Values are a key component. Harvard professor Lynn Sharp Paine makes the point: '[M]any have come to regard a value system based on sound ethical principles as a foundation of *organizational* excellence'[20] [emphasis supplied]. We are speaking not just of 'ethical excellence' but of something far larger, something that determines how successful the entire organization will be.

## Challenge puzzle

It has been widely praised as a 'gold standard' business ethics decision: Johnson & Johnson's (J&J) choice to recall world-wide all Extra-Strength Tylenol capsules on store shelves or already sold to customers. The reason was that police had notified J&J that seven people died in separate incidents in the Chicago area, apparently from ingesting Tylenol capsules containing cyanide.

No law required J&J to recall the Tylenol and the cost to the company would be more than $100 million. In fact, the FBI asked J&J to do nothing because recalling the product could give copycats reason to do similar crimes in the future. But in a very short time, J&J considered the situation and decided to recall the Tylenol because their number one corporate value was 'responsibility to doctors, nurses and patients, to mothers and fathers and all others who use our products and services'. Jim Burke, J&J CEO at the time, said 'there really was only one decision'. The basic tenet of medicine is 'do no harm'. People trusted Tylenol but people had died taking the product. 'We needed it to get off the shelves. It was the right thing to do.'[21]

Meanwhile, roundly criticized as a bad decision was Ford Motor Co.'s choice to build and sell the Pinto automobile despite discovery that its fuel tank often ruptured in a rear-end collision. Studs protruding from the rear of the axle housing punctured the tank and the fuel filler neck sometimes ripped. Spilled gasoline could ignite.

No law required Ford to fix the problem. Several modifications were possible, but all added $11 or more to the cost of manufacturing each car and therefore conflicted with a goal that total cost of the car must not exceed $2,000. Ford studied the issue for years and used a cost-benefit analysis approved by a US government agency, the National Highway Traffic Safety Administration (NHTSA), to calculate that making the $11 fix would cost $137 million and only prevent an estimated 180 deaths (each life valued at $200,000) and 180 burn injuries (each injury valued at $67,000) and 2,100 burned cars (each car valued at $700), for a total benefit of $49.53 million. Ford chose not to fix the gas tank problem.

Years later, the NHTSA formally determined that the Pinto was defective and Ford recalled the cars. Ford also was indicted for reckless homicide after three teenage girls died in a fire after a rear-end collision – reportedly the first time a corporation was tried for alleged *criminal* conduct – but was found not guilty by the jury.[22]

Laws didn't resolve the issues facing either J&J or Ford. It's a puzzle: act on values like J&J did, or act on a carefully studied, rational decision like Ford did? How can a company decide which to do?

---

[1] Lincoln, A 1861, *First Inaugural Address*, Washington, DC.

[2] Robin, D, Giallourakis, M, David, FR & Moritz, TE 1989, 'A different look at codes of ethics', *Business Horizons,* 32 (1): 66-73.

[3] Daly, FJ 2002, *Commonwealth North Forum Proceedings*, 5 April 2002.

[4] Daly, FJ 1998, 'The ethics dynamic,' *Business and Society Review* 102/103 (1): 37-42.

[5] Hosseini, K 2007, *The Kite Runner,* illustrated edn, Riverhead, New York, 46.

[6] Gove, PB ed, 1965, *Webster's Third New International Dictionary of the English Language Unabridged*, G. & C. Merriam, Springfield, MA.

[7] Holland, JH 1998, *Emergence: From Chaos to Order*, Perseus, Cambridge, MA, 123.

[8] 1991, *Guidelines Manual*, United States Sentencing Commission, Washington, DC, §8.

[9] 2004, 'Corporate Governance Rules,' *NYSE Listed Company Manual,* New York Stock Exchange, New York, §303A, 16-17.

[10] Ethics Officer Association 2002, 'Letter to James L Cochrane', in *New York Stock Exchange Corporate Accountability and Listing Standards Committee Report*, viewed 21 January 2012, www.iasplus.com/resource/nysegovf.pdf.

[11] 2009, 'Government Update on Mandatory Disclosure Program', *Federal Ethics Report,* 16 (11): 7-8.

[12] Conaboy, RP 1995, 'Welcome and Conference Overview', in *Corporate Crime in America: Strengthening the 'Good Citizen' Corporation, Proceedings of the Second Symposium on Crime and Punishment in the United States*, United States Sentencing Commission, Washington, DC.

[13] Oliver, CR 2004, *Looking For a HERO? Four Public Policy Initiatives on Business Ethics,* unpublished manuscript.

[14] Weick, KE & Sutcliffe, KM 2001, *Managing the Unexpected: Assuring High Performance in an Age of Complexity,* Jossey-Bass, San Francisco.

[15] Szumal, JL 2003, *Organizational Culture Inventory Interpretation and Development Guide,* Human Synergistics, Plymouth, MI.

[16] 2006, *Zero Tolerance Policies Are Not as Effective as Thought in Reducing Violence and Promoting Learning in School, Says APA Task Force (press release)*, American Psychological Association, Washington, DC.

[17] Treviño, LK & Brown, ME 2004, 'Managing to Be Ethical: Debunking Five Business Ethics Myths', *Academy of Management Executive,* 18 (2): 69-81. Toffler, BL with Reingold, J 2003, *Final Accounting: Ambition, Greed, and the Fall of Arthur Andersen,* Doubleday, New York.

[18] Toffler, BL with Reingold, J 2003, *Final Accounting: Ambition, Greed, and the Fall of Arthur Andersen,* Doubleday, New York.

[19] Hersey, P & Blanchard, KH 1982, *Management of Organizational Behavior: Utilizing Human Resources,* 4th edn, Prentice-Hall, Englewood Cliffs, NJ.

[20] Paine, LS 1997, *Cases In Leadership, Ethics, and Organizational Integrity: A Strategic Perspective,* Irwin/McGraw-Hill, New York, 1.

[21] Burke, J quoted in Finney, DP 2002, *Tylenol Hero Tells CEOs to Develop, Follow Ethical Code,* McClatchy-Tribune Business News.

[22] Gioia, DA 1992, 'Pinto fires and personal ethics: a script analysis of missed opportunities', *Journal of Business Ethics,* 11 (5, 6): 379-389.

Chapter 3

# The foundation

## A vision

### LEARNING OBJECTIVES

By the end of this chapter you should:

- □ be able to create a leadership vision that makes business ethics effective.
- □ know the fundamental purpose of business ethics.
- □ understand the difference between policing and mentoring.
- □ understand that business ethics should focus on prevention.
- □ know the importance of an appreciative vision.

## FALLACY 2: ETHICAL DECISION-MAKING IS COMPLICATED AND REQUIRES EXPERTISE

From a practical business viewpoint, this fallacy may not qualify as a 'self-defeating statement', but if it were always true it would raise the difficulty level for company ethics programs. Two aspects of truth lie behind it. The first is that everyone can think of an ethics dilemma that is difficult or impossible to solve. Philosophers and academics debate such dilemmas. The second is that ethical decision making sometimes *can* be complicated and *can* require special expertise.

Effective leadership can counter both problems — leadership is a critical factor. We mean leadership by executives, by managers, by supervisors and by hands-on employees when circumstances and expectations require them to step up to a leadership role. Leadership must create an environment that helps people make good decisions and take ethical actions the first time and every time.

Effective leadership can achieve this because the overwhelming majority of ethics decisions in business are not 'impossible dilemmas'. As we said in Chapter 1 most ethics decisions in business are merely 'choices' people can learn to make adroitly because, although they have ethical implications, they are like other choices people have to make in everyday life. As for those rare 'impossible' dilemmas, we all need to develop the ability to identify such situations quickly and protect everyone by sending them straight to the most senior leaders so the company can call up every available resource to resolve them wisely.

A William Shakespeare comment about leadership:

> *What impossible matter will he make easy next?*
>
> — *The Tempest, Act II, Scene I*

The foundation of business ethics is getting its leadership vision statement right. The vision — the fundamental purpose of business ethics — is to build trust, to help people make wise choices that prevent problems and to protect people from harm.

A leadership 'vision statement' must meet three criteria:

- it must be accessible to all members of the organization;
- it must provide an image of the future organization, a direction or goal for everyone to work toward; and
- it must provide an attractive improvement over perceived alternatives.

Barney Rosenberg, vice-president of ethics at a multinational corporation, described a telephone call he received from one of his company's managers. The manager was proud. He had recognized an ethics issue and felt he handled it well because he had paid attention during the company's ethics training. A landlord had offered him two tickets to a hockey tournament.

*I turned them down!*

The manager had recognized that the landlord and the company were re-negotiating a lease and that accepting the tickets would create a conflict of interest. It was a choice, not a dilemma. The choice protected both parties and allowed lease negotiations to continue without risk of scandal for either side. The choice fulfilled the company's (and the manager's) vision of high ethics.

## Rowboat analogy

A rowboat analogy may help clarify the principle. If you were in a helicopter hovering high over any corporation – Microsoft, IBM, Exxon – and looked down through an 'ethics lens' that revealed the company's business ethics culture, you would see rowboats. Depending on the size of the company, you would see dozens, hundreds or even thousands of rowboats. Each employee of the company would be rowing her or his own ethics rowboat (hopefully in the proper direction).

The rowboat analogy highlights that each of us, as an individual, chooses our own ethical direction. Two other important lessons that emerge are:

- If all of us in the company – say 50,000 of us – choose to row in the same direction (the ethically right direction, of course) then our paths will be smooth. But if one, two or three of the 50,000 choose to row in a different direction then conflicts arise, boats will collide, some may sink, and people may get hurt.
- The first people to detect ethics boats that are off course will be employees rowing their own boats nearby, people within hollering range who can sound the alarm and call for an immediate course correction before any boats collide, before any boats sink and before anyone gets hurt. That is why one, two or a few people can save a company from ethics disaster or, alternatively, sink it.

An effective corporate ethics program organizes all employees to encourage each other to live up to the values we aspire to, let the better angels of our nature surface and prevent people who are less than noble from carrying out schemes for nefarious purposes.

Until 2006, Hewlett-Packard had a long-established reputation for gold-standard business ethics. But as you read the following information from the record of a Congressional hearing, ask yourself if every element of the company – board of directors, senior management, middle managers and employees – had the same vision of what business ethics should be.

Here was the situation: Rules required everyone in the company to keep confidential what happened in meetings of the Board of Directors ... but information was leaking out. Board chair Patricia Dunn said, 'The Board's most sensitive discussions kept ending up in the newspapers.' Nothing stopped the leaks – not repeated reminders to directors about confidentiality, not expectations voiced that the responsible person should come forward, and not repeated notifications that the leaks were being investigated.

Telephone records might show which director had talked to journalists, but the phone company would release records only if requested by a subpoena or by the subscriber. In late spring 2005, Dunn became aware that the investigators were accessing telephone records 'obtained from publicly available sources in a legal and appropriate manner'.[1] In essence, an investigator called the telephone company and pretended to be a board member asking for his own telephone records. This investigative technique was called 'pretexting'.

Hewlett-Packard employees Vince Nye and Fred Adler deserve credit. They saw a rowboat going in the wrong direction, as it were. On February 7, 2006, Nye spoke up in an email to Anthony Gentilucci, manager of global security investigations for HP.

> *I have serious reservations about what we are doing. As I understand Ron's methodology in obtaining this phone record information it leaves me with the opinion that it is very unethical at the least and probably illegal. If [it] is not totally illegal, then it is leaving HP in a position ... that could damage our reputation or worse. I am requesting that we cease this phone number gathering method immediately and discount any of its information. I think we need to re-focus our strategy and proceed on the high ground course.*[2]

That same day, Fred Adler also raised the issue with management. Asked later, during the Congressional hearing, '[D]id anyone say, what we are doing is just crazy?' Adler responded:

> *Essentially, myself and Mr. Nye did. We went to – we went to – Mr. Nye went to Mr. Gentilucci. ... I went to my manager late on the 6th or early on the morning of 7 February, 2006, and told them I was deeply troubled and concerned about what happened. Shortly thereafter, Mr. Nye also contacted my manager after not receiving satisfaction through his manager, Mr. Gentilucci.*[3]

The investigation continued. A Hewlett-Packard attorney obtained assurance from the contract investigators who were actually doing the pretexting that 'there are no laws against pretexting'[4] and, through Gentilucci, obtained a Boston attorney's consultant's assurance that pretexting of phone records is legal.[5] The method Nye objected to was described by Gentilucci:

> *[I]nvestigators call operators under some ruse, to obtain the cell phone records over the phone. ... In essence the operator shouldn't give it out, and that person is liable in some sense. ... I think it's on the edge, but above board. We use pretext interviews on a number of investigations to extract information and/or make cover purchases of stolen property, in a sense, all undercover operations.*[6]

Nye and Adler spoke up to management when they saw the company doing something they believed was possibly illegal or, at best, unethical. A widely recognized problem is that employees sometimes choose to remain silent about suspected wrongdoing because they fear retaliation if they speak up. They worry they might get fired.

In days of yore, when company founders David Packard and Bill Hewlett were active in the business, they established Hewlett-Packard's original gold-standard ethics reputation by deliberately building the climate and culture of their company to encourage employees to speak up. It was their vision of what business ethics should be:

> *[T]his policy is aimed at building mutual trust and understanding, and creating an environment in which people feel free to express their ideas, opinions, problems, and concerns. … We've found that people do not seem to be particularly averse to bringing up any problems or concerns they may have, and managers usually are able to find satisfactory solutions fairly quickly. It must be clearly understood by supervisors and managers that people using the open door are not to be subjected to reprisals or to any other adverse consequences. … [The policy] is used quite frequently.*[7]

Nye and Adler apparently shared that vision and felt safe from retaliation. Not only did they speak up the first time, both continued to express concern about the issue. On March 17, 2006, Nye wrote:

> *If one has to hold his nose and then conduct a task, then [it] is logical to step back and consider if the task or activity is the right thing to do. In this matter, collecting cell phone call data in my opinion was a nose closer.*[8]

Hewlett-Packard's senior management focused on lawyers' assurances that pretexting was legal (and not on Nye's view that even if it was legal it was unwise). Hewlett-Packard got the telephone records and Congress subsequently held public hearings about whether that violated individuals' privacy. Patricia Dunn, board chair, told Congress:

> *I relied on trusted people who were lawyers and investigators … and received assurances that the investigation was both legal and compliant with HP's Standards of Business Conduct. … I urge Congress to consider legislation that would provide not only clear-cut rules on 'pretexting' or any other threat to individual privacy, but … ways of pursuing [companies'] responsibility to protect their intellectual property and confidentiality.*[9]

## The importance of mentoring

'Business ethics' can be defined simply: it is how society expects business people *should* behave. Ethics in business includes — but goes beyond — compliance with laws. Ethics in business is what each of us chooses to do: judgments and decisions we make even when clear-cut laws and rules don't exist (or we don't know them). Deciding to park beside a fire hydrant is a law compliance ethics issue. Deciding to run a personal errand while out of the office on company business is a judgments-and-decisions ethics issue.

People usually believe they have high ethics. If asked, they'll say, 'Of course I'm an ethical person and I want to do the right thing.' The story of a company trying to rate ethics in annual performance reviews illustrates this. The ratings were designed to be made on a five-point scale ranging from 1 (unethical, needs remediation) to 5 (exemplary, rarely equalled), so of course a midpoint 3 would be 'average' and 4 would be 'above average'. Under those guidelines, managers felt they were generous giving 4 ratings, but the employees who received a 4 felt that because they did not get a 5 someone was suggesting they were less than ethical – unethical. The company had to discard numerical ethics ratings and switch to a narrative description of the employee's ethical behavior. We bring good ethics from home to work with us. We come to work as angels.

> *But a baby food company sold millions of bottles labeled apple juice which contained water, sugar, flavoring and coloring – and little or no apple juice. Some of the employees of that company must have known ...*

Some people – perhaps most people – seem to want to focus on outliers when they are designing a corporate ethics program. 'Outliers' are people suspected of ethics violations or perhaps even actual violators. A focus on outliers reacts to problems. It creates rules and laws that might have prevented what the outliers already did. That approach focuses on compliance. 'Compliance' is what authorities order us to do. Compliance is laws, rules, power and policing. It is a minimum standard that must be met. Unquestionably, in every company every employee, manager and executive should clearly understand that compliance is a ground rule: nothing the company does requires anyone to break a law.

Where we have worked, allegations identified less than one percent of the employees as outliers. The reality where others work is possibly different. Lynn Brewer, who worked for Enron and then became an independent ethics consultant, said that her experience indicates that up to 20 percent of the employees in companies she has worked with may be outliers. The important point is that, either way, the alleged violators are a minority.

Criminologist James Q Wilson highlighted this reality in explaining his studies of crime. He said, 'What most needed explanation, it seemed to me, was not why some people are criminals but why most people are not.'[10]

Yes, outliers must be attended to. 'Wrongdoers', even if they are a minority of employees, should not be ignored, but our message is different: every company should design its ethics program to help all of its employees go beyond mere compliance with laws to achieve the high ethics they aspire to in a world that is full of 'gray areas' not clearly addressed by laws.

Companies should not allow their ethics standards to be set by wrongdoers – or in response to what wrongdoers do. Instead, companies need to invest in helping every one of us think clearly, eliminate uncertainty and do things right – make good decisions in the face of ethics surprises and confusion we encounter every day. A company's ethics process should enable each employee to get ethics out of the realm of dreams and imagination and into daily practice, and should foster both an organizational climate and an organizational culture designed to help all employees achieve a high standard of ethics.

Mentoring means helping people succeed. Business ethics is not a *police* function. It is *not* about catching and punishing wrongdoers.

> *Ethics is not about policing. It is about creating the kind of climate in which people are encouraged to make the right decisions in the first place.*
>
> – *Kent Kresa, CEO*[11]

Newspapers today publish stories demanding that people be taught 'ethics', and what they mean is 'teach people the rules then catch and punish anyone who violates them'. That defines ethics as compliance. Policing is a good thing to do, but we should not design company ethics and company culture to catch wrongdoers and punish them. Policing is someone else's role.

Business ethics is a *mentoring* function. Design it to help people make good, ethical decisions in the first place, and thereby prevent wrongdoing, eliminate ethics failures and eliminate the need to punish anyone. Capitalize on the good values and goodwill that the vast majority of employees bring to the job.

Ethics is a tool leaders use to build mentoring relationships and a trust system throughout their organization. Ethics does not require us to catch others making mistakes so much as it requires us to promote doing the right thing the first time every time. Yes, we should anticipate what might go wrong and, mentor-like, coach ourselves and others around us to prevent mistakes or, failing that, to detect and fix mistakes as early as possible. But our primary concerns should be envisioning the right thing to do and making it happen.

## Foster mindfulness

Mentoring means fostering mindfulness. US society expects business leaders to foster mindfulness throughout their companies. Mindful people are alert for what they did not expect. They are sensitive to ethics issues and concerns. They notice, they communicate and they respond quickly. The key principles and practices of mindfulness belong to the company ethics program.

Even the most ethical, the most honorable, the most mindful people find themselves in circumstances from time to time where they feel it is difficult to make a good decision. We think we'll have no influence. Or we've never seen this situation before. Or events surprise us. Pressures imposed by time or other people force us to act too fast. It is not always easy to make an ethical decision, even if it's true that most are just 'choices'. For example, put yourself in the shoes of this captain of a navy ship, alone, far from home base. You decide if what the captain did was ethical or not.

> *A US Navy sailor was jailed by local police while on shore leave in a small, unstable nation. A local merchant offered to get the sailor out of jail and deliver him to his ship if its captain would discreetly add an extra $3,000 to the merchant's contract to deliver provisions to the ship. [US policy is to favor US justice over foreign justice for US military lawbreakers.] Whether the $3,000 was a bribe or ransom, the captain paid it from US government*

*funds [lawyers say that was illegal], the sailor arrived, the ship sailed on time and the captain meted out punishment to the errant sailor.*

A management principle and a leadership competency emerge. The management principle is that mindful companies strive to create an organizational climate that allows — indeed encourages — people to behave ethically, even when circumstances seem to make ethical decisions and ethical behavior difficult. The leadership competency is that mindful leaders strive to inspire employees to be mindful. To be an effective leader, being technically competent and dynamic is not enough. An effective leader must also be seen as 'someone who can be trusted, who has high integrity and who is honest and truthful'[12] — a poster person inspiring high ethics.

Hallmarks of mindfulness are openness, kindness, compassion, appreciation, avoidance of blame and willingness to listen, to learn and to improve continuously. Some say traits like these are indicators of good management and ethical behavior. Mindfulness recognizes that change constantly presents new opportunities and new challenges. Mindfulness appreciates the strengths an organization and its people already have. Mindfulness builds upon those strengths. For leaders, mindfulness means keeping the organization wakeful and nimble rather than trapped in a bureaucracy dedicated to repeating the past.

A mindful organization has an abundance mentality. It focuses on the assets it has rather than the assets it lacks. It is like asking for a departmental budget of $1.2 million but receiving an allocation of only $1 million. In this situation, mindful people do not deplore what must be sacrificed due to the $0.2 million shortfall but instead focus on best using the $1 million they were given to work with.

## Focus on prevention

A good corporate ethics program counters surprises and pressures, making it possible for ethical people to make a good decision even when it could be difficult to make a good decision. It helps us be better angels.

To paraphrase Smokey Bear: only you can *prevent* ethics disasters. Unethical conduct by one, two or a few people can destroy a company. Ethical conduct by one, two or a few people can save it.

A company's ethics telephone started ringing one morning. You know the telephone we mean — the number a company encourages its employees to call when they spot a business ethics problem. The company assured its people they could feel safe calling this number.

*Safe? Don't we all know that people who raise an ethics issue lose their jobs? Okay. Ethics matter. I should speak up when I see something going wrong. But there are reasons I can't. My boss will be angry. The people I work with won't like me. I'll be called a troublemaker and pretty soon I'll be out of a job.*

The first call came from employee Able [pseudonym], who had submitted the company's form requesting reimbursement for travel expenses. Able's manager refused to sign it until Able claimed *more* money spent on meals and tips, not the actual costs. The manager wanted Able to claim as much money as possible. The manager apparently felt he was looking out for the employee's 'best interests' by helping Able collect the maximum allowable *per diem*.

> *More money in Able's pocket? Who would know the claim was padded? Usually you don't need receipts for meals and tips.*

About six more calls followed, all from Able's colleagues. News travels fast.

They knew the manager had asked Able to pad the reimbursement request. Padding wouldn't cost the company anything because the cost of this travel would be passed on to the customer. In fact, this might be a cost-plus contract giving the company additional profit when costs increased.

The company's ethics process handled the situation in two steps. First, Able (and the colleagues) got immediate reassurance that company policy required reporting actual costs and prohibited padding costs. Second, a senior manager met with Able's manager, who was a new hire.

> *I knew it. Here comes trouble. It will flow downhill.*

The tone of the meeting between those managers was mentoring: here's how things work in this company. Other companies may pad expenses; we don't. Other companies may retaliate against employees who call the ethics telephone line; we don't. Integrity is a core value our employees widely share; we formally adopted it as an official company value, and we encourage employees to speak up quickly when they feel violation of any value, not just this one, might occur. In this case, the company's ethics process has been protective, as it is designed to be. It prevented filing a false expense report. No crime occurred. No violation of the values occurred. Everybody is safe. No harm done.

> *Is this story true?*

Yes. And here is another.

Some years ago, when desktop computers first appeared in business offices, three US Air Force organizations began using them at the same time. One, we'll call it the test group, mentored its employees. It proclaimed an ethics vision based on the value of integrity (always to practice crime-free computing), brought all employees together to discuss and refine a group view of proper computer uses (creating an open environment, where people felt able to speak up and feel safe), published its final rules as policy, then followed a rule that *every* deviation from the norm and every suspected abuse would be investigated promptly, thoroughly and impartially. Policy was that violators would be disciplined, not overlooked, and discipline would be commensurate with the seriousness of the misconduct.

In the first year, the test organization uncovered four incidents reported as possible computer abuse. Investigation disproved one allegation and corrected the other three early, before they became actionable violations. In the same time frame at the other two organizations (we will call them the control groups because they had no mentoring), one suffered repeated incidents of malicious tampering with program code and the other suffered the theft of two modems with cables and cards, theft of compiler software and copying of software without permission of the copyright owners.[13]

> *Integrity is important. Being able to speak up and feel safe is important. I wish my company worked that way.*

So do we. We all need to make that happen.

## Build culture

Mentoring means building a good corporate culture. People come to work with different backgrounds and perspectives. Perhaps a few want to do wrong. Most want to do right but are uncertain … they sometimes wonder … they ask themselves, 'In this situation, what exactly is the right thing to do?' The corporate culture should answer that.

> *A factory in New England received a customer order to build gyroscopes. In the contract negotiations, the customer noted it had not taken all of the similar units ordered in a previous contract. The customer acknowledged it had not claimed those units in the time specified by the old contract, despite reminders from the New England firm to do so.*
>
> *Company employees and their supervisor realized they could book a profitable new sale. However, they worked in a high-ethics corporate culture. They felt the customer had some moral claim to the value of the gyroscopes ordered but not claimed under the old contract even if the customer did not have a legal claim because of failure to request those units before the old contract expired. They agreed to allow the value of those units as a factor in new negotiations.*

Stanford University psychologist Philip Zimbardo believes too many people work in organizations where 'the system' – the culture – actually encourages good people to do evil things, which he labeled 'the Lucifer effect'.[14]

> *I always used to feel frustrated with how organizations operate. People at the lowest level always knew what had to be done, and I always asked myself, why did bright people do stupid things? Then I realized that the management structure imposed organizational stupidity.*
>
> – *Roger E Meade, CEO*[15]

For example:

> *The California Bureau of Automotive Repairs (BAR) found the largest auto service business in California had instructed its employees to sell a specified number of alignments, springs, brake jobs and shock absorbers during every eight-hour shift. BAR investigators, posing as customers, brought cars (carefully inspected by BAR mechanics and known to be in good condition except for worn brake pads) into those shops and documented that employees recommended and performed unnecessary service, made unneeded repairs*

*and replaced parts that were in good condition, even parts that were nearly new.*

Brian Cruver painted Enron as a poster child epitomizing the wrong kind of corporate culture. When he worked there, Cruver said, Enron sometimes was referred to as 'the dark side' because it was powerful and relentless, gobbled up other businesses, and could manipulate markets, regulators and politicians.

*The dark side? Some employees of the company must have known.*

Cruver didn't mind joining the dark side because Enron offered great pay, benefits and prestige – its employees were perceived as 'the best and the brightest'.

*Lots of people look to their job for income, personal advancement, prestige, and maybe some thrills. But they also want to work for a company they can be proud of, a company that is a good place to work, a company that both thrives and survives.*

When the end came for Enron, Cruver got 30 minutes to pack up and leave the building. One thing he left behind was his Enron *Code of Ethics* handbook.

When he arrived home at midday, Cruver felt exhausted and overwhelmed. His boys and the puppy sensed something was wrong. He couldn't eat. He wanted to know who deserved the blame. Enron's espoused core values were Respect, Integrity, Communication and Excellence (RICE, for short). How amazing, he thought, that Enron drilled that acronym into their employees' minds but failed so miserably to actually live up to those values. Cruver decided the company he wants to work for will be like Enron should have been, but not too much like Enron actually was.[16]

A graduating senior at the University of Redlands asked an ethics symposium panel, 'As a job applicant, how do I tell the difference between a company that is ethical and one that is not?'

What questions do you ask and what answers do you hope for when trying to recognize an ethical company? Consider those companies where business ethics clearly failed: Enron, Arthur Andersen LLP, Global Crossing, Tyco and a host of other companies. From the outside, they looked like very successful corporations. But when their ethics issues exploded, nothing could save them.

*Effective* business ethics would have built a vision and corporate culture that would prevent the explosions. Over at Enron, the company did have a code of conduct, a corporate ethics officer, a 'hotline' and other trappings of a formal ethics program. Over at Andersen LLP, according to alumna Barbara Ley Toffler, Andersen gave each new employee a thick binder titled *Independence and Ethics*. Moreover, as a powerhouse business consultant, Andersen sold business ethics advice and training to other companies.

If we agree that *effective* business ethics is important, how do we implement it? How can we get ethics out of the realm of 'public relations' and into daily practice? This is not to demean public relations. Public relations is a good thing when its goal is to present a true image of the company. But if its goal is to present a false image, that is problematic. We all are concerned that our reputation is true to whom we think we are. That is so for individuals, and also for companies and other organizations. We need to ensure that our ethics reputation is a true image based on what we actually do, not a false image claiming we are doing good because that is socially desirable when actually we are pursuing an unpublicized less-than-noble agenda.

At a national level the US Government regulators have recognized and adopted this vision of business ethics before much of the business community has. By stereotype, regulators should write and enforce rigid rules that govern what companies are allowed to do. Yet US regulators are writing broader policies that explicitly encourage companies to foster corporate cultures which encourage employees to voluntarily live up to their own high values.

In companies, ethics work not only can but must be done at several organizational levels. At corporate-wide level, the best corporations build a vision, climate and culture where high ethics thrive day in and day out throughout the entire company. Support from the very top of the company is critical. While people are capable of a lot of good things even if support from the top is not there, the lack of it will make the company's ethics anemic.

At a lower level, departments need to take charge of their own ethics efforts. Departments usually have a sub-culture, operating within the overall corporate culture but tailored to the department's particular situation. The practice of allowing company units to have stricter but not looser policies and practices in some areas than others has some merit. For various reasons, like mergers, acquisitions, geographic separation, demographics and the type of work performed, some departments may demonstrate different approaches to ethics than others. We've seen differences between departments staffed by construction engineers versus departments staffed by computer engineers. What matters to one group is different from what matters to the other. Sometimes it is differences in what people value; sometimes it is differences in the work situation.

At grassroots level, an individual or a small group of co-workers often will sense that they need to set their own vision and high ethics standards, lead the way, model good ethics and mentor colleagues.

## An appreciative vision

Professors David L Cooperrider and Leslie Sekerka identified two approaches to creating organizational culture:[17]

- Deficit focus – detecting errors, analyzing root causes, planning remedies and implementing corrections. This approach is primarily reactive, racing to fix worrisome, distracting and sometimes crippling problems that have already struck the company. It is policing and punishing wrongdoers. This approach is common at Stage 1 of the Ethics Dynamic.

- Appreciative focus – an appreciative and positive focus seeks to draw out human strengths so the organization self-organizes to be even better. This approach primarily emphasizes prevention and mentoring the majority of employees to be successful. This approach is required to achieve Stages 2 and 3 of the ethics dynamic.

The leadership vision should build on appreciative focus, using corporate climate to create a corporate culture that helps every employee achieve the high ethics he or she already aspires to. 'Climate' is expectations, policies, procedures and methods a company uses to influence employee behavior. 'Culture' is what employees believe, value and actually do. If they are different, culture always trumps climate. Climate and culture are most powerful when they are congruent.

The leadership vision required for good ethics is a vision of mutual trust, a climate and culture valuing open communication without fear of retaliation, so everyone can make good decisions the first time, and where bad news, like good news, will rocket to top management so full company resources can resolve problems when they are smallest.

CEO Roger Meade is right. People usually know the right thing to do, and management structure should strengthen their good instincts by providing organizational wisdom. Management structure should not cause good people to do bad things by imposing organizational stupidity on them. Convergence means that a company's management style and its ethics program should reinforce each other. Convergence is one of the often unstated themes of business: some of the more positive management trends and business ethics are moving in the same direction, creating a synergy that brings more power to both of them.

Shouldn't managers listen when employees raise ethics issues? Isn't that a core need? Shouldn't managers realize that employees who are afraid of them or feel it is useless to speak up won't tell them important news? Basic manager training should explicitly achieve that 'Aha!'

People should aspire to work for a company that appreciates the high ethics they already have and want to bring to their jobs, a company whose ethical standards are set by its ethical people – the majority of its employees, a company smart enough not to set ethical standards primarily by reacting to a small minority who are outliers. People's ethical vision should be that their company enables each of its employees to get ethics out of the realm of dreams and imagination and into daily practice. People should expect their company to foster an organizational climate begetting an organizational culture which helps every employee achieve high ethics, the reputation most employees and most companies already aspire to. Ultimately, the vision is an appreciative corporate culture where open communication and values-based trust abound.

## Challenge puzzle

It is a puzzle: What best fosters workplace safety … and why does it work best?

Maslow's famous hierarchy of needs begins with physiological needs and then advances next to safety needs.[18] This suggests that safety in the workplace is a widely shared value among employees.

Enforcement of safety regulations like those required by OSHA clearly is a police function. It promotes compliance, not ethics. It has its place, but a paragraph in letters OSHA writes to businesses implies that enforcement and good intentions are not enough:

> *We recognize that an elevated lost work day injury and illness rate does not necessarily indicate a lack of interest in safety and health on the part of your business. Whatever the cause, however, a high rate is costly to your company in both personal and financial terms.*[19]

Think twice about OSHA's point that a high injury and illness rate impacts a business in 'both personal and financial terms.' As CEO of Alcoa, Paul O'Neill felt strongly that the driver for safety should be 'personal terms', not 'financial' issues:

> *I told the financial staff that if anyone ever calculated how much money we were saving by being safe, they were fired. ... I didn't want [employees] to think they were being asked to do something because management was trying to think how to save money. I didn't care, and I was prepared to accept the consequences of spending whatever it took to become the safest company in the world.*[20]

Under O'Neill's leadership, Alcoa framed safety as an ethical value. People injured were not statistics. They were humans with faces, names, families, and friends. At the start of O'Neill's initiative, Alcoa's annual lost workday rate already was exemplary, only 1.86 cases per 100 employees, even less than the industry average. Four years later, the rate was down to 0.14 cases per 100 employees – better than a 92 percent improvement – and people credited a 'culture shift', because managers and employees understood that safety was about values, not money, and every employee knew to prevent injuries by fixing any safety issue without delay and without explicit instructions to do so, no matter what the cost.[21]

Financial concerns, human resources concerns, compliance concerns, values concerns – what best fosters workplace safety ... and why?

---

1 Dunn, P 2006, 'My Role in the Hewlett-Packard Leak Investigation', in Hewlett-Packard's Pretexting Scandal, Hearing Before the Subcommittee on Oversight and Investigations of the House Committee on Energy and Commerce, 109th Cong. 44-76 (September 28, 2006), serial no. 109-146.

2 Nye, V 2006, 'Re: Privileged Communication' [email to Anthony R. Gentilucci, February 7, 2006], in Hewlett-Packard's Pretexting Scandal, Hearing Before the Subcommittee on Oversight and Investigations of the House Committee on Energy and Commerce, 109th Cong. 362 (September 28, 2006), serial no. 109-146.

[3] 2006, Hewlett-Packard's Pretexting Scandal, Hearing Before the Subcommittee on Oversight and Investigations of the House Committee on Energy and Commerce, 109th Cong. 113 (September 28, 2006), serial no. 109-146 (testimony of Fred Adler).

[4] DeLia, R 2006, 'Privileged Communication' [email to Kevin Hunsaker, February 7, 2006], in Hewlett-Packard's Pretexting Scandal, Hearing Before the Subcommittee on Oversight and Investigations of the House Committee on Energy and Commerce, 109th Cong. 375 (September 28, 2006), serial no. 109-146.

[5] Seyedin-Noor, B & Lain, T 2006, 'Interviews of Kevin Hunsaker' [draft memorandum, August 21, 2006], in Hewlett-Packard's Pretexting Scandal, Hearing Before the Subcommittee on Oversight and Investigations of the House Committee on Energy and Commerce, 109th Cong. 661 (September 28, 2006), serial no. 109-146.

[6] Gentilucci, AR 2006, 'Re: Phone Records' [email to Kevin Hunsaker, January 30, 2006], in Hewlett-Packard's Pretexting Scandal, Hearing Before the Subcommittee on Oversight and Investigations of the House Committee on Energy and Commerce, 109th Cong. 306 (September 28, 2006), serial no. 109-146.

[7] Packard, D 1995, *The HP Way*, Harper Business, New York, 157.

[8] Nye, V 2006, 'Cell Phone Information (Call Data)' [email to Ted Crawford, March 17, 2006], in Hewlett-Packard's Pretexting Scandal, Hearing Before the Subcommittee on Oversight and Investigations of the House Committee on Energy and Commerce, 109th Cong. 464 (September 28, 2006), serial no. 109-146.

[9] 2006, Hewlett-Packard's Pretexting Scandal: Hearing Before the Subcommittee on Oversight and Investigations of the Committee on Energy and Commerce, House of Representatives, 109th Cong. 2 (September 28, 2006), serial no. 109-146.

[10] Wilson, JQ 1993, *The Moral Sense*, Free Press, New York, 24.

[11] 2001, 'A Message from the Chairman and Chief Executive Officer,' Standards of Business Conduct, Northrop Grumman Corporation, Century City, CA, 1.

[12] Kouzes, JM & Posner, BZ 2003, *Credibility: How Leaders Gain and Lose It, Why People Demand It*, Jossey-Bass, San Francisco, 24.

[13] Oliver, CR 1985, 'A psychological approach to preventing computer abuse – a case history,' *Computer Security Journal*, 3(2): 51-56.

[14] Zimbardo, PG 2007, *The Lucifer Effect: Understanding How Good People Turn Evil*, Random House, New York.

[15] Meade, RE 2009, email to authors.

[16] Cruver, B 2002, Anatomy *of Greed: The Unshredded Truth from an Enron Insider*, Carroll & Graf, New York.

[17] Cooperrider, DL & Sekerka, LE 2003, Toward a theory of positive organization change, in KS Cameron, JE Dutton & RE Quinn *Positive Organizational Scholarship: Foundations of a New Discipline*, Berrett-Koehler, San Francisco.

[18] 'Maslow's Hierarchy of Needs', 2011, viewed 21 January 2012, www.abraham-maslow.com/m_motivation/Hierarchy_of_Needs.asp.

---

[19] 'OSHA Identifies 13,000 Workplaces with Highest Injury and Illness Rates,' OSHA Workplace Injury Statistics and News, 2011, viewed 21 January 2012, www .ehso.com/OSHA_Injuries.htm.

[20] O'Neill, PH quoted in Lagace, M 2002, 'Paul O'Neill: Values Into Action,' Working Knowledge for Business Leaders, Harvard Business School, Cambridge, MA, viewed 21 January 2012, http://hbswk.hbs.edu/archive/3159.html.

[21] Thomas, T, Schermerhorn, JR Jr, & Dienhart, JW 2004, 'Strategic leadership of ethical behavior in business', *Academy of Management Executive*, 18(2): 56-66.

# Chapter 4

# The strategy

## Culture trumps climate

### LEARNING OBJECTIVES

By the end of this chapter you should:

- □ be able to use policies, training, guidelines – anything employees can see, touch or hear – and values to create a corporate climate that builds a culture of trust and high ethics.
- □ understand three types of trust.
- □ know how to measure trust.
- □ be familiar with a 'complex adaptive system' (CAS) perspective of trust in business.
- □ be familiar with 'dissatisfiers'.

## FALLACY 3: BAD PEOPLE CAUSE ALL BUSINESS ETHICS FAILURES

Business ethics can fail due to bad apples (less-than-noble individuals), bad cases (difficult moral issues) or bad barrels (sour organizational culture). But when you drill down to basics, the trigger for an ethics violation in every instance is an individual's behavior. Too often that is a *good* individual trying to live up to expectations of the corporate climate (what the company does and expects) and the corporate culture (what employees collectively do and expect). Too often that is a *good* individual trying too hard to do 'a good job', a good individual trying to give a company 'help' the CEO did not ask for and would not want (or at least *should* not ask for or want), a good individual trying to contribute to company success and profits … but in the wrong way. Good distance, wrong direction.

Research provides useful insight into what can make good people do – or *not* do – bad things. Three research studies are explained below. Professor Philip Zimbardo's Stanford Prison Experiment provided an excellent example of good people behaving unethically because they were trying too hard to do a good job. Stanley Milgram's obedience experiments demonstrated that virtually all of us will violate our personal values and ethics if we think our employer expects us to do so and that the violation will serve a worthy purpose. David Bersoff's experiment showed that companies can deliberately do things that influence people to avoid wrongdoing.

The participants in Zimbardo's experiment fit into three categories: volunteer prisoners who tried too hard to perform the prisoner role, volunteer guards who tried too hard to perform the guard role and professional psychologists who tried too hard to perform the researcher role.

Zimbardo assigned nine male volunteers to be 24-hour-a-day prisoners in a simulated jail guarded by male volunteers who worked eight-hour shifts. All were college age. The guards adopted a domineering role and harassed the prisoners by using tactics similar to fraternity hazings: line up and count off, do push-ups and jumping jacks … They tried too hard to do a 'good job' as guards. The prisoners – who knew they were free to quit the experiment at any time – stayed to play their role, accepted the harassment, and suffered. They tried too hard to do a good job as prisoners. The psychologists focused on gathering data from the experiment and worked too hard at doing that. Zimbardo later said this was one of the most unethical psychology experiments ever conducted because by the end of five days the guards were severely tormenting the prisoners. '[I]t was terrible what I was allowing to be done to those innocent boys.'[1] He cut the experiment short, saying he had been blind to the reality of the destructive system he had created and should have terminated the experiment much earlier.

Everybody in Zimbardo's experiment – guards, prisoners and psychologists – was trying too hard to do a 'good job' and get the results they thought the research project expected. Zimbardo concluded from this and other events that too many people work in organizations with 'systems' – organizational climate and culture – that encourage good people to do evil things.

Milgram's research showed we all probably are willing to do 'evil' if we think 'the system' requires it. In his experiment, Milgram assigned volunteer 'teachers' to administer what appeared to be increasingly painful electrical shocks to punish a volunteer 'learner' when he answered questions incorrectly. Milgram justified the shocks as legitimate research aimed at improving how people learn. The 'teachers' showed stress and distress. When they expressed concerns, the experiment supervisor ignored their issue and said the 'experiment' required them to continue. All of the 'teachers' obediently delivered shocks until eventually most (65 percent) reached some internal ethical limit and refused to deliver shocks anymore, saying shocking the 'learner' *violated their personal values and ethics*. (For the record, the 'teachers' believed the shocks were real but they were not; the 'learner' was a confederate of Milgram who only pretended to receive shocks.)[2]

After watching a film showing Milgram's research, one college student said, 'I cannot imagine what kind of mental breakdown I would experience if I had actually been one of those [people] in the study. If I was in their shoes, I would probably obey the experimenter until I heard the 'learner' scream for the first time, at which point I would refuse to continue shocking him and probably start crying on the spot.'[3]

*Everyone* in Milgram's experiment was willing to violate personal values and ethics, at least for a while, because their job expected them to do so and the results appeared worthy.

David Bersoff[4] explored what companies could do to make employees unwilling to commit wrongdoing. He built on research by professors Gresham Sykes and David Matza,[5] who had identified five ways people justify their own wrongdoing: by denying personal responsibility (uncontrollable outside forces made it happen), by denying injury (no one got hurt), by denying there were 'victims' (they deserved what they got), by criticizing critics (they are misguided) and by appealing to higher loyalties (serving a worthy purpose – the Milgram scenario). 'Five ways people justify actions ...', said a student who asked that her name not be used. 'I believe most people have used them at one point in their lives or another.'[6]

Bersoff tested 'employees' by paying people too much money for participating in a psychology laboratory experiment and then watched to see who would take the extra money and who would try to give it back.

He found people were significantly more likely to report the overpayment if the experiment included events that helped people recognize they would be taking the money from a real person (there is a victim), or gave them practice handling an ethics scenario (someone may get hurt), or directly asked if the payment was correct (personal responsibility).

People in Bersoff's experiment responded to 'interventions' any company can use to improve its climate and its culture.

## Improving climate and culture

Every company and every organization has both a climate and a culture. Most people accept whatever climate and culture exist at a company: 'It is what it is.' However, people do aspire to be ethical and to work for an ethical company. They want to work for a thriving company they can be proud of. They want their work to feel meaningful, productive, contribute good to the world and promote values they hold dear. If a company's climate and culture do not meet those needs, people look for work elsewhere.

This is an important truth. A few years ago, at a company ethics meeting, an employee of a *Fortune* 500 manufacturing company volunteered the following experience. The employee said when he went to a neighborhood Christmas party in previous years, a number of people said how lucky he was and what a great company he worked for. 'That made me feel really good.' Recently his company came into the public eye for an ethics scandal. This year, people were coming up to him and saying, 'What the hell is going on with your company?' Needless to say, he did not feel good about that.

It is wise company strategy to appreciate that people bring good ethics from home to the workplace. It is good practice to consciously develop the organizational climate and culture to support employees' aspirations. Do this by involving all leaders in constantly encouraging employees to feel it is safe to live by their personal ethics and to believe it is safe to openly approach leaders and 'challenge up' to prevent an ethics failure.

Right here some people raise an objection: 'Let employees live by their *personal ethics?* Some people have ethics I would not feel comfortable with!'

We are not talking about instant coffee. We are talking about developing sustainable organizational climate and culture. To do that, adjust and shape personal and corporate ethics through the influence of laws, personal and company values, corporate policies and the expectations of co-workers so that climate, culture and personal ethics have high congruence.

As noted earlier, 'climate' is the expectations, policies, procedures and methods the company uses to influence employee behavior. 'Culture' is what employees believe, value and actually do. Culture always trumps climate. Climate and culture are most powerful when they are congruent. Design them to prevent wrongdoing, to eliminate ethics failures and to eliminate the need to punish anyone.

Useful concepts come from Professor Edgar Schein, who analyzed culture at three levels:

- artifacts, which are things people can see, hear or touch;
- espoused values, which are what people and companies say they value and which translate into artifacts; and

- underlying beliefs and assumptions, some unconscious, which translate into the espoused values.[7]

To shape its organizational climate, a company can create artifacts, espouse values, listen to employees' own espoused values and endeavor to identify and reinforce widely shared values and honor the beliefs and assumptions that underlie them. A company that does not deliberately build, monitor and adjust its climate is at high risk of an ethics failure.

To shape its organizational culture, a company must depend on its employees choosing to 'do the right thing'. With respect to business ethics, what most needs explanation is not why some people violate rules and ethics but why most people work so hard to do the right thing. Employees are not inherently bad; in truth, most employees come to work inherently good. What organizational climate can do is reinforce employees' opportunities and capabilities to achieve the high ethics they already aspire to, thus involving employees in creating the corporate culture the company aspires to have.

## Build a trust system

Chapter 3 identified the fundamental purpose of business ethics as building trust, helping people make wise choices that prevent problems, and protecting people from harm. This chapter defines the fundamental purpose of a corporate business ethics *program:* to build a trust system – that is, to create a corporate climate that fosters a culture of trust and high ethics. The inputs to the trust system are artifacts and values that create an organizational climate helping people make good, ethical decisions, pulling 'bad apples' up to ethical norms and providing help to handle 'bad cases'. The output from the trust system is organizational culture – people willing, able and doing ethical things.

What we expect to emerge from a trust system is high ethics, morale and loyalty, plus credibility, effectiveness, personal satisfaction and competitive edge. Research indicates people who come together with trust resolve problems faster than people who come together without it.[8]

What we can expect to emerge when trust is absent is disaster. For example, look at what happened at a lightning-caused wildfire on the north side of Mann Gulch, Montana, on August 5, 1949.

Fifteen US Forest Service smokejumpers parachuted onto the south side of Mann Gulch and met up with a ranger who had already arrived on site. As the jumpers hiked toward the fire, foreman 'Wag' Dodge saw flames cross to their side of the gulch. The wildfire now was burning toward them, about 200 yards ahead.

Dodge ordered the jumpers to escape by turning around and running up a steep hill through 2½-feet-tall grass. They could see 30-feet-high flames racing behind them, overtaking them. As a last resort, foreman Dodge lit a new fire directly in front of the jumpers and ordered them to lie down where it had burned. Dodge set the example by lying down in the hot ashes.

After the wildfire had passed, Dodge rose out of those ashes and began searching for members of his crew. Instead of following his order and his example, all of them had tried to outrun the flames, to reach the top of the ridge before the fire did. Only two succeeded. The other 13 died because, under the stress of that situation, they 'were unable to make any sense whatsoever of the one thing that would have saved their lives, an escape fire'.[9] For whatever reasons, they did not trust their leader.

'They trust me ... don't they?' That is a powerful question to ask and intuitively we know it speaks to the heart of company ethics. It is difficult, perhaps impossible, to be successful without having the trust of people both inside and outside the organization. Francis Fukuyama, a scientist at the Rand Corporation, saw trust as rising from shared values that give people ability to work together for common purposes and to subordinate individual interests to the good of larger groups. Fukuyama wrote a book titled simply: *Trust.* He believed trust is critical not only to an organization but also to society in general and to every aspect of economics.[10]

## Three types of trust

The three types of trust in the business environment are institutional, relational and calculative.[11] 'Institutional trust' is organizational reputation. 'Relational trust' is people's feelings of identification with a group. 'Calculative trust' is people's judgment that others will cooperate.

### Institutional trust

People trust organizational reputation and trust you because you are a member of that organization. Imagine what reception a new college graduate would get if he or she appeared in New York City asking to rent a theatre. Would the reception be different if that graduate said at the outset, 'Hello, I'm from The Walt Disney Company'? People who start new jobs at 'a good company' expect to be able to trust its managers. Customers who place orders with 'a good company' trust it to deliver the right goods or service at the right time.

For some years, *Fortune* magazine has published an annual list titled 'The 100 Best Companies to Work For'. Although not every company chooses to be considered for inclusion, the very existence of this list highlights a truth: people want to work for a 'good company'. They will quit a company they find lacks institutional trust; high employee turnover often marks an untrustworthy firm.

Society has created organizations specifically to provide institutional trust: certified public accountant and bar association recognition create initial trust for CPAs and attorneys, although subsequent experience may lead people to adjust their level of trust.

Other organizations provide institutional trust as a by-product, incidental to their primary purpose. Since 1909, *Good Housekeeping* has issued its seal of approval for products accepted for advertising in its magazine. Since 1957, the American

Meteorological Society has issued its seal of approval to bolster trust for TV weather forecasters.

Companies sometimes reorganize specifically to create institutional trust, as when companies that have experienced a public ethics disaster replace the old managers with new ones. A highly visible example was Hewlett-Packard. Following its 2006 ethics disaster, Hewlett-Packard replaced the chair of its board of directors, its chief ethics officer and its general counsel.

Research shows that to generate the most institutional trust, organizations should value effectiveness more than efficiency.[12] In terms of the well-known business trilogy – cost, schedule and quality – effectiveness equates to quality while cost and schedule both relate to efficiency. Quality is really another side to ethics because quality is a promise and keeping promises generates trust, just as the opposite also is true.

Companies deliberately invest in building institutional trust. Witness the common thread linking these historic slogans:

> The Quality Goes In Before the Name Goes On. (Zenith)
>
> Quality Is Job 1. (Ford)
>
> We Bring Good Things to Life. (General Electric)
>
> Breakfast of Champions. (General Mills)
>
> Don't Leave Home Without It. (American Express)

All are aimed directly at winning the trust of customers and simultaneously the trust of employees, potential employees and the community. The effect is stronger than some imagine: to its own surprise, Intel's advertising sticker, 'Intel Inside', was widely credited with creating trust for any computer it appeared on.

Our college students see huge institutional trust problems in today's world. 'Top executives of [redacted] spent the weekend … at the lavish St. Regis resort in Monarch Beach, California,' said Jenny. 'This retreat occurred just days after the [company] was granted millions and millions of [financial bailout] dollars by the federal government. This retreat cost $44,000 … executives pampered themselves without any remorse for their behavior that paraded their affluence at the taxpayer's expense. … The excessive spending did not end. … [A]n additional $86,000 was spent on four executives' deluxe English hunting trip. … [then] they spent $343,000 on yet another executive retreat in Phoenix, Arizona.'[13]

'What if I told you that there is a business out there that knowingly sells harmful products to the public?' asked Arash. 'What if I told you that the products that this business sells have been conclusively proven to cause aneurysms, leukemia, cataracts, various cancers, periodontium disease and pneumonia? What would you say about that, I wonder? What I am talking about, if you have not guessed it by now, are the cigarette companies.'[14]

## Relational trust

When people identify with a group, they feel relational trust. What people have learned about the group makes them feel a 'personal connection' to their manager or other group members. *Esprit de corps* highlights relational trust. It underlies school spirit and the spirited names chosen by youth sports teams. The converse also appears true: human resources professionals say people quit managers, not companies, which implies that absence of relational trust of the manager poisons people's relationship with an otherwise trustworthy company.

The relational aspect, the group 'gestalt', needs to be emphasized. Atul Gawande, a physician who has won recognition for writing about healthcare in *New Yorker* magazine and *Slate* online magazine, marveled at a simple research discovery: surgeons who chose members of their operating team 'almost randomly', used different members – competent professionals all – for each operation, and held no team meetings were observed to not perform as well as surgeons who picked team members they had worked well with before, who used the same professionals every time and who convened team meetings both before and after the operation – working as a partner with the team.[15]

'Partnership' is a key concept. Research shows people are more willing to accept a supervisor's decisions if they believe that supervisor is their friend or believe the organization's values agree with their own, personal values.[16] How to maximize relational trust? '[E]mployees' trust is higher', reported one research team, 'when they are satisfied with their level of participation in decisions. ... When managers share control, they demonstrate significant trust in and respect for their employees. ... The emphasis in communication is on sharing and exchanging ideas.'[17] Organizations should value open communication among supervisors and employees so everyone feels listened to and no one fears retribution for having spoken up.

'We want good news to travel fast and bad news *even faster* up the line,' Ron Sugar told managers and employees when he first took charge as CEO of a *Fortune* 100 corporation. 'We need to be mindful of honestly communicating problems as well as breakthroughs. The sooner we communicate a problem, the easier it is for us to marshal our company's resources to solve it.'[18] Open communication allows problems to be identified and corrected when they are small, before they have time to grow into catastrophes that overwhelm corporate resources.

As evidence that companies invest in building relational trust, consider how many create formal or informal 'teams' to jointly deliver high quality results. So, the dealership that services your car organizes a team linked to each service-writer to encourage the mechanics to feel mutually accountable for delivering good results. The company that manufacturers airplanes organizes a product team to encourage everyone designing the plane, buying parts for it and assembling those parts to feel mutually accountable for building a great airplane.

People are aware of a common problem that interferes with relational trust. 'Workplace bullying is sad and pathetic,' said our student Veronica. 'It is childish and should have no place in a working environment. Colleagues should respect each other and work together to be productive and efficient. Personal problems should be checked at the door before walking into the building, but if that cannot be done then people should seek help to resolve them.'[19]

Recognition of bullying as a workplace problem is recent. Previous generations urged each other to be 'thick skinned' so as to endure it. European nations, Australia and Canada are trying to legislate against it, much as legislation confronts sexual harassment and discrimination. Similar efforts in the United States have not yet created anti-bullying laws.

Many behaviors constitute bullying, e.g. yelling, name-calling, micromanaging and withholding information.[20] A Columbia University survey indicated 33 percent of employees have been bullied. The World Health Organization (WHO) identified many impacts: confusion and embarrassment that undermine self-confidence and cause anxiety, depression, panic attacks, high blood pressure, migraines, fatigue, muscle pain and ulcers.[21] Compliance laws may prove capable of eliminating bullying in the workplace someday; business ethics has potential to eliminate it much faster.

In sum, relational trust has long been recognized: all for one, one for all; united we stand, divided we fall.

## Calculative trust

People's judgment that others will cooperate is calculative trust.

In social terms, what people have learned about each other gives them feelings about what other people may do based on appreciation of their values, experiences, goals and abilities.[22] Real people making real decisions often do this by choosing a solution that will suffice (accepting a choice that may not be perfect but in their experience will be 'good enough'), or discarding solutions that fail a particular test (never buy a bright red car), or by using bias and shortcuts such as choosing a solution that looks similar to a previous success (this worked last time).[23]

Calculative trust frequently surfaces as a problem in companies when people lack positive expectations. Consistently, across all types of corporations that operate ethics call centers, about 60 percent of the calls report a breakdown in this type of trust. These problems lie in the human resources–employee relations domain. The most common phrase is, 'It's not fair'. Sometimes the complaint is that a supervisor acts unfairly; sometimes it is that a co-worker behaves unfairly. The underlying issue is lack of trust that a supervisor or a co-worker has cooperated, is cooperating, or will cooperate.

'Fairness' is a sensitive issue. Research indicated many children (60 percent) develop preference for equal treatment by age eight,[24] but by age 17 recognize altruism and at times are willing to accept unfair treatment if it seems reasonable.[25] In a *New York Times* article, one of the researchers said teenagers' tolerance of inequality has limits. ''One for me, two for you' may not be too bad, but 'one for me, five for you' would not be accepted.'[26]

In this arena, government legislation created compliance rules focused on correcting some of the trust problems: requirements not to discriminate based on race, religion, gender and so forth, and requirements to investigate every complaint of sexual harassment. This governmental approach encourages people to appreciate and respect diversity.

How to maximize calculative trust? Appreciate that trust is a psychological state, a person's willingness to be vulnerable to actions of another person based on positive expectations about that person.[27] The key term, we think, is 'positive expectations'. For success in building calculative trust, it is not enough for a person to be personally trustworthy; a person must be able to create an environment of positive expectations.[28] Similarly, it is not enough for a business leader to be personally ethical; the leader must be able to create an environment that enables and encourages ethical activity by all members of the organization.

Here are two stories shared by college students about failure of calculative trust. Rosalie said, 'One of my very close friends and her male co-worker arrived late to work one day, at the exact same time. Instead of both of them getting in trouble, the manager only asked her to go back home. She was punished for arriving late, but her male co-worker was able to stay at work and was not punished at all. … A moral manager would have given both equal punishments for arriving late, instead of letting the male get away with it.'[29]

'The first job I ever had,' recalled Brittany, 'I worked at [redacted], and I had a very money-driven manager who made some poor decisions when serving food. When preparing the sandwich toppings for the day, we were never allowed to throw out expired vegetables … he always required us to use old lettuce, avocados and tomatoes if they were still somewhat presentable. I always had a hard time bringing myself to do this, so I would throw it out in a very discreet manner. One time he caught another food preparer doing this and fired her. So I contacted the health inspector … my manager was finally caught.'[30]

Returning briefly to the Mann Gulch disaster, Professor Karl Weick's analysis indicated that institutional trust should have been high. At that time, the Forest Service's four principles for dealing with fire emergencies were to start a backfire, get to the top of a ridge where fuel is thinner, turn into the fire and try to work through it and pick the spot where the fire hits you (do not let the fire pick the spot). Weick opined that Dodge trusted those principles: he led his jumpers toward the top of a ridge, picked a spot to face the oncoming flames and lit an escape backfire. What broke down primarily, according to Weick's analysis, was relational trust. The smokejumpers had not established a sense of team in advance and they did not keep each other informed of what they were doing and why.[31] To cope with this emergency, relational trust needed to already exist because when you are running from flames that are licking at your back, it is too late for much talk. The other two jumpers who survived demonstrated calculative trust;

they 'stuck together' and were lucky to find a 'crack in the ridge' to escape through.

Calculative trust is not blind. It is a person's judgment that available information warrants the risk of placing trust in another person.

## Measuring trust

Measuring trust is subjective. Unlike the output of a manufacturing system that can be objectively counted, perhaps the number of shoes completed each day, the output of a trust system is likely to vary by individual and certain to vary by viewpoint. The president of a company probably has very different expectations of a good company trust system than does the ordinary entry-level employee, the mailroom or office clerk.

Subjectivity explains why employees award low grades to a company's trust system if they simply perceive that their supervisors do not teach and enforce compliance rules which everyone must follow to stay out of trouble.

As a practical approach to measuring trust that any company's own staff can use at virtually no cost, we suggest the following two-step process.

### Step one

Convene at least two 50-minute focus groups (of five to ten employees each), or individually interview at least ten employees, to discuss several topics drawn from the following questions. Good practice would ensure the participants include a cross-section of employees at all levels and are chosen at random.

- What kind of example do managers set at all levels? Do they model the company's values?
- What job performance expectations increase the possibility of unethical activity?
- Are company values integrated into work (and if so, how?) or are they an occasional add-on?
- Is company data presented frankly and honestly, or is it 'tweaked' to make someone look good?
- How are the company's values used to plan work strategies and implement human resource policies?
- How does the company maintain a work environment that places high value on, and promotes, ethical behavior and integrity?
- How do the company's operational and performance requirements put pressure on you to cut corners? Would quality be sacrificed for schedule?
- Are companies that sell supplies to our company treated like partners and are they expected to meet the same ethical requirements we do?

- What impact does the company's attitude towards ethics have on employees' or on managers' behavior?
- What is the one thing the company could do to make you feel it really values ethical behavior?
- What anecdote or key indicator sends you a message about our company's actual ethical climate?

With respect to this last question, one of the authors asked a senior vice-president for finance, 'Is there some example you can give in which the company sacrificed financial gain for principle?' Without hesitation he answered, 'The company had a building it no longer needed. It had been on the market for a long time when someone brought an offer of $500,000. I agreed and we shook hands.' Between the handshake and closing, another potential buyer brought an offer of $1 million. 'I went to the [company] president, told him the story and that we had nothing signed or legal but that I had given my word and I thought we should sell to the first buyer. The president agreed and we did.' While the company in fact lost money, it preserved its reputation and, given the fact that we are relating it many years later, the value that the company got from this decision that burnished its reputation is of considerable value.

## Step two

After the focus groups or interviews have been completed, analyze the information obtained to answer the following questions.

- Do employees show familiarity with the company's values?
- Are ethics important to employees?
- Is a company message that ethics and compliance are important coming across clearly?

A thoughtful critic might ask, 'How do those questions measure trust?' The answer is that they probe members of the organization for what they have learned about behaviors evidencing trust or revealing symptoms of trust problems, much as a physician probes for indicators of possible heart disease by asking a patient, 'Do you often feel colder than other people? Can you walk for 30 minutes? Do you often feel out of breath?' To sharpen the ethics focus, the following three questions could be asked directly during focus groups and interviews or answered as part of the post-session analysis.

- Do employees feel the company values effectiveness more than efficiency? (An institutional trust probe)
- Do employees feel supervisors encourage open communication and listen to everyone? (A relational trust probe)
- Do employees have positive expectations about other people in the company? (A calculative trust probe)

## Complex adaptive systems

Climate, culture, customs, rules, laws and influences from outside and inside the company – it is very complex and a trust system needs to be sensitive to all of them and prepare employees to respond effectively to all of them.

A goal is to reach the point where customs, values and beliefs have been communicated so clearly that employees know what is expected of them without having to be told. Compliance programs are necessary but not alone sufficient to achieve that. Employees will not trust a company that does not protect them from trouble, so supervisors at each management level must teach and enforce the compliance programs or the trust system will receive low grades because employees will not trust the supervisors.

But the trust system needs to be built on more because compliance programs are controls, not trust, and it is impossible to create enough controls to handle every situation employees face. The trust system needs to be built on leadership. Leaders are supervisors and managers as well as executives. In fact, leadership ought to be a company value and employees at all levels ought to be expected to exercise it.

A trust system clearly is a complex adaptive system (CAS) and that proves to be good news because, surprisingly, research shows that CAS are governed by simple sets of rules.

In the mid-1980s, researchers at the Santa Fe Institute in New Mexico began to study 'the spontaneous self-organizing dynamics of the real world', which they called CAS.[32] A major discovery was that a small set of simple, well-chosen rules can govern a large, complicated system. Craig Reynolds showed how a flock of birds can soar together, swooping through the sky, frequently and rapidly changing directions, with no apparent leader. Reynolds was able to simulate the same behavior on a computer using just three rules: (a) every bird maintains a minimum distance from other objects and birds, (b) every bird tries to match the velocity of nearby birds, and (c) every bird tries to move toward the center of nearby birds.

Margaret Wheatley observed similar patterns in business ethics, saying that if an organization has strong commitment to values, then you can observe any employee and 'tell what the organization values and how it chooses to do its work'. Such coherence, she said, 'is achieved not through compliance to an exhausting set of standards and rules, but from a few simple principles that everyone is accountable for, operating in a condition of individual freedom.' For organizations with integrity, Wheatley said, values 'are truthful representations of how they want to conduct themselves, and everyone feels deeply accountable to them'. She emphasized that trusting each person to work freely with those values, to talk about them, interpret and learn from them, will result over time in a pattern of ethical behavior 'recognizable in everyone, no matter where they sit or what they do'.[33]

Corporate values now become a powerful influence because they are the 'few simple rules' that drive the CAS, the company's trust system. In summary, corporate values often include such characteristics as quality, people, integrity and leadership. When applied to current problems, for example, a CAS can self-organize to build institutional trust by practicing knowledge management so the company does not lose the lessons learned (the quality value). A CAS can self-organize to build relational trust by developing participative management and honoring due process in human-resource practices and dispute resolution (the people value). A CAS can self-organize to build calculative trust; the CAS achieves this because individual employees assess their colleagues' capabilities, competence and performance, apply penalties when trust is not reciprocated or fulfilled, and reward achievement by granting trust (the integrity value).

Efforts to influence trust systems, to maximize trust, are smoothed by 'equifinality', a characteristic of a company's ethics system. Equifinality means desired results can be reached from many different starting points and by using many different methods.[34] It allows people to explore an array of acceptable solutions and not demand that everyone use a single, rigid approach. People should recognize and appreciate that no single, universal best solution exists and the best solution to choose depends on the situation, the specific need and the environment.

## Dissatisfiers

Years ago, management professor Frederick Herzberg and his colleagues discovered that people associated distinctly different events with job satisfaction and job dissatisfaction.

The satisfiers were things like achievement, recognition and advancement. Managers turned their attention to how companies could best deliver satisfiers because they were 'motivators' that caused employees to perform better work.

The dissatisfiers were things like policies and administration, supervision and relationships with other people at work – categories that well describe the majority of 'business ethics complaints'. Herzberg labeled these dissatisfiers as 'hygiene factors'. Hygiene factor failures make a company a bad place to work, create an unethical corporate climate and culture, and can lead to misconduct which damages or destroys a company.

> *Wait a minute …*
>
> *This discussion is focused on 'employees' – regular people. Weren't the ethics scandals that made certain corporations infamous, the scandals we've all heard about, caused by executives rather than by working-level employees? The rogues were executives and managers who violated laws and company policies, who violated the trust the company places in supervisors and who took advantage of customers, employees and other people.*

Exactly right: hygiene violations. Trust is a hygiene element.

Actually, the image of ethics scandals as caused by executives is only a half-truth, because executive scandals tend to draw publicity and prosecutors try to catch the big fish. When working-level employees make an ethical misstep, the incidents often are hidden from public view by privacy protections afforded by the normal course of business.

At any level, hygiene violations damage trust and degrade organizational climate and culture. Hygiene violations contribute significantly to confusion about ethics and its role.

## Challenge puzzle

Consider the puzzle faced by Coca-Cola Co. Why were there different outcomes in Belgium and India?

In June 1999, Belgium banned Coke products because more than 240 people in Belgium and France reported health problems possibly caused by Coke. Complaints included headaches, dizziness and stomach upset.

The company recalled beverages – 17 million cases – from five European nations, the largest recall in the company's history. It also offered to cover healthcare costs for anyone affected. The recall cost about $250 million. CEO Douglas Ivester said the company's 'success has been based on the trust that consumers have … that trust is sacred to us'.

Investigation determined that Coke products did not cause the health problems. Coke sales in Belgium recovered after the recall was lifted and three years later sales were better than ever.

In August 2003, an environmental group in India alleged that Coke and other soft drinks contained high levels of pesticides. Coke and other soft drink makers made public data refuting those allegations.

Beverages were not recalled. India's health minister questioned the validity of the environmental group's research and tests by both government and independent laboratories cleared Coke. Nevertheless, Coke sales dropped and after three years Coke reported sales were continuing to decline.[35]

Why different outcomes?

---

[1] Zimbardo, *The Lucifer Effect*.

[2] Milgram, S 1963, 'Behavioral Study of Obedience', *Journal of Abnormal and Social Psychology* 67(4): 371-378. Milgram, S 1974, *Obedience to Authority*, Harper & Row, New York.

[3] Veronica [Redacted], email to authors, October 3, 2008.

[4] Bersoff, DM 1999, 'Why Good People Sometimes Do Bad Things: Motivated Reasoning and Unethical Behavior', *Personality and Social Psychology Bulletin* 25(1): 28-39.

---

[5] Sykes, GM & Matza, D 'Techniques of Neutralization: A Theory of Delinquency', *American Sociological Review* 22(6): 664-670.

[6] [Redacted], email to authors, October 12, 2008.

[7] Schein, *Organizational Culture and Leadership*, 17.

[8] Meyerson, D, Weick, KE & Kramer, RM 1996, 'Swift Trust and Temporary Groups', in RM Kramer & TR Tyler (eds), *Trust in Organizations: Frontiers of Theory and Research*, Sage, Thousand Oaks, CA, 166-195. 'The Gurus Speak: Complexity and Organizations' 1999, *Emergence*, 1(1): 73-91.

[9] Weick, KE 1993, 'The Collapse of Sensemaking in Organizations: The Mann Gulch Disaster', *Administrative Science Quarterly* 38(4): 628-652 at 634.

[10] Fukuyama, F 1995, *Trust: The Social Virtues and the Creation of Prosperity*, Free Press, New York.

[11] Rousseau, DM, Sitkin, SB, Burt, RS & Camerer, C 1998, 'Not So Different After All: A Cross-Discipline View of Trust', *Academy of Management Review* 23(3): 393-404.

[12] Whitener, EM, Brodt, SE, Korsgaard, MA & Werner, JM 1998, 'Managers as Initiators of Trust: An Exchange Relationship Framework for Understanding Managerial Trustworthy Behavior', *Academy of Management Review* 23(3): 513-530.

[13] Jenny [Redacted], 2008, AIG Rescue Fund Spending, unpublished manuscript.

[14] Arash [Redacted], 2008, Ethical Dilemmas that We Face with Cigarette Companies, unpublished manuscript.

[15] Gawande, A 2002, *Complications: A Surgeon's Notes on an Imperfect Science*, Picador, New York, 29-30. Pisano, GP, Bhmer, RMJ & Edmondson, AC 2001, 'Organizational Differences in Rates of Learning: Evidence from the Adoption of Minimally Invasive Cardiac Surgery', *Management Science* 47(6): 752-768.

[16] Tyler TR & Degoey, P 1996, 'Trust in Organizational Authorities: The Influence of Motive Attributions on Willingness to Accept Decisions', in RM Kramer & TR Tyler (eds), *Trust in Organizations: Frontiers of Theory and Research*, Sage, Thousand Oaks, CA, 331-356.

[17] Whitener *et al.* 'Managers as Initiators of Trust'.

[18] Sugar, RD 2003, *Business Conduct Officer Handbook*, 4th edn, Northrop Grumman Corporation, Los Angeles, CA.

[19] Veronica [Redacted] 2008, email to authors.

[20] Meyers, L 2006, 'Still Wearing the 'Kick Me' Sign', *Monitor on Psychology* 37(7): 68-70.

[21] Stambor, Z 2006, 'Bullying Stems from Fear, Apathy', *Monitor on Psychology* 37(7): 72-73.

[22] Doney, PM, Cannon, JP & Mullen, MR 1998, Understanding the Influence of National Culture on the Development of Trust', *Academy of Management Review* 23(3): 601-620.

[23] Scholars of decision theory call the 'good enough' approach 'satisficing' and the discard of solutions that fail a particular test 'elimination by aspects.'

[24] Fehr, E, Bernhard, H & Rockenbach, B 2008, 'Egalitarianism in Young Children', *Nature* 454(7208): 1079-1084.

[25] Fehr, E, Rützler, D & Sutter, M 2011, 'The Development of Egalitarianism, Altruism, Spite and Parochialism in Childhood and Adolescence' (Discussion Paper No. 5530, 2011), Institute for the Study of Labor website, viewed 21 January 2012, http://ftp.iza.org/dp5530.pdf.

[26] Angier, N 2011, 'Thirst for Fairness May Have Helped Us Survive', New York Times, viewed 21 January 2012, www.nytimes.com/2011/07/05/science/05angier.html.

[27] Rousseau *et al.*, 'Not So Different After All.'

[28] Treviño, LK & Brown, ME 2004, 'Managing to Be Ethical: Debunking Five Business Ethics Myths', *Academy of Management Executive*, 18(2): 69-81.

[29] Rosalie [Redacted] 2008, Untitled, unpublished manuscript.

[30] Brittany [Redacted] 2008, Untitled, unpublished manuscript.

[31] Weick, 'The Collapse of Sensemaking.'

[32] Waldrop, MM 1992, *Complexity: The Emerging Science at the Edge of Order and Chaos*, Simon and Schuster, New York.

[33] Wheatley, MJ 2006, *Leadership and the New Science: Discovering Order in a Chaotic World*, 3rd edn, Berrett-Koehler, San Francisco, 129.

[34] Cummings, TG & Worley, CG 1993, *Organization Development and Change*, 5th edn, West, St. Paul, MN, 89.

[35] Ivester, D 1999, quoted in 'Coca-Cola 'Regrets' Contamination', viewed 21 January 2012, http://news .bbc .co.uk/2/hi/europe/371300.stm. Pirson, M & Malhotra, D 2008, 'Unconventional Insights for Managing Stakeholder Trust', *MIT Sloan Management Review*, 49(4): 43-50. Leith, S 2002, 'Coke's European Challenge: 3 Years After Recall, Sales in Belgium at Their Best', Atlanta Journal-Constitution, 1A.

# Chapter 5

# The 'campaign'

## Low cost or no cost

### LEARNING OBJECTIVES

By the end of this chapter you should:

- □ be able to use a catalyst model to organize a business ethics function.
- □ understand strengths and weaknesses of various approaches to ethics training.
- □ know the role of an organization's code of ethics.
- □ be familiar with a process for analyzing ethics training needs.
- □ be familiar with conflict of interest certificates.

## FALLACY 4: COMPANY ETHICS PROGRAMS ARE EXPENSIVE, TIME-WASTING, AND OF LITTLE PRACTICAL VALUE

About $7.6 million – that is how much the Boeing Company budgeted for one year of its ethics program, according to Warren Rudman, the attorney and former US Senator who assembled a team to act as external, independent examiners of Boeing's ethics program. And that same year, Boeing expected its ethics program to be over budget, to actually spend about $9.2 million.

A number of people – not a scientific sample – have commented that their company (not necessarily Boeing) schedules them for ethics training once a year. 'We show up, play a game about ethics and then return to work like we did before.' Anecdotes like these give people the idea that corporate ethics programs are expensive, of little practical value and time wasted. Obviously they can be, but they do not have to be. A company's business ethics 'campaign' can be low-cost or even 'no-cost' and effective – perhaps more effective than a high-cost campaign would be.

The notion of 'low-cost or no-cost' can be misleading. There is actually no scenario where an ethics effort is completely no cost, but there are scenarios where the effort involves only money already spent (sunk costs) and no new funding (prospective costs). The important idea is that an effective ethics effort can be accomplished by respecting and conserving the business resources (time and money) that every other effort (marketing, manufacturing, research, human resources, finance, etc.) is asked to conserve.

Three guiding principles are useful to recognize from the outset.

- Leaders must create and promote the high ethics environment. That role is theirs.
- Employees need easy access to a local, front-line ethics specialist – someone well respected and able to make a connection with employees as well as administer the ethics process.
- Public policy expects the company to specify a high-level person responsible for the compliance and ethics program corporate-wide and to provide the resources necessary for success. In addition, it expects the company to specify individuals within the organization who are responsible for day-to-day ethics program operations.

It is a mistake to think that specifying 'a high-level person' to be responsible allows a business to delegate ethics to an ethics officer or an ethics function. At all levels, it is leaders – all of them – who are responsible for creating an open environment that allows and encourages employees to surface problems, big or small, and challenge conduct they believe is illegal, in violation of company policy, inconsistent with company values or not in the best interests of the company. Sometimes companies express that thought by saying that employees should 'respectfully' surface problems. 'Respectfully' imposes a burden. Employees should feel there are no requirements to surface a problem except truth and an honest motive.

Leaders set the tone. It is easy to spot commitment when you see it – and even easier when you do not. Leaders should be models of behavior so employees can easily recognize their leaders' commitment to company values, both in word and in deed. Simply put, an ethics program cannot succeed if the leaders' commitment to ethics is not real and obvious.

## Organizational design

How a company should organize to ensure ethical excellence does not have a simple answer. Two organizational design macro issues are (a) what role an ethics function should perform, and (b) who should lead the ethics function.

### The role

Is an ethics program a funnel or a catalyst? People sometimes think the ethics office is a funnel through which an organization channels all of its ethics work. Not true. That violates a key principle: leaders must create the ethics environment. Realistically, the ethics office is a catalyst fostering everyone's ability to independently initiate good ethics work. When an ethics program is working really well, leaders and employees throughout the company visibly take responsibility for making good ethics decisions quite independently every day in every way.

Independence in decision-making does not mean employees act entirely alone – they do consult with each other – but ethics decisions must be decentralized. They cannot all be routed through the ethics office because there are not enough ethics officers. Span-of-control realities are clear. Companies with 100,000–200,000 employees may have roughly 60–130 ethics officers. Some may work ethics full-time, some 'part-time' as a major component of their job, and some address ethics as an 'additional duty' – an occasional task – which is common at small sites. At best (130 ethics officers for 100,000 employees) the ratio is one ethics officer for each 769 employees. At worst (60 for 200,000) the ratio is one ethics officer for each 3,333 employees. Either way, ethics officers would be overwhelmed if they were expected to directly manage every ethics decision by every employee.

The same companies with 100,000 to 200,000 employees typically also have a manager-to-employee ratio of about 1:6, so managers have genuine opportunity to influence many ethics decisions by many employees. It is vital that all managers be ethics leaders, not just the top managers. Still, can managers be everywhere all the time? People sometimes must – or choose to – make decisions independently. This reality supports the premise that every employee must learn to handle ethics issues.

An ethics office is only a facilitator, a helper. The role of actually building a culture that expects and encourages managers and employees to successfully handle ethics issues independently belongs to all leaders in the company. Those leaders must focus on helping all employees achieve their goal of highly ethical behavior.

## Ethics function leadership

Uncertain about who is competent to lead business ethics, companies have tested several solutions. Today, a person appointed chief corporate ethics officer might be in the finance, audit, law, engineering, contracts, human resources, diversity, or corporate public relations department, and a person with any of those backgrounds might handle ethics really well. However, every placement has a reasonable rationale but, on further examination, also has a reasonable objection. Four examples are law, finance, public relations and training.

*Law*

Looking at what so many companies do, apparently it is difficult to overcome a penchant for placing the ethics function in the law department or general counsel's office. Ethics does require, at a minimum, compliance with the law, but some critics object that corporate lawyers are advocates whose role is to protect a company from legal problems by using the law to a company's advantage.

An individual lawyer could be a good ethics officer — we know some who are — just as a human resources, contracts, finance or other employee could be. But the function, no matter who does it, should not be located in the law department or the company's legal operation (general counsel's office, etc.), whatever it is called, because of potential for conflict of interest between the company's ethical best interests and legal best interests. One CEO who encountered such conflict said severe criminal allegations sent the company into defensive mode in a legal sense, but that hindered the ability of managers to look at the situation, perhaps change what the company was doing, and thereby prevent recurrence of the events that allegedly were criminal. In that instance, the management decision was to be open enough to fix the problem, and thereafter deal with the legal aspects as best as possible.

Michael Josephson was a law school professor undertaking to teach a course on ethics exactly the way he would teach any other law school course: by focusing on how to make issues narrow and discover loopholes — here are the rules and how to get around them. Then the light dawned! A new father, he asked himself, 'Do I want my son to grow up in a world where people think about ethics the way I teach the subject?' His answer: No! That was not the ethical world he or his son should live in.[1] Laws and ethics are not alien to each other, but they are not the same.[2] Now Josephson, a prominent full-time ethics teacher and consultant, focuses not on laws, rules and loopholes but on inspiring, developing and honoring strong character. Do other lawyers experience the same epiphany?

Professor Linda Treviño warns companies not to focus too much attention on laws and rules and forcing people to conform to standards. She says too little attention is given to the 'aspirational element' – fostering a culture that allows people to perform at the high ethical levels they want to achieve.[3]

### *Finance*

A reason to appoint a finance or audit manager to be company ethics officer is that some companies have long relied on those functions to identify and enforce compliance requirements in their particular regulated industry. This view was reinforced by the role of the finance department in implementing Section 404 of the *Sarbanes-Oxley Act* of 2002. One objection raised in finance circles is that it is difficult to find a finance or audit manager who is proficient in all of the compliance requirements in all of the functional realms (which include human resources, safety, finance and technical functions) and proficient in managing human relationships, investigation of violations, consistency in discipline and coordination with the board of directors.[4]

### *Public relations*

Because ethics and corporate reputation go hand-in-hand, corporate public relations representatives may be appointed to be the company's ethics officer. The International Association of Business Communicators Research Foundation reported that 1,827 public relations professionals responding to a survey said they are expected to advise management on ethics issues. One objection noted by those same survey respondents was that more than 70 percent claimed they had no ethics education or training.[5]

### *Training*

Education and training are important components of the business ethics environment. Should trainers be in charge of ethics? Popular recommendations are to 'send everyone through ethics training' and to 'require annual ethics training for all employees'. Professional trainers often label that approach 'sheep dip training', characterizing it as a bath everyone is sent through to 'disinfect' them and satisfy some administrative checklist. Realistically, sheep dip training does not change the hearts, minds or behaviors of employees because it only exposes information to people. They may not be interested and listening. It violates a fundamental principle: people must buy into and own the ethics process if it is ever to become effective.

Analyze the options: ideally, business ethics operates across silo functions, is multi-disciplinary and includes elements of law, accounting, public relations, education, training, organizational development and management. That analysis suggests that business ethics is a general management role. Leadership must draw together the functional expertise of many people. So the chief ethics officer might best be located in the organization responsible for developing, maintaining and promoting the company culture. In small companies that would mean a general manager. In large companies, it might mean a fifth option: put organizational development professionals in charge of ethics because developing corporate culture and getting people to 'buy in' is what they do.

A corollary is that below corporate level, at department or individual level, business ethics also calls for general management skills — exactly the skills that managers at those levels have, or at least need and are developing.

## Ethics committees' role

The purpose of an ethics committee is to build a high ethics culture by wisely applying the gamut of resources available to the company. Therefore, the members of the committee should be the key, senior functional *leaders* of the business unit or site. Even in very small organizations where the owner or lead executive performs the ethics officer role part-time such person should have an advisory group of trusted associates to perform the ethics committee tasks.

How many ethics committees a company should have is uncertain. Major business units should have one, and we have seen sites with a history of ethics problems benefit from at least temporarily having one. Each committee's charter should focus on four tasks:

1. first and foremost, to use the full resources of the company to foster interventions that establish ethics policy, deliver a consistent and integrated ethics message and build a high ethics climate and culture;
2. to monitor ethics problems to learn what broad issues need to be addressed somehow by interventions;
3. to oversee and ensure that people with appropriate expertise expeditiously resolve problems surfaced by the ethics process and apply analysis and corrections to ensure similar problems do not recur; and
4. to support and guide the work and decisions of individuals assigned the task of ethics officer.

For example, the committee is using full resources of the company and building ethics culture if it gets all managers out of their functional silos by bringing them together for collective leadership discussions, education and training. We have heard graduates say such conferences focused on everything a leader needs to know for success and conclude in retrospect, 'That was *all* about ethics!' This can create peer influence at its best. One leader said, '[This company] spent a lot of money sending all the managers through leadership training. We did surveys and … we all had our heads screwed on the right way.'

### *Front-line ethics officers*

Some controversy exists about which leader the local, front-line ethics officer should report to. If leaders throughout the company truly are responsible for creating the ethics of their organization, then the front-line ethics officer might serve as the operational agent of, and be hard-lined to, the business unit/site manager and have a dotted-line relationship — for technical, professional direction and support relevant to ethics – to the high-level person assigned overall responsibility for the entire corporation's compliance and ethics program.

In our experience, that organizational design works well. An alternative design sees front-line ethics officers as agents of, and hard-lined to, the high-level person assigned overall responsibility for the entire corporation's compliance and ethics program with a dotted-line relationship to their business unit/site manager who provides support to them in matters relevant to ethics.

Boeing Corporation is a noteworthy example of the controversy. It was in 2003, after Boeing experienced several very public ethics scandals, that the US Air Force barred three Boeing units from federal government contracting and assistance. Boeing did not contest the suspensions. Instead it undertook to regain its customers' confidence. To that end, the company's board directed Boeing to engage Warren Rudman, then a lawyer in private practice and formerly a United States Senator from New Hampshire, to independently study the structure and organization of Boeing's company ethics and compliance programs, the overall ethics culture at Boeing and Boeing policies for handling competitors' proprietary information.[6]

At the conclusion of that study, the Rudman report first emphasized the principle that leaders should take responsibility for ethics, saying, 'We cannot stress enough how important it is for senior executives to incorporate into their everyday planning and communications the unambiguous message that ethics, integrity and compliance are at the core of Boeing's corporate culture.' Then it recommended Boeing reorganize its ethics function: ethics staff assigned to business units 'should report directly up through the ethics office, with "dotted line" reporting/support responsibility ... to management of the relevant business unit'. The aim of hard-lining all ethics officers to the senior corporate ethics officer – a silo ethics organization – was so that employees would see the ethics staff as independent.[7]

The principle of equifinality – the ability to achieve desired results from many different starting points and using many different methods – probably means a company could build an effective ethics program using either the decentralized (catalyst) or centralized (funnel) organizational design. But the decentralized approach seems to encourage leaders to take personal responsibility for building the corporate ethics culture and the centralized approach seems to encourage them to delegate ethics to a silo ethics organization instead.

Front-line ethics officers often have other, major, primary job assignments to perform at their sites and hold the ethics role as a part-time additional duty. Nevertheless, the company and employees depend on them to *connect* with employees, to so manage the ethics program at their location that they open two-way channels for ethics information between the company and employees. They ensure the integrity of channels for ethics information: they make all ethics issues visible to senior leaders at both local and corporate levels so 'cover-ups' by any single, misguided leader become procedurally impossible. That protects both the company and its leaders from suspicions of intentional wrongdoing.

Front-line ethics officers provide leadership in coordinating and passing down ethics policies, procedures, plans and training materials to leaders and employees, and they are a resource people can turn to for assistance or when an issue needs elevation to a higher level of attention. They advocate using the ethics contact telephone line, promote the company values, facilitate ethics and compliance training by competent authorities and do the hands-on ethics administration.

Front-line ethics officers coordinate investigation, analysis and disposition of alleged violations of compliance rules or the code of conduct. To do so, they need analytical skills. Ethics issues can surface in many ways, so for problems revealed by the ethics process or brought to them in any way they must be able to identify systemic problems that need correction, identify and refer to high levels of management issues that may warrant intense professional investigation or reporting outside the company, and efficiently refer non-ethics issues to the responsible function (e.g. employee relations, benefits, security, law).

Front-line ethics officers need to participate in staff and other meetings at all levels to increase the ethics and compliance program's visibility and to discuss relevant ethics issues. Periodically, as function professionals, they need to convene as one group with the high-level person assigned overall responsibility for day-to-day direction of the entire corporation's compliance and ethics program to exchange ideas, to make plans, to share experience and to support each other.

To help open all doors for two-way communication, the training and communication facilitated by front-line ethics officers should include briefings for new employees, temporary employees and consultants. It should include information on the company's ethics contact telephone line as a resource available to help answer ethics questions and concerns, and on the company's values and code of conduct that should guide them as long as they are acting on the company's behalf.

To support tone-at-the-top, front-line ethics officers advise corporate executives on ethics issues and advocate inclusion of the ethics message in speeches — both internal and external — and in other communications, such as the annual report, marketing brochures and memos to employees.

The front-line ethics officer should coordinate with the procurement staff to ensure ethics program expectations and materials reach the company's suppliers. Close contact with the procurement staff can uncover opportunities to emphasize the ethics message, for example, by presenting at supplier conferences, by sending periodic reminder letters, and by creating specific publications — both hard copy and electronic — for suppliers.

Expect each supplier to have and abide by its own code of conduct, a code that is consistent with the customer corporation's and with the US Sentencing Guidelines for Organizations and other public policy expectations. In the past, several large companies asked suppliers to contractually promise to abide by the customer company's own code of conduct, a request impractical for suppliers that serve *many* large companies.

*High-level responsible person*

The title given to the corporation's high-level person responsible for day-to-day ethics operations varies by company. Recently, the title of 36 percent of the Compliance and Ethics Leadership Council membership list showed 'vice president' or 'senior vice president'. Other titles included 'head' or 'global head', 'general manager', 'chief', 'director' and 'deputy'. What drives the position is the corporation's own need for an erudite ethics leader and the public policy expectation that the corporation will designate a specific individual and provide adequate resources, appropriate authority and direct access to the governing authority.[8]

This high-level person – for convenience we will call the position the corporate ethics director – plays a key role by providing technical direction and support that set the corporation's ethics self-image, the attitude everyone connected with the corporation will take toward ethics and the ethics program as a symbol of the entire company. Here is where key issues are raised and resolved, where executives are inspired to 'walk the talk' and also to 'talk the walk'.

The corporate ethics director has four missions: program oversight, policy guidance, company-wide goals and strategies and education.

'Program oversight' means supporting company leaders in their advocacy of the company values and establishing consistent, efficient processes to handle ethics issues across the corporation. That includes formal monitoring and evaluation of ethics based on information from the ethics contact telephone line, fostering adherence to regulatory obligations and consultation on consistent discipline for code of conduct violations. The director periodically briefs the corporation's board of directors or a committee thereof.

'Policy guidance' means serving as a point to clarify ethics-related policy. It ensures the implications of ethics policies are clearly and specifically communicated in the code of conduct and that geographically separated site procedures are consistent with corporate procedures. Working with the law department, the corporate ethics director updates ethics policies to meet new or amended requirements.

'Company-wide ethics and compliance goals and strategies' are developed in concert with company leaders, including the corporation's board of directors as now expected by several public policy documents – the *Sarbanes-Oxley Act* of 2002, the US Sentencing Guidelines for Organizations, and the Delaware court's Caremark decision – and front-line ethics officers. Annual targets and plans are made compatible with the company's business strategies. Key planning elements include management interviews, annual audit results, employee surveys, conversations with customers, input from front-line ethics officers and collateral coordination with other functions throughout the corporation.

'Ethics education' responsibility requires the corporate ethics director to identify best practices and trends inside and outside the company and provide that information to management and front-line ethics officers. The director acts as a source of internal ethics expertise and the clearing house for initiatives on ethics programs, process and delivery. The director leads training to develop front-line ethics officers and oversees both the needs analysis and the guidelines for ethics training for the workforce.

Generally, the corporate ethics director supports senior management's creation of company ethics in every respect, develops the skills of front-line ethics officers, communicates to leaders appreciation of their work in the ethics arena and ensures employees have the information and awareness they need to make ethical decisions.

### *Qualifications to be an ethics officer*

Any representative of the ethics program needs to be an approachable person employees will trust and will perceive as fair and responsive. At one time or another, the ethics officer is asked to assume the role of counselor, teacher, or investigator. The ethics officer needs talent as a communicator — a listener, a speaker and a writer — to constantly reiterate the ethics message with innovation and creativity to keep it fresh in employees' consciousness.

### *Strategic concerns*

Five strategic concerns deserve ethics officers' continuing attention:

- *Coordination.* The ethics office does not replace other functions. When employee concerns are received at the ethics contact telephone line but are not ethics-related, the normal procedure is to refer them to the function that has responsibility for the topic and the expertise to address the concerns. However, those functions often are not organized to systematically receive, process and respond to employee concerns, so the company must build initiative into the ethics process to ensure those functions work on the issue and give the employee an adequate response.
- *Prevention.* Analysis to identify patterns, trends, new risks and root causes is required. Investigation of ethics concerns is vital and management action to resolve them is important but both are episodic, like a physician prescribing medicine to alleviate symptoms of an illness. What remains are the necessary analytical steps to cure the root problem to prevent recurrence of the same or foreseeable problems.
- *Protecting reputation.* In every inquiry, truth, objectivity, impartiality and protection of privacy are paramount. People's reputations and futures are at stake. It is just as important to prove people innocent when that is true as it is to prove people guilty when that is true.
- *Keeping employees.* The 'hanging tree' is not the only option when a person is found culpable of a mistake. Punishment can serve four ends:

prevention (a painful consequence to motivate everyone to avoid future mistakes), rehabilitation (a lesson to teach the person how to work properly), incapacitation (firing people so they cannot hurt the company again) and retaliation (imposing suffering as a consequence for misdeeds). Removing an employee from a job sometimes is necessary, but rehabilitation is culturally preferred and deserves to be maximized. In business, imposing painful consequences to motivate people or retaliating to cause them suffering are unwise strategies. Stanford professor Jeffrey Pfeffer reported that at the Men's Wearhouse company policy was to not routinely fire employees caught stealing, but instead to have a discussion about obligations and offer them a second chance, to give them opportunity to develop their own human potential.[9]

- *Effective investigation.* When an allegation is raised, the company needs an objective, thorough and reliable investigation – fully coordinated with the law department – to resolve it. Fundamentally, this requires four steps: (a) interview the complainant when possible (do not rely on just a written report describing the initial telephoned complaint); (b) find physical evidence if it exists (usually business records); (c) interview all 'eyewitnesses'; and (d) interview the individual accused of the wrongdoing to hear that person's side of the story.

A frequent flaw in investigations, something the front-line ethics officer may be able to prevent, is inadequate investigation by a well-intentioned person who takes shortcuts. Especially to be avoided is the inquiry that skips straight to step (d), an inquiry that consists only of asking the accused the leading and self-defeating question, 'You didn't do this ... did you?'

No single best practice prescribes how to organize the ethics office. Companies should choose the best practice for their particular company in its particular situation. A fault visible today, and one the US Sentencing Guidelines for Organizations discourages, is the number of companies that fail to provide any visible ethics organization.

## Approaches to ethics training

Promoting an ethical climate and culture requires a communication plan which encompasses training. Three approaches are 'annual', 'periodic', and the 'campaign model':

- 'Annual training' appears to be a stereotype of how required training should be forced on an organization and its employees. It is a convenient way to check off 'training completed' on paper, and people typically respond to it with token compliance and little behavior change. Typically it is one training session per year, of 1–4 hours, and frequently that is imposed as a standard as part of the company's legal agreement settling a government complaint.

- 'Periodic' is a better phrase to recognize need for refresher training from time to time and to formally allow flexibility in the training schedule by not being locked into an annual cycle.
- The 'campaign model' adds even more flexibility because it aims to constantly pepper employees with ethics messages, realistically engage and refresh their active interest and achieve real behavior changes. This approach takes lessons from successful political campaigns: be 'on message', be repeated, and be delivered by multiple vehicles.

## Campaign model

Research shows the campaign model works best when it reinforces people's pre-existing attitudes,[10] so it fits hand-in-glove with a positive organizational development environment that believes most employees already have high ethics and work hard to be ethical. Research also confirmed that printed communication contributes most to the campaign model when supplemented by face-to-face communication such as ethics instruction that leaders personally give to their direct reports.

To enhance successful use of the campaign model for ethics:[11]

- Encourage intensity in people's belief in high ethics, values and trust for the corporation.
- Give people a clear vision of how to achieve the high ethics goal.
- Develop the visibility and ability of the ethics staff to help people achieve the goal.
- Create psychological 'short-distance' — people's perception that their investment of a little energy will yield large progress toward the high ethics goal.
- Put eye-catching posters everywhere, especially in lobbies, conference rooms, cafeterias and break rooms and change them periodically to draw fresh attention by showing a fresh face. Posters should promote the company's values and promote the ethics contact telephone line.
- Publish ethics messages in company newsletters. They demonstrate tone-at-the-top and familiarize people with how workplace scenarios might relate to company values, or to the company's code of conduct, or to laws, rules and regulations the company must comply with.
- Discuss ethics scenarios in staff meetings and embed ethics principles in other meetings and training courses of all sorts, for example, as a module in the company's annual internal audit meeting. This is face-to-face communication to supplement printed communications and a tone-at-the-top message: this company takes business ethics seriously. Issues discussed in a particular work group are apt to be most relevant to their work setting. People may not get an hour of 'training' at one sitting but much more than an hour if they spend 15 or 20 minutes discussing ethics

at multiple regularly scheduled meetings, such as staff meetings. Also relevant to such discussions is the notion of 'piggyback', where the ethics office gets a place on the larger agenda at various corporate-wide meetings or function-wide meetings (finance, quality, marketing, audit and so forth).

- Leaders should include references to ethics in their talks and speeches both inside and outside the company. They should seize opportunities to be active participants and presenters at industry and business-wide ethics and compliance conferences, as Ron Sugar did speaking as CEO of Northrop Grumman at the US Naval Academy in 2003 and again in 2007, as Josue 'Joe' Robles Jr did speaking as CEO of USAA insurance at the ECOA Sponsoring Partners Forum, and as Jim Skinner did speaking as CEO of McDonald's Corporation to the Society of Corporate Compliance and Ethics conference.

Warren Rudman's report on Boeing provided an important clue in effectively developing ethical climate and culture at low cost or no cost. At Boeing, in-person training in a group format led by the employees' manager with give-and-take discussion appeared to effectively impart information and ensure employees perceived managers as serious about ethics. This is a low-cost or no-cost effort: when company managers take charge of ethics and train their direct reports to make ethical decisions independently, business ethics becomes part of day-to-day operations, a mentoring approach that requires little or no special time and expense. Research shows employees learn best from their own managers.

## Needs analysis

The starting point for training is a 'needs analysis'. It is an iterative process to focus training effort on the most important topics. Like a financial budget determines how the limited resource called money should be spent to fill the most important purchasing needs, a training needs analysis determines how the limited resource called training – money, staff, time and perhaps other limitations as well – should be spent to fill the most important training needs.

The needs analysis process steps are:

1. identify possible objectives;
2. prioritize: identify important objectives;
3. assess current resources;
4. identify final objectives; and
5. repeat from Step 1.

Inputs for all steps can come from multiple sources. For ethics training we look especially for inputs from the experience of front-line ethics officers, from evaluation of recent ethics investigations, from search of the business ethics literature, and from the perspective of the company's leaders.

The ethics officer's needs analysis basically addresses four major topics:

- awareness (compliance training);
- values (as a basis for decision-making);
- service (the ethics contact telephone line, inquiries and investigations); and
- skills (for front line ethics officers)

Typically, the management and organizational development component within the training department addresses the category of topics the ethics office is interested in. They do not automatically know what ethics training to offer. Their question, like the ethics officer's, is what training is needed for good business reasons? To the extent that the ethics office can help them answer that question objectively, the ethics office can influence what they teach.

Examples of training sponsored jointly by the ethics and organizational development functions include corporate-wide leadership feedback (sometimes called 360-degree or multi-level feedback) and leadership training seminars.

## Online training

A word about online training: on its face it appeals to the cost-conscious and it has its uses, but be careful. While we are not fans of online training, it may be getting cheaper to develop it effectively in-house. In any case, while it is administratively easy to track and check, it is not as effective as in-person training can be and certainly not recommended as the sole training solution.

For a large corporation with employees scattered around the world, online training allows courses to be delivered to all employees, including people working alone or at small, remote sites. All employees are given the same message, and completion can be perfectly documented by name, date, time and who completed exactly what training (and who failed to). Costs for classroom space, training publications and instructor travel are avoided.

But from an effectiveness viewpoint, if online courses are purchased from a vendor, then the content may not match the company's environment. Developing custom software is typically time-consuming and expensive. And employees who see online, brochure, or game-based training as unappreciative of what they already know may be sufficiently uninterested that they learn little or nothing.[12]

In 2007, a number of Illinois state employees were asked to repeat mandatory ethics training they had 'completed' online. Supervisors said some employees finished too quickly – 80 computer screens of information in three or four minutes.[13]

At dinner recently, the dean of a major business school mused that some well-known universities have experimented with online courses, and even online master's degrees, but have pulled back because they perceived negative impacts on the quality of learning and their school's reputation. Some courses, he said, lend themselves more to online courses – accounting, for example. Courses that require extensive reasoning and values-based decision-making benefit from face-to-face classes. Business ethics is a prime example. Online training for business ethics appeals to people who simply want to check off completion of an annual requirement. Effective training for business ethics requires face-to-face discussion.

But what about reaching those isolated employees that some companies have working alone in 'remote' locations around the world? For speedy briefings, online training may work. But for effective training, the company needs to deliver face-to-face training when the isolated employees are pulled back to company headquarters for periodic coordination meetings. Where resources permit, consider personal visits to small, isolated company sites. Personal experience in visiting 10 sites was that the 'ethics guy' was the only visitor from corporate most of them ever had. The visit elevated the ethics profile at those sites and opened their two-way ethics communication channel with corporate by making them feel comfortable because they knew they could chat with a friend.

Online training, brochures and games usually are closed-end training interventions based on sets of rules (ethics dynamic Stage 1). They have pre-determined answers that experts defined as right, partially right, or wrong and may not fit the complexity of a current situation.

## Small group discussions

Scenarios for in-person small group discussions have potential to rise above other training methods by encouraging participants to explore what might change decisions about what is the right thing to do. 'Book answers' become only starting points for serious discussions (ethics dynamic Stage 2).

Everybody brings values to discussions. 'Values' essentially are individuals' sense of what 'ought to be', which they often compare with 'what is'. Everyone also brings tacit wisdom to discussions. 'Tacit wisdom' is the sum of their life experiences that tells them what will or will not work.

By appreciating the values and tacit wisdom participants bring to work, group discussions build on human strengths, help the organization to self-organize around shared values and, through peer influence, draw outliers toward group norms.

If a few trained facilitators must lead all discussions face-to-face, reaching all employees of a large corporation could take months, if not years, and be expensive. But if the training is designed to be delivered simultaneously by all of the corporation's managers, reaching all employees face-to-face can be accomplished quickly at low or no cost.

Three fundamental principles of adult learning are worth keeping in mind:

- Adults want to learn what they believe they need to use now.
- Adults retain best what they learn through personal experience and discovery.

- Adults perceive themselves as busy. They want to minimize the time spent to learn anything.

Rudman's blue-ribbon report to Boeing said that the give-and-take of group discussions led by employees' own managers 'is most effective, not only in imparting information, but in ensuring that management at all levels is seen to view these issues with the utmost seriousness'.[14]

Feedback from employees indicates they find scenario training at staff meetings memorable. A number indicated they worked one scenario per meeting throughout the year, thus elevating ethics to continuing education rather than once-a-year training.

What succeeds is to position each manager as a discussion administrator or facilitator rather than as a subject-matter expert. Have the managers conduct the training as an agenda item in a normal business meeting. Provide the small groups ethics scenarios as discussion prompts and 'book answers' to score their own results. Encourage them to discuss why their answer, if it varied from the book answer, might be more correct. To use this well, managers receiving the scenarios also need to receive a clear, uncomplicated lesson plan, and a channel to elevate special questions to corporate experts. It helps managers who are not strong communicators. In extreme cases, an ethics officer can offer to help lead this kind of training, but only with a commitment from the manager that he or she will be present throughout the training program.

## Conflict-of-interest training

Conflict of interest is one of the most prevalent ethical problems in society. It rears its head in politics, local government, education, business hiring and even in youth sports programs. Every business faces potential conflict-of-interest situations. So companies should ask employees to sign a conflict of interest certificate when hired and periodically thereafter. Lawyers look upon the certificates as valuable to use in an internal investigation or even in court. They confront an accused employee with the document, asking 'Is this your signature?' Only a few certificates ever will be used in this fashion. It is best for the ethics officer to look upon the certificate as an educational tool and as much as possible give clear guidance to employees who sometimes can fall unwittingly into a conflict of interest.

Sometimes explaining and clarifying can be the most difficult part of conflict-of-interest training because people have a hard time understanding that simply the appearance of conflict can be a real issue. A prominent example became news in the OJ Simpson trial. Although Judge Lance A Ito was criticized for the way he conducted the trial, one thing he got right was an exquisite understanding of conflict of interest. Prosecutor Marcia Clark indicated she might want to call as a witness Los Angeles Police Department Captain Margaret York to testify about her dealings with Detective Mark Fuhrman, who at one time worked under her supervision.

The problem? Captain York was the wife of Judge Ito, the trial judge. In chambers and on the record, Judge Ito told attorneys for prosecution and defense:

There is potential that one side or the other may wish to call my wife as a witness with regard to Mr. Fuhrman. If that happens, then under the code of civil procedure section 171.1, sub (a) sub (1), I'm required to disqualify myself as the trial judge in this case.

Judge Ito declared that he had no 'personal knowledge of my wife's dealings with Mr. Fuhrman while she was a lieutenant at West LA and the watch commander back in 1985'. But the problem was appearances, not what Judge Ito actually knew. The problem was whether people would believe he could make decisions faithful to the requirements of law, and the possibility that some would believe he could not. In the interest of the institution of justice, Judge Ito asked for another judge to rule on whether 'my wife is a material witness, whether or not she has any relevant, admissible or material information to offer'.[15]

Judge John H Reid ruled there was 'no reasonable expectation' that Captain York could contribute anything relevant to the trial, she was not called as a witness and Judge Ito was not disqualified and remained trial judge.

View the conflict-of-interest certificate as a communication and training tool. It alerts employees to what conflicts look like in a way that is hard to ignore. It can alert employees to possible conflicts that they may have and surface those potential conflicts in a non-threatening way so the employee and the company can work together to shield the employee from work assignments that would create an actual conflict of interest and possibly lead to wrongdoing.

The certificate needs to be tailored to the company's business, but as a minimum probably should ask:

1. Are you or any member of your family an employee, officer, or director of any company that does or seeks to do business with our corporation? ('Family' means spouse, parent, siblings, children, grandparents and grandchildren, and in recent years has been broadened to include 'significant others'.)

2. Do you or any member of your family own, directly or indirectly, a substantial financial interest in any supplier or prospective supplier? ('Substantial' means ten percent or more of your own net worth, at least five percent interest in a publicly-traded company, or any interest in a non-publicly-traded company.)

3. During the last year, have you or any member of your family received, directly or indirectly, from a supplier or prospective supplier anything which has a value in excess of ten dollars? ('Anything' includes travel, entertainment, gifts, gratuities, cash, free or discounted services, free or discounted use of facilities, compensation, commissions, fees, services, honorariums, or payments of any kind.)

4. Has a debtor/creditor relationship existed at any time in the last year between you or any member of your family and a supplier or prospective supplier? (Excludes loan or credit transactions at current market rates.)
5. Have you directly or indirectly revealed company proprietary matters to any unauthorized persons or have you used company proprietary information in any way to promote your own business or personal interests?
6. Do you or any member of your family have any other interest or arrangement which may violate the company's standards of conduct or may otherwise result in an actual or perceived conflict of interest?

What to do with completed forms? While it is tempting to file them in employee personnel records, experience indicates it is better to have the company's ethics office keep them together, grouped by year of completion and alphabetized. This facilitates an annual audit, by the ethics office, comparing employee rosters to certificate lists to ensure that every active employee has signed a certificate sometime during the year.

## Codes of ethics

An organization's code of ethics should be a vision statement defining *how* a company aspires to conduct business. It is a communication document with legal implications, not a legal document. See it as composed of multiple documents: an easy-to-read vision statement that steers readers to details in laws, policies and governance documents. Some company codes are excessively detailed. Others are excessively simplistic. Many are so preoccupied with law enforcement and legal self-defense that they poorly articulate the values, beliefs and precepts of a desirable corporate culture.

A code of ethics need not spell out every rule and detail. It should express goals employees set for themselves. People invest enormous energy to achieve such goals; they are virtually unstoppable. A code should include general values and behaviors that employees are apt to encounter. For example, it should be clear that as a general rule all employees should avoid accepting gifts from anyone doing business or seeking to do business with the company, and this is especially so for those in areas like procurement who are more apt to receive offers of gifts from suppliers. Where exceptions are necessary, they should be detailed in company policies and procedures.

## Challenge puzzle

It is called 'OCI' – organizational conflict of interest. It arises when (a) an organization (b) has a business interest in a situation and (c) a business responsibility to a third party. If the business interest and the business responsibility even appear to possibly conflict, then an OCI exists.[16] Here are four examples.

1. Under contract to the government, Company A (pseudonym) prepared specifications for radio equipment. The government used those specifications to advertise for companies to supply that equipment. Company A submitted a bid.[17]

2. Under contracts to the government, Company B (pseudonym) manufactured undersea systems and is developing more undersea systems that may supplement or replace systems manufactured by competitors. The government wants to contract for Company B to assess the performance of undersea systems the government already has deployed. (A complication may be that any company capable of assessing the performance of such systems probably is a manufacturer of systems already deployed or being developed for future deployment.)[18]

3. The Environmental Protection Agency wanted to contract for Company C (pseudonym) to study the economic and environmental impacts of the Clean Air Act's provisions regulating acid rain. Company C had unrelated contracts with electric utilities and a coal company, industries already identified as prime contributors to acid rain.[19]

4. The Defense Industry Initiative (DII) and the US Federal Sentencing Guidelines for Organizations ask companies to police themselves to eliminate unethical behavior within their own organizations. Does this encourage companies to eliminate visibility of unethical behavior rather than eliminate the behavior itself?[20]

It's a puzzle: How to deal with OCI when the best bidder(s), the companies most competent to do the work, have or appear to have such conflicts?[21]

---

[1] Josephson, M n.d., personal communication. Accord in Morris, T 1997 *If Aristotle Ran General Motors: The New Soul of Business*, Henry Holt, New York, 143.

[2] Daly, FJ 1998, 'Rules and values are ethical allies', *Center for Business Ethics News* 6(2): 3, 7.

[3] Treviño, L 2006, 'The Honorable Student', *BizEd* 5(6): 26.

[4] Krell, E 2006, 'Compliance watch: the walking, talking compliance risk', *Business Finance*: 17.

[5] Communicators Divided Over Role as Ethics Counsel to Management: New ABC Study, 2006, *PRWeb*, viewed 22 January 2012, www.prweb.com/pdfdownload / 38419.pdf.

[6] Rudman, WB *et al.*, 2003, A Report to the Chairman and Board of Directors of The Boeing Company Concerning the Company's Ethics Program and Its Rules and Procedures for the Treatment of Competitors' Proprietary Information, Boeing, Chicago, IL, viewed 22 January 2012, www.boeing.com/news/releases/ 2003/q4/rudman.pdf.

[7] Rudman *et al.*, 'A Report'.

---

[8] 2004, Guidelines Manual, United States Sentencing Commission, Washington, DC, §8B2.1.

[9] Pfeffer, J n.d., personal communication. O'Reilly, CA III & Pfeffer, J 2000, *Hidden Value: How Great Companies Achieve Extraordinary Results with Ordinary People*, Harvard Business School Press, Boston.

[10] Kotler, P & Roberto, EL 1989, *Social Marketing: Strategies for Changing Public Behavior*, Free Press, New York.

[11] Kotler & Roberto, *Social Marketing.*

[12] Brown, KG 2001, 'Using computers to deliver training: which employees learn and why'? *Personnel Psychology* 54(2): 271-296.

[13] State Employees Fail Ethics Test by Going Too Fast, 2007, Associated Press, viewed 27 January 2012, www.pantagraph.com/news/state-employees-fail-ethics-test-by-going-too-fast/article_6d96ea47-d64b-5a48-b443-e0ca2ba15770.html.

[14] Rudman *et al.*, 'A Report. '

[15] Los Angeles County Superior Court, 'In Camera Hearing on Furman Tapes, Disqualifying Ito ' [transcript], 1995, viewed 22 January 2012, www.lectlaw.com/files/cas48.htm.

[16] Gordon, DI 2005, 'Organizational Conflicts of Interest: A Growing Integrity Challenge' (Public Law and Legal Theory Working Paper No. 127), George Washington University Law School, Washington, DC, viewed 22 January 2012, http://papers.ssrn .com/so13/papers.cfm?abstract_id=665274.

[17] 'Lucent Technologies World Services Inc., 2005, GAO Decision B-295462.

[18] 'PURVIS Systems, Inc., 2004, GAO Decision B-293807.3; B-293807.

[19] 'Selected Agencies' Efforts to Identify Organizational Conflicts of Interest', 1995, GAO Report to Congressional Committees GAO/GGD-96-15.

[20] 'Conflict of Interest', Wikipedia, 2011, viewed 16 October 2011, http://en .wikipedia.org/wiki/Conflict_of_interest.

[21] Brodsky, R 2010, 'Defense Scales Back Organizational Conflict-of-Interest Rule', Government Executive, viewed 22 January 2012, www.govexec.com/story_page.cfm?articleid=46798.

# Chapter 6

# The expectations
## Public policy

### LEARNING OBJECTIVES

By the end of this chapter you should:

- understand developments in three approaches to public policy on business ethics: compliance, corporate codes and self-regulation.
- be familiar with the US *Foreign Corrupt Practices Act* and the UK *Bribery Act* of 2010.
- be familiar with the Defense Industry Initiative and the US Sentencing Guidelines for Organizations.
- know the USSG standards for an effective ethics program.
- be familiar with the Caremark decision, New York Stock Exchange requirements and the *Sarbanes-Oxley Act* of 2002.

### FALLACY 5: ONE ETHICS PROGRAM IS AS GOOD AS ANOTHER — NO UNIFORM STANDARD EXISTS

In the United States, a public policy has been emerging that today provides a uniform standard for business ethics programs to meet. The policy has three interrelated tracks: compliance, codes of conduct and self-regulation. Comparison will help discern the trend and forecast future developments in public policy on business ethics.

# Compliance expectations

## US expectations

The first track may be considered 'traditional', and is how government usually addresses a business ethics problem: enacting a law to prohibit the bad action. A chain of compliance laws shaped the US business ethics policy into the 1980s.

For example, the *Sherman Act* of 1890, an 'antitrust' law, responded to concerns that corporations were trying to eliminate competitors and become monopolies. The *Sherman Act* and those that followed, such as the *Clayton Act* of 1914 and the *Robinson-Patman Act* of 1936, made illegal various actions that businesses might take to become monopolies.

Another influential law, the *Foreign Corrupt Practices Act* (FCPA) of 1977, responded to admissions by more than 400 US companies in the mid-1970s that they had paid bribes to foreign government officials, politicians and political parties to win contracts and facilitate their business. The FCPA aimed to prohibit public sector bribes. Originally the FCPA made it illegal for US persons to bribe foreign officials. In 1998 the law was extended to companies and people of any nationality while in the US, making it illegal to bribe foreign officials.

## International expectations

The international compliance effort was extended significantly by the UK *Bribery Act* of 2010. Broader and stricter than the FCPA, it aims to prohibit both public and private sector bribes. The UK *Bribery Act* (a) applies to behavior inside the UK or outside by a person/entity with a 'close connection' to the UK — citizen, resident, corporation or having any business operations in the UK, and (b) prohibits giving a bribe, receiving a bribe, bribing a non-UK public official and — for a business — failing to prevent a bribe.

The United Nations Office on Drugs and Crime (UNODC) advocates that 'businesses should not go below international standards contained in the United Nations Convention against Corruption'.

There are three myths about corruption:

1. *It wasn't me – it was the other guy.* That is wrong. Corruption involves two parties – someone offering money and someone else accepting it. Both are guilty.

2. *Corruption is a victimless crime – it is just a lubricant to grease the wheels.* No, corruption erodes integrity, undermines trust, is a hidden overhead cost and can destroy reputations.

3. *There is nothing that can be done about it – it is a part of doing business.* Wrong again. There is nothing inevitable about corruption. The less it is tolerated, the more a culture of cheating will be replaced by a culture of integrity.

As an example of what would be below United Nations standards, UNODC points to 'facilitation payments' – money that companies pay to accelerate a governmental process such as issuing drivers licenses or clearing customs inspections. UNODC laments:

> *For example, a facilitation payment is just a fancy name for a bribe, yet some companies allow them up to a certain threshold or under certain circumstances – or even consider them tax deductible.*[1]

## Enforcement

Compliance laws and regulations use government power to dictate what businesses may not do. Their strength is that they are enforceable; offenders can be taken to court. A major weakness is 'policing'; government must dedicate people, time and money to detect, investigate and prosecute offenses. From 1978 to 2000, the US prosecuted about three FCPA cases per year, which some characterized as ineffective enforcement – a wink and a nod. By 2008, the US Department of Justice (DOJ) had 60–100 investigations under way, and by 2010 had more than 130. This increase in the number of investigations is because of an initiative to eliminate corruption in business.

DOJ official Lanny Breuer said the US goal is to create 'global consensus that corruption is unacceptable'.[2] A DOJ press release said enforcement of the FCPA aims to maintain the integrity of US markets and create a level playing field for companies that want to 'play by the rules'. Clearly the *U.K. Bribery Act* supports the same goal, although it is too new to have established an enforcement pattern.

The business academic literature contains numerous articles calling US the 'lone voice' in 1977 for bribery reform as a moral duty. Other countries were called reluctant. Beverley Earle, in 1996, said that 'bribes are listed as a business expense' in Germany and reported that the German State Secretary of Finance, Joachim Grunewald, had stated that prohibiting bribes 'would damage German firms in the international market and threaten jobs'. According to Earle, a German industry spokesman said they are not bribes – they are marketing costs.[3] About the same time, Nora Rubin reported that cross-border bribery is tax-deductible in Germany, France and several other countries.[4]

In 1997, the OECD (Organisation for Economic Cooperation and Development), a successor to the OEEC (Organisation for European Economic Cooperation) that ran the US-financed Marshall Plan for reconstruction after World War II, undertook to influence other countries to adopt laws similar to the FCPA to combat bribery of foreign public officials in international business.

The OECD plan was ratified by enough countries so as to take effect on February 15, 1999. By 2011 a total of 38 countries had signed it, with Germany and France among them, and both countries adopted stricter anti-bribery laws.

Germany's progress has been documented in particular. Where Germany once allowed companies to deduct bribes as a business expense, it now prosecutes companies that pay bribes.[5] OECD examiners reported that Germany now prohibits deduction of unlawful payments, encourages companies to comply and has reported increased number of cases of bribery that have been detected and investigated. The examiners believed this has had a deterrent effect on companies.[6]

Trace International, a non-profit membership association based in the United States of America and organized to develop effective anti-bribery resources for member companies, studied international anti-bribery enforcement trends. It found that 'most countries' have passed their laws prohibiting foreign bribery since 2000. How many of those countries enforce those laws? Trace opines that secrecy by governments and companies appears to hide many enforcement events. The information that is publicly available indicates that in the last 34 years just 24 nations showed enforcement of their foreign bribery laws and just 40 showed enforcement of their domestic bribery laws against foreign citizens or companies. US led the way, showing 3.5 times more foreign bribery actions than all other nations combined, followed by the United Kingdom.[7]

## Code of conduct expectations

The second track may be considered 'cultural'. Businesses have responded to the ethical climate they operate in by publishing their own corporate code of ethics. Recent research showed companies in the US publish ethical codes more often than companies elsewhere in the world.

By 1989, *Business Horizons* reported that 'management has responded to business scandals with company 'codes of ethics',' but found it difficult to analyze the 84 codes that were obtained from organizations listed in the *Business Week* 1000 because they were either: '(1) very different; (2) often similar; (3) not connected with ethics; (4) perceived as an important tool for fostering ethical conduct; and (5) not very effective in a broad ethical sense' — a welter of contradictions.[8]

In another study, Professors Cecily Raiborn and Dinah Payne wrote, 'Some codes are excessively detailed while others are excessively simplistic.'[9] Professor Betsy Stevens said, 'While ethical codes should promote law-abiding behavior, it appears they are preoccupied with law enforcement and self-defense and often do not rise above this plateau to successfully articulate the values, beliefs and precepts of a desirable corporate culture.'[10] Indeed, some long and detailed corporate codes of conduct look like they were written by lawyers and only for lawyers. Research has shown some that companies do not even distribute their codes to all their employees,[11] an error incredible at its face value as an indicator that the company never expected employees to know and abide by its code.

A strength of a corporate code of ethics is that it is – or should be – a readable, practical guide that a company can tailor to fit its particular organizational climate and culture, its particular values and the fundamental beliefs underlying those values, and the laws, policies and rules that because of its particular type of work deserve employees' special sensitivity and attention. A weakness of a corporate code is that people may not pay attention to it. An unread code influences and inspires no one.

Another code expectation is imposed by the New York Stock Exchange (NYSE) on its listed companies. Its influence on large companies has been sufficiently pervasive to indicate public policy. The NYSE expects listed companies to meet its corporate governance standards, which include a requirement for a code of business conduct and ethics. Generally, the code must encourage fair dealing and actively promote ethical behavior. Specifically, the code must include conflicts of interest, confidentiality, protection of company assets, compliance with laws, rules and regulations and company procedures to encourage good-faith reports indicating violations without fear of retaliation.

For perspective, when codes were first written in the 1980s, they were mostly written by lawyers; there was no understanding that 'code' in the ethics sense did not mean a code like the motor vehicle code or the criminal code. In a number of cases, these ethics codes were unreadable by most employees.

The need to make ethics codes accessible and useful to all employees redefined what 'code' means in the business ethics setting. It is important that a good code provides guidance consistent with the company's values in those areas that apply to all or a large number of employees. Loading it up with provisions and laws that apply to only limited areas of work is a recipe for making it irrelevant for the overwhelming number of employees. Without overdoing it, it is good to provide references to other documents – policies and procedures – that explain details and exceptions. The relationship between the ethics code and policies and procedures is important.

## Self-regulation expectations

The third track may be considered 'innovative' – an initiative government has taken to address business ethics problems more effectively: encourage self-regulation. This began in the 1980s and appears to be both successful and developing further.

Self-regulation was triggered by corruption in the US defense industry where, as of May 1985, the federal government was investigating a maelstrom of scandals, improprieties and allegations: 131 allegations against 45 large companies, allegations that included defective pricing, mischarging of costs and labor, unauthorized product substitutions, kickbacks and false claims.

A blue-ribbon commission headed by David Packard — the well-known co-founder of the Hewlett-Packard Company who had served from 1969 to 1971 as US Deputy Secretary of Defense — led the defense industry into a self-regulation plan that has strongly influenced US public policy. Officially titled The President's Blue Ribbon Commission on Defense Management, but informally known as the Packard Commission, its 16 members were appointed by President Ronald Reagan by executive order in July 1985. The commission's June 1986 report said:

> *Widely publicized investigations and prosecutions of large defense contractors have fostered an impression of widespread lawlessness, fueling popular mistrust of the integrity of [the] defense industry. A national public opinion survey, conducted for the Commission in January 1986, revealed that many Americans believe defense contractors customarily place profits above legal and ethical responsibilities. The following specific conclusions can be drawn from this survey:*[12]
>
> - *Americans consider waste and fraud in defense spending a very serious national problem and one of major proportions. On average, the public believes almost half the defense budget is lost to waste and fraud.*
> - *Americans believe that fraud (illegal activity) accounts for as much loss in defense dollars as waste (poor management).*
> - *While anyone involved in defense procurement is thought likely to commit fraudulent and dishonest acts, defense contractors are widely perceived to be especially culpable for fraud in defense spending.*
> - *In overwhelming numbers, Americans support imposition of the severest penalties for illegal actions by contractors — including more criminal indictments — as a promising means to reduce waste and fraud.*
> - *Nine in ten Americans believe that the goal of reduced fraud and waste also could be served through development and enforcement of strict codes of conduct. Americans are almost evenly divided, however, on whether defense contractors can be expected to live up to codes they develop for themselves.*
> - *Four in five Americans think that defense contractors should feel an obligation, when doing business with [the Department of Defense], to observe ethical standards higher than those observed in their normal business practices.*

The Packard Commission faced a conundrum: it was 'critically important' for the US government to fix defense contractor ethics, but 'no conceivable number of additional federal auditors, inspectors, investigators and prosecutors' could police them, nor had criminal sanctions worked in the past to ensure contractors' ethics.

## The defense industry initiative (DII)

The solution that emerged was a new approach called the DII on Business Ethics and Conduct. It required no new government police. Instead, the burden of policing contractor ethics was placed on the contractors themselves – self-regulation. By June 1986, 32 major companies signed up to self-regulation. The Packard Commission reported that each company pledged to meet seven standards:

- have and adhere to written codes of conduct;
- train their employees in such codes;
- encourage employees to report violations of such codes, without fear of retribution;
- monitor compliance with laws incident to defense procurement;
- adopt procedures for voluntary disclosure of violations and for necessary corrective action;
- share with other firms their methods for and experience in implementing such principles, through annual participation in an industry-wide 'Best Practices Forum'; and
- have outside or non-employee members of their boards of directors review compliance.[13]

For the defense contractors, signing up to the DII was not entirely altruistic. The companies hoped that effective self-policing would prevent the US government from pursuing a 'first track' solution: enacting additional compliance laws. Industry executives foresaw the government was likely to adopt extensive, stifling, rigid, complex, detailed and onerous ethics regulations to control defense companies. To head off such legislation, a number of defense companies encouraged the DII approach that committed them as formal signatories to a pact to stringently regulate themselves.

Since 1986, contractors and the US government have agreed that the DII has worked effectively. The industry-wide Best Practices Forum has 'leveled' the ethics playing field by giving every company in the industry equal access to business ethics ideas and methods that work well for other companies. If imitation is the sincerest form of flattery, perhaps the strongest endorsement of the DII is an effort in the US healthcare industry, in response to discussions with the US Department of Health and Human Services, to establish an ethics initiative modeled largely on the DII. Companies are better off collaborating with each other on ethics. Each company's ethics effort will have more punch if it is part of an industry-wide effort. Leaders in the industry talk and word gets out that your company has credible ethics without you having to engage the media.

In March 2010, the DII updated its core principles. The first six remain DII principles, although they were reworded and are now counted as five principles. Two major changes were (a) addition of a vision statement 'to uphold the highest ethical standards in all our business dealings with the government', and (b) elimination of the seventh principle, 'Have outside or non-employee members of their boards of directors review compliance.'[14] The intent of the update was to retain core elements of the original principles while 'the modified language … more forcefully conveys DII's commitment to ethical business and its focus on the key concepts of promoting ethical 'values' and 'culture''.[15]

The DII set a new direction for business ethics in the US by making companies responsible for policing themselves. Realistically, it recognized that government cannot afford to hire enough police to watch every company all of the time. Instead, it cast government as an over-the-shoulder auditor to judge whether companies' own ethics processes work effectively. It made government an on-call only-when-needed auditor to judge how well the companies were doing the ethics job.

## The US sentencing guidelines (USSG)

Within a few years, the US developed an even broader initiative by which the government encourages companies and other organizations in general — not in any particular industry — to voluntarily create high-ethics organizational culture programs and keep government in the over-the-shoulder as-needed auditor role.

In 1991, the US Sentencing Commission published guidelines for federal courts to help standardize punishment of corporations and other organizations convicted of crimes. The USSG extended general principles of the DII to all 'organizations' in the United States — corporations, partnerships, associations, joint-stock companies, unions, trusts, pension funds, unincorporated organizations, governments and political subdivisions of governments and non-profit organizations.

Because the DII gave defense companies a 'head start' on developing business ethics programs, those programs became models for all sorts of businesses and industries. The DII provided 'consulting' to the US Sentencing Commission, although what is not clear in the printed record is how strong the DII influence on the USSG was. What is clear is that the guidelines framers' thinking evolved from an 'optimal penalties' approach (companies caught in crime must pay fines calibrated to induce crime avoidance) to a crime prevention approach (guidelines so companies would know that living up to good citizenship would allow them low penalties if crime occurred despite their best efforts).[16]

The general design of the guidelines paralleled the DII plan: companies should voluntarily organize corporate ethics programs and police themselves. Only if the company was accused of a crime would the government look to see if the corporate ethics program met standards to be considered 'effective'.

This approach was based on three assumptions:

- Some companies are convicted of crimes even though their managers did everything reasonably possible to prevent and uncover wrongdoing —

employees broke the law despite the company's best efforts; while at other companies managers encouraged or directed the wrongdoing.

- Actions by managers can significantly reduce the likelihood and impact of corporate crime and, if crime does occur, identify and hold accountable the perpetrators and make other corrections that will prevent similar crimes in the future.
- The sentencing guidelines can provide incentives, a carrot-and-stick. If a violation occurs, a company with a good ethics program in place can receive a reduced punishment (the carrot) but a company with a bad ethics program or no ethics program will receive heavy punishment (the stick).

The USSG is not a mandate. It does not *require* any company or other organization to do any particular thing. Organizations may choose to voluntarily comply with the guidelines and potentially reap rewards, or they may choose to ignore the guidelines and potentially suffer draconian fines as consequences. Government takes the role of an over-the-shoulder auditor to judge whether organizations' own ethics processes work effectively.

As a practical matter, the USSG carrot-and-stick incentive offers three increasingly advantageous options. 'Good' is federal judges' authority to dramatically reduce fines if a company can prove that it already had an effective ethics program when a violation occurred. 'Better' is that discretion allowed US attorneys to not even take companies to court if they had an effective ethics program. 'Best' is the possibility that companies' effective ethics programs can prevent violations from occurring at all.[17]

## The uniform standard

The USSG, by defining an effective ethics program, established a uniform standard for business ethics programs to meet. It frequently has been described as 'seven steps', although it has always had more. It was amended in 2004 to add more characteristics. The standards are summarized below. They have been described by Win Swenson, one of the key people developing the guidelines, as not being a 'superficial checklist requiring little analysis or thought' and as being drafted somewhat generally so each can be satisfied by a range of possible approaches — 'a framework, not a highly specific course of action that companies can simply 'adopt''.[18]

1. A qualifying program has been 'designed, implemented and enforced' so that it generally will be effective. The company must have exercised diligence.
2. Establish standards and procedures to prevent and detect criminal conduct.
3. The organization's governing authority shall be knowledgeable about the content and operation of the program and exercise reasonable

oversight of its implementation and effectiveness. High-level personnel shall ensure the organization's program is effective, and specific high-level personnel shall be assigned overall responsibility for it. Specific individuals within the organization shall be delegated day-to-day operational responsibility, report periodically to high-level personnel and have adequate resources, appropriate authority and direct access to the governing authority.

4. Do not give substantial authority to anyone the organization knew, or should have known, has engaged in illegal activities or other conduct inconsistent with an effective ethics program.

5. Conduct periodic, effective training programs and otherwise disseminate information to members of the governing authority, executives, managers, employees and agents.

6. Ensure the ethics program is followed, including monitoring and auditing to detect criminal conduct. Periodically evaluate the effectiveness of the program. Publicize a system, which may allow anonymity or confidentiality, enabling employees and agents to report or seek guidance regarding potential or actual criminal conduct without fear of retaliation.

7. Promote and enforce the program consistently throughout the organization. Provide appropriate incentives to be ethical and appropriate discipline for criminal conduct and for failing to take reasonable steps to prevent or detect criminal conduct.

8. After criminal conduct has been detected, respond appropriately to that conduct and prevent similar conduct in the future.

9. Periodically assess the risk of criminal conduct and design the program to reduce the risk of that conduct.

10. Consider particular features of the company — size, kinds of business it conducts, prior history — to determine what actions are needed for an effective program.

11. Look to the company's external environment — to regulatory requirements and what others in the company's industry do — to ensure the program 'measures up'.

12. Promote an organizational culture that encourages ethical conduct and a commitment to compliance with the law.

Especially significant in the 2004 revision was the specification that companies should 'promote an organizational culture that encourages ethical conduct'.[19] The 1991 guidelines emphasized compliance (ethics dynamic Stage 1) and the 2004 revision implied recognition of values and trust (Stages 2 and 3). The advisory committee recommending the revisions wanted the word 'ethics' included in the guidelines. Some commission members felt including that word was not consistent with the original legislative intent and charter on compliance. A number of leaders in the ethics community got together to lobby the commission and members of Congress to include the word 'ethics', and it happened.

## Parallel expectations

Since the early 1900s, major US businesses – more than half of the *Fortune* 500 companies – have preferred to incorporate in Delaware, so its laws have major impact on US corporations. The Delaware Chancery Court expressed public policy in what is widely known as the Caremark decision. In that case, the court considered whether members of a board of directors failed to exercise oversight where employees were involved in criminal activities. The court said directors who in bad faith failed to act where due diligence would have prevented the harm could be held personally liable. A presumption of law is that business decisions – good or bad – are made by informed directors acting in good faith. To show 'bad faith' requires evidence that directors knew they did not uphold their fiduciary obligations or that they demonstrated conscious disregard of their responsibilities. The impact of the Caremark decision was to alert board of directors' members to the need to ensure their company has a reasonable system to detect, report, investigate and correct illegal activities – an effective business ethics process.

The *Sarbanes-Oxley Act* (SOX) of 2002 is Congress' response to the collapse of responsible financial corporate governance at Enron and a number of other corporations. SOX fits the compliance law method government traditionally used to attack business ethics problems, but it has an interesting self-regulatory undertone: if executives could have known about a financial ethics problem, then they should have known and should have fixed it. SOX requires public corporations to install controls to prevent financial ethics failures and to alert executives to any adverse information with significant financial consequences, and it requires the CEO and CFO of public corporations to assess the health of at least part of the ethics element of their corporation quarterly: the internal controls established for financial reporting processes.

As a practical matter companies have focused on responding to SOX by actions outside their ethics program, primarily by defining financial processes and installing control procedures to detect, limit and correct problems seriously affecting company finances.

Table 6.1 compares the expectations documented in three key public policies and organizes them in seven topic categories. The original documents are all easily available on the internet. In Table 6.1, the USSG specifications appear most complete, but companies are on their own and no mechanism for coordinating companies' actions exists. The DII, on the other hand, brings coordinators from member companies together for an annual Best Practices Workshop (to compare what they are doing in the realm of business ethics and share ideas about what works best), holds other meetings each year, and oversees annual self-audits of each member company's ethics program. For firms outside the defense industry and for firms outside the US, various business ethics organizations – such as the Ethics and Compliance Officer Association (ECOA), the Society of Corporate

Compliance and Ethics (SCCE), the Health Care Compliance Association (HCCA), the Institute of Business Ethics (IBE) of the United Kingdom, the Cercle d'Éthique des Affaires-Cercle Européen des Déontologues (CEA-CED) of France, and the European Business Ethics Network (EBEN) — organize periodic professional conferences to share best practices. SOX, by imposing legal requirements, created a business opportunity for accounting and law firms to sell and administer extensive SOX compliance programs to corporations. So in responding to SOX, companies are not coordinating with each other so much as they are following protocols the accounting and law firms have created to market as proprietary products.

**Table 6.1** Ethics expectations and requirements of three public policy documents

| Category | Defense industry initiative | Federal sentencing guidelines | Sarbanes-Oxley |
|---|---|---|---|
| Tone-at-the-top | Company lives by ethics that preserve integrity of the defense industry | Governing authority knows and oversees compliance and ethics program | Chief executive and chief financial officer(s) certify that each quarterly and annual report is complete, true, fair and that internal controls to notify officers of material problems were evaluated in the past 90 days; deficiencies, weaknesses and changes in the controls reported along with fraud discovered |
| Ethical organizational culture | Culture encourages employees to report violations without fear | ▪ Promote an ethical organizational culture<br>▪ A system for employees and agents to report or seek guidance about ethical conduct without fear of retaliation, and possibly anonymously or confidentially | The audit committee will establish a way to receive and process complaints, including anonymous or confidential concerns, about accounting or auditing |
| Culture development | Train employees on code of ethics | ▪ Effective training and communication on compliance and ethics delivered to governing | Promote honest and ethical conduct, full disclosures, and |

| Category | Defense industry initiative | Federal sentencing guidelines | Sarbanes-Oxley |
|---|---|---|---|
| | | authority, high-level personnel, substantial authority personnel, employees, and agents<br>▪ Promote and enforce compliance and ethics consistently throughout the organization; use incentives, and use discipline for criminal conduct or failure to reasonably prevent or detect criminal conduct | compliance with rules and regulations |
| Policies and procedures | Written code of ethics | Standards and procedures to prevent and detect criminal conduct | A code of ethics for senior financial officers and immediate disclosure of any change in or waiver of that code |
| Effectiveness evaluation | Company publicly accountable for commitment to DII principles [annual audit] | ▪ Periodically evaluate the effectiveness of the compliance and ethics program<br>▪ Periodically assess risks of criminal conduct and act to reduce those risks | Quarterly evaluation, see tone-at-the-top |
| Organization | Requires multi-company 'Best Practices' workshop annually | ▪ High-level person responsible for compliance and ethics program<br>▪ Specific individual(s) responsible for day-to-day operation of compliance and ethics program and given adequate resources, authority, and direct access to the governing authority<br>▪ No substantial authority given to any person who engaged in illegal acts or other inappropriate conduct | Only independent members of the board of directors will comprise the audit committee |

| Category | Defense industry initiative | Federal sentencing guidelines | Sarbanes-Oxley |
|---|---|---|---|
| Operations | Monitor compliance and disclose violations of federal procurement laws | ▪ Monitor and audit to detect criminal conduct<br>▪ Due diligence to prevent and detect criminal conduct<br>▪ Respond to criminal conduct and prevent its recurrence | Promote honest and ethical conduct, full disclosures, and compliance with rules and regulations |

## Challenge puzzle

Companies understand they should follow the laws of the nation(s) where they do business. What additional standards should they live up to? Do universal values exist that are relevant for business?

International values have been proposed but not universally adopted. Noteworthy have been:

- the United Nations Global Compact, consisting of a single page, focused on human rights, labor, the environment, and anti-corruption and reportedly endorsed by at least 2,000 businesses;[20]
- the OECD (Organisation for Economic Cooperation and Development) Guidelines for Multinational Enterprises, consisting of 95 pages and promoted by 42 national governments;[21]
- the Global Sullivan Principles, consisting of a single page and designed to advance human rights and social justice;[22] and
- the Caux Principles, consisting of 8 pages and formulated by business leaders to reduce social and economic threats to world peace and stability.[23]

**Table 6.2:** Summary comparison of these four global value statements

| UN Global Compact | OECD Guidelines | Global Sullivan Principles | Caux Principles |
|---|---|---|---|
| Protect human rights | Cooperate and refrain from bribery and improper politics | Promote equal opportunity | Respect stakeholders beyond shareholders |
| Not be complicit in human rights abuses | Provide meaningful information | Respect employees' voluntary freedom of association | Contribute to economic, social, and environmental development |
| Uphold freedom of association and | Respect employee rights to | Compensate employees to meet | Build trust by going beyond the letter |

| UN Global Compact | OECD Guidelines | Global Sullivan Principles | Caux Principles |
|---|---|---|---|
| collective bargaining | representation, refrain from unfair influence in labor negotiations, negotiate constructively on employment conditions | at least basic needs; provide opportunity to improve skill and capability to raise their social/economic opportunities | of the law |
| Eliminate forced labor | Mitigate adverse effects on employees of changes in business operations | Provide a safe and healthy workplace; protect health and the environment; promote sustainable development | Respect rules and conventions |
| Abolish child labor | Observe standards of employment and industrial relations not less than those of comparable employers in the host country | Promote fair competition, respect intellectual and other property rights, avoid bribes | Support responsible globalization |
| Eliminate discrimination in employment/ occupation | Use, train, and upgrade the labor force | Improve quality of life in communities where the company does business | Respect the environment |
| Support a precautionary approach to environmental challenges | Refrain from discrimination in employment | Promote the application of these principles by people with whom the company does business | Avoid illicit activities |
| Promote greater environmental responsibility | Conform to countries' competition policies | Be transparent in implementing these principles | |
| Encourage environmentally friendly technologies | Protect the environment and avoid environmentally related health problems | | |

| UN Global Compact | OECD Guidelines | Global Sullivan Principles | Caux Principles |
|---|---|---|---|
| Work against corruption, including extortion and bribery | | | |

Searching for greater simplicity, for a universal code, a common core of values that people from various cultures actually share, Rushworth Kidder, founder of the Institute for Global Ethics, interviewed 24 people in 16 countries whom he chose because their peers believed they represented clear ethical thinking. What emerged were the following eight global core values: love, truth, fairness, freedom, unity, tolerance, responsibility and respect for life.[24]

It is a puzzle: how can a business implement those eight values?

---

1 UNODC [United Nations Office on Drugs and Crime] in Cooperation with PricewaterhouseCoopers Austria, 'Anti-Corruption Policies and Measures of the *Fortune* Global 500,' vol. 1, section 1.1, 2011, viewed 22 January 2012, www.unodc.org/documents/corruption/PWC_report/Report_Volume_1.pdf.

2 Brzezinski, M 2010, 'Obama's Foreign Bribery Crackdown', *Washington Post,* A23.

3 Earle, B 1996, 'The United States' Foreign Corrupt Practices Act and the OECD Anti-Bribery Recommendation: When moral suasion won't work, try the money argument', *Dickinson Journal of International Law,* 14: 207-242.

4 Rubin, NM 1998, 'A Convergence of 1996 and 1997 Global Efforts to Curb Corruption and Bribery in International Business Transactions: The Legal Implications of the OECD Recommendations and Convention for the United States, Germany, and Switzerland', *American University International Law Review,* 14(1): 257-320.

5 Huskins, PC 2008, 'FCPA prosecutions: liability trend to watch', *Stanford Law Review,* 60(5): 1447-1457.

6 'Germany: Phase 3,' Directorate for Financial and Enterprise Affairs, OECD, 2011, viewed 22 January 2012, www.oecd.org/dataoecd/6/46/47413672.pdf.

7 Trace International, 'Global Enforcement Report ', 2011, viewed 22 January 2012, www.traceinternational.org/.

8 Robin, D, Giallourakis, M, David, FR & Moritz, TE 1989, 'A different look at codes of ethics', *Business Horizons,* 32(1): 66-73.

9 Raiborn, CA & Payne, D 1990, 'Corporate codes of conduct: a collective conscience and continuum', *Journal of Business Ethics,* 9(11): 879-889.

10 Stevens, B 1994, 'An analysis of corporate ethical code studies: Where do we go from here?', *Journal of Business Ethics,* 13(1): 63-69.

11 Weaver, GR, Treviño, LK & Cochran, PL 1999, 'Corporate ethics practices in the mid-1990s: an empirical study of the *Fortune* 1000', *Journal of Business Ethics,* 18(3): 283-294.

[12] President's Blue Ribbon Commission on Defense Management 1986, *Conduct and Accountability: A Report to the President,* Author, Washington, DC.

[13] President's Blue Ribbon Commission on Defense Management, *Conduct and Accountability.*

[14] 'The DII Principles,' Defense Industry Initiative on Business Ethics and Conduct, 2010, viewed 22 January 2012, www.dii.org/files/DII-Principles.pdf.

[15] 2011, *Public Accountability Report 2010,* Defense Industry Initiative on Business Ethics and Conduct, Washington, DC, 15.

[16] Swenson, W 1995, 'The Organizational Guidelines' 'Carrot And Stick' Philosophy, and Their Focus on 'Effective' Compliance,' in RP Conaboy, *Corporate Crime in America: Strengthening the 'Good Citizen' Corporation, Proceedings of the Second Symposium on Crime and Punishment in the United States,* United States Sentencing Commission, Washington, DC, 28-29.

[17] Thompson, LD 2003, *Principles of Federal Prosecution of Business Organizations,* Department of Justice Memorandum, US.

[18] Swenson, 'The Organizational Guidelines' 'Carrot And Stick' Philosophy.'

[19] 2004, *Guidelines Manual,* United States Sentencing Commission, Washington, DC, §8B2.1.

[20] 'The Ten Principles,' U.N. Global Compact, n.d., viewed 22 January 2012, www.unglobalcompact.org/AboutTheGC/TheTenPrinciples/index.html.

[21] 2011, *OECD Guidelines for Multinational Enterprises,* Organisation for Economic Cooperation and Development, Paris, France. 'The OECD Guidelines for Multinational Enterprises: Summary of the Guidelines', viewed 22 January 2012, http://actrav.itcilo.org/actrav-english/telearn/global/ilo/guide/oecd.htm.

[22] 'The Global Sullivan Principles of Social Responsibility' n.d., Leon H Sullivan Foundation, viewed 22 January 2012, http://lhsfound.accountsupport.com /sample-page/global-sullivan-principles. 'Sullivan Principles', Wikipedia, 2011, viewed 22 October 2011, http://en.wikipedia.org/wiki/Sullivan_Principles.

[23] Caux Round Table, 'Principles for Responsible Business', 2009, viewed 22 January 2012, www.cauxroundtable.org/view_file.cfm?fileid=143.

[24] Kidder, RM 1996, *How Good People Make Tough Choices: Resolving the Dilemmas of Ethical Living,* Fireside, New York, 91-92.

# Chapter 7

# The heart

## Open communication

### LEARNING OBJECTIVES

By the end of this chapter you should:

- □ be able to open ethics communication channels.
- □ understand strengths and weaknesses of an OpenLine.
- □ know make-or-buy considerations for an OpenLine.
- □ understand how to operate an OpenLine.

## FALLACY 6:
## RAISING ETHICS ISSUES IS CAREER SUICIDE

If it is true where you work that raising an ethics concern is career suicide, then company ethics are already broken. When companies begin a serious and effective discussion about ethics, they soon find that the 'genie is out of the bottle'. Employees define ethics broadly. Efforts to limit discussion to one area of concern quickly become futile. Organizational climate and culture must help employees raise ethics concerns safely and productively. Open communication is the heart of successful business ethics in any company.

Companies traditionally have a well-established channel for handling employees' concerns. Sometimes called 'chain of command', it applies the company's hierarchical management structure to hear and resolve issues at the lowest possible level. Any company's code of ethics should plainly state that 'employees are encouraged to raise issues with their manager first' and make it safe and effective to do so. You want to bring managers into the ethics process seeing it as an ally, not perceiving it as a threat or as competition to their leadership role.

A way to do that is to encourage use of the Wait-a-Minute! process to raise concerns in a non-confrontational, non-threatening way. While people are in a meeting, plans and decisions are being considered and made, unexpectedly, someone – always from the back of the room – says, 'Wait a minute!' A hush falls over the room. All eyes turn to the speaker, who now must say something useful. What the speaker should say is:

1. There might be a problem about [fill in the topic].
2. What is unclear to me is ... or What possibly is missing is ... or What other people have said about that is [fill in what you recall from experience].
3. What experience do you have about this? [Ask others at the meeting to share their knowledge. Two outcomes are possible: people will speak or people will not. If people speak, then discussion is under way.]
4. [If people do not speak, or if the speaker is asked for her/his own opinion:] My suggestion is [the right thing to do].

One day, at a meeting of about 150 managers, the senior site manager announced plans to implement a bad idea. Cynthia, representing Human Resources, jumped to her feet and said, 'Wait a minute!' She used the process to turn the meeting around, to reach a decision to do the right thing, and achieved the result without embarrassing anyone, causing anyone to feel threatened or committing career suicide.

Still, employees may worry about raising the most troublesome issues with their own manager, and those issues may be just what senior company leaders most need to hear, whether they want to or not. Four problems that may deter employees from communicating openly, four problems that may block the chain-of-command channel, are:

- *Attitude.* We have all heard of managers whose attitude is 'my way or the highway', 'don't rock the boat', 'I don't want to hear bad news', or 'just do what you're told — you're not paid to think'.
- *Behavior.* Some managers seem unavailable — they are 'always' in meetings, or traveling, have their doors closed, are too busy to listen, or are uninterested.
- *Wrongdoing.* Some managers have actually done something wrong — 'ship it anyway and we'll fix it if they reject it', 'I don't care how you do it; just make the numbers look good'. Another face of wrongdoing is that the manager is aware of a problem but washes her or his hands of it by passing the problem to someone else. People feel that voicing a concern to that manager will do no good.
- *Fear.* Retaliation can often be too wily and subtle to prove but may nonetheless be real and painful.

## Open ethics communication channels

If a company wants to hear people's concerns, if it wants the 'Wait-a-Minute!' process to work, then it must open up the ethics communication channels. It needs to do two things: (a) open the traditional, hierarchical, chain-of-command channel by ensuring that managers listen to the concerns and respond appropriately to them (and sanction them if they do not); and (b) open one or more alternative channels so that people can use them instead.

### Open management channels

A company should train, coach and mentor managers — and train, coach and mentor specialists in the functional organizations — so that they create trust and listen to employees.

A way to get managers to perform the listening role effectively is to involve them in personally teaching company values and ethics to those who directly report to them. This is an organizational climate initiative. Such teaching offers three hidden benefits. First, the best way for managers to learn values and ethics themselves is to teach it and engage in discussion with those who report to them. That can change the managers' behavior and make them more open to listening to 'bad news'. Second, teaching those who directly report boxes the manager in. Once the manager makes this public presentation on ethics, he or she endorses it and implicitly commits to employees that her/his own behavior will reflect the highest ethical standards. Third, when company managers personally deliver ethics training to their subordinates, they open a communication channel that should allow their employees to feel safe — and actually be safe — when giving the manager an early warning of 'bad news'. People can thereafter go to the manager and say, 'Remember when you were teaching us ethics and we talked about [fill in the topic], well something similar has come up and I thought you would want to know about it: [state the concern].'

### Open alternative channels

Ombudsman offices, front-line ethics officers and other opportunities provide channels for employees to express concerns when they feel it is unwise to contact their own manager because of one of the risks listed above. Some alternative channels are routinely built into the company structure. Employees are expected to take questions directly to human resources, payroll, safety, security and law. But these functional channels will not appeal to some employees or fit some issues. The channel will fail and employee displeasure will fester.

Laws or regulations sometimes mandate alternative channels. The *Sarbanes-Oxley Act* of 2002, for example, requires public corporations to provide a channel that any employee can use to present an accounting or audit issue to the board of directors' audit committee. This requirement is designed to detect financial mistakes and misconduct early, before the situation deteriorates to the level of Enron, WorldCom and their ilk. Where we have worked, the channel we provided worked well: employees could contact the Chair of the Audit Committee of the Board directly by addressing a letter to her/him at the ethics office. Our commitment was to deliver that letter to the Chair unopened. In fact, the Chair would have wanted to know why it was opened, if it was.

Mandated or not, every company today needs to establish an appropriately named ethics assistance telephone line, and the company must undertake to operate it scrupulously. For many people the ethics assistance line will be a symbol of the legitimacy of the organization's entire ethics effort. Advertise the telephone number widely using posters, flyers, websites, newsletter notices and through briefings. One of the best tools is the full-size, scenic calendar pioneered by TRW and continued by Northrop Grumman after the companies merged. Employees loved to post it on their wall in the office and at home, putting the company's ethics assistance phone number in front of them day-in and day-out. Encourage employees with a question or concern to contact their manager or any manager as first choice, or to contact a functional expert if feasible or to call the ethics office. If it could be measured, the greatest value of an ethics office would be the violations and improper actions that are avoided because employees seek and obtain advice.

## The OpenLine

Ethics office channels open an alternative communication channel at the level of institutional trust. We have lost count of the number of calls we have received from employees who say, 'This is a really good company, but things are going wrong and I don't trust anyone who works at this site. Can I tell you about it … anonymously?' That is an expression of institutional trust. For convenience, we will refer to the ethics office channel as the 'OpenLine' and the person who uses the channel as the 'caller' whether the communication arrives by telephone, letter, email or in a face-to-face meeting.

We choose the name 'OpenLine' for a reason. In part, the spelling is an attempt to brand the ethics contact line and draw attention to it as something distinctive. In addition, research at 30 *Fortune* 500 corporations discovered the name given to the line made a significant difference in employees' willingness to use it and also what they used it for. Lines named 'hotline' or 'alert line' received few calls – about four calls per year per 1,000 employees on the company's payroll. Lines with those names apparently were seen as '9-1-1' emergency lines that only welcomed calls about crimes in progress. In contrast, lines with 'friendly' or 'invitational' names like 'help line' or 'open line' received dramatically more calls, about 23 per 1,000 employees each year, and those called 'assist line' or 'guide line' or 'advice line' received still more calls, about 43 calls per year per 1,000 employees, and callers often expressed milder concerns or asked for information.[1]

A stereotype is that people use such telephone lines to anonymously 'drop a dime' on someone. Internationally, France and Germany prohibit companies from operating telephone lines to receive anonymous complaints because of those nations' historic experience with Nazi police.

Reality is that an OpenLine rarely receives 'drop-a-dime' calls – and those are obvious when they do come in. Instead, people use the OpenLine to ask questions because they want to do the right thing. They use the OpenLine to express concerns because they want to work for a company that does the right thing. Our own experience, and experience at some companies we know, is that most callers identify themselves, some ask that their identity be kept confidential, and only a very low percentage ask to remain anonymous (less than two percent at the Jet Propulsion Laboratory).

For many organizations, a very real issue is whether to accept anonymous OpenLine calls or to protect identity if callers ask for confidentiality. A concern is that it feels wrong to not be able to face your accuser. In the US, public policy recognizes that circumstances of the workplace mean important tips would not be received without affording the protections of anonymity and/or confidentiality. So accepting anonymous and confidential callers has become common; in fact, US law currently expects or requires companies to do so.

The more important issue is institutional trust. The OpenLine must emerge as a communication and mentoring channel that employees can trust. Such a line will naturally meet with a dose of cynicism from some employees and a healthy skepticism from more. It is important to address the skepticism and not worry about the cynicism. While a resource like this will always be subject to distrust by a percentage of the population, the opinion of such a minority will not tarnish the OpenLine if the company takes great care to operate it scrupulously, adhering to the best practices.

The primary focus of the OpenLine should be mentoring: to allow senior management to hear people's concerns and answer their questions. A secondary focus should be to identify problems the company needs to look into and resolve. Inquiry should be concerned with *what happened* and fixing process, not with *who* called or *who* did it. The goal is to create good climate and help people, not create fear and punish people. Inevitably, some inquiries will determine that individuals need to be held accountable for their behavior. When that situation arises, the company needs to rely on its procedures for dispute resolution and adverse personnel actions, with all of the notifications – including legal ones if criminal activity or regulator violation is involved – due process, and privacy protections that routinely are built into those procedures.

## Types of OpenLine calls

OpenLine calls basically are of three types.

- Type 1 is a *question* the ethics officer can directly respond to, usually on the spot. For example, 'Widget Company, one of our suppliers, mailed me season tickets for the local National Football League games, can I accept them?' The ethics office provides guidance to the caller. Rarely should this be a decision that allows the caller to say, 'The ethics office said it is (or is not) OK.' Better is guidance to the company's policy or code of conduct so the caller is led to make her/his own decision and say, 'Company policy 2006-ABC says it is (or is not) OK.' An executive who calls with a question expects nothing less; why should any employee receive lesser service? All questions must be fairly answered because employees tend to have an expanded view of ethics, especially involving anything that can be considered unfair. Responding 'we only deal with fraud, waste, and abuse' will not satisfy them. It will make them brand the OpenLine as useless and discredit the ethics process.
- Type 2 is an *issue* the ethics system has no policies to answer and another function of the organization has policies for or handles routinely. For example, 'I'm supposed to be entitled to a pay raise because I completed a quality inspection training course plus 500 hours of practical experience performing inspections, but my paycheck hasn't changed.' The ethics office refers the issue to a responsible functional expert for response. It is important to note that this referral is not simply an uninterested handoff. The ethics office follows progress of the resolution effort because while the ethics office may think 'it is out of our hands' the caller may still hold the OpenLine accountable, so whether human resources or other functions handle the issue fairly has potential to reflect on the OpenLine process. This argues for a high profile for the ethics process and the need to establish good working relations with other functions, convincing them they have a stake in resolution of ethics issues that goes beyond the immediate scope of their normal role. The ethics office also makes an initial judgment as to whether Type 2 issues have special circumstances that indicate need for immediate law department involvement because, despite surface appearances, the issue has potential to significantly impact the company.

- Type 3 is a *suspicion or allegation* that requires an ethics-oriented investigation. For example, 'My manager has season tickets and is going to all of the local National Football League games. I turned those tickets down when Widget Company offered them to me. I suspect Widget offered them to my manager and he accepted them.' The ethics office coordinates the investigation and monitors corrective actions.

The OpenLine derives from 'hotlines' originally defined as a mechanism for 'internal reporting of alleged misconduct' anonymously or confidentially and without fear of retaliation. Some companies, when they first introduced 'hotlines', limited calls they would accept to 'fraud, waste and abuse'. It did not take long before employees made it clear that you cannot limit ethics by simple declaration. 'If you want to talk ethics,' they said, 'you must listen to all of my ethical concerns, including, for example, that I was treated unfairly by my supervisor in a recent assignment change. If you don't then the 'hotline' isn't credible for anything.' Ethics is any issue involving fairness and justice.[2]

## Wikis, social media and whistleblowing

In the digital age, a hot topic is how business ethics should relate to the internet and social media. The issue is a two-sided coin: on the positive side, how blogs and social media can improve business ethics; on the negative side, the damage information posted to blogs and social media can do.

*Positives*

Ethics officers are exploring ways to appreciate the strengths of blogs and social media and how companies can use them to achieve ethics and compliance goals.

Our experience is that posting the company's code of conduct, its values, and its OpenLine phone number to its public website creates a plus for the company's organizational climate and culture. Some companies post ethics training modules to the public internet; we posted ours only to the company's private intranet. Blogs, Twitter, Facebook and other social media carry informal conversations and our ethics officers made no effort to monitor them or participate — *except* when a caller alerted us that someone had posted an OpenLine type of concern. In that case, we would look to see if any participant in the conversation had suggested calling the OpenLine and, if not, we would log on simply to suggest doing that.

A social media consultant recommends companies create a plan to ensure that the company and employees both use social media effectively. That plan aims to explain what the company hopes to achieve by being accessible on social media, to clarify who employees are representing when they use social media, and to detail what social media sites employees will be expected to use as part of their jobs, how to handle common occurrences, and what to do about unusual incidents. These issues belong to several functions: brand image to corporate communications, job design and training to human resources, and unusual incidents to line managers and security. None belong to the ethics office.

## *Negatives*

Inspired by WikiLeaks, news organizations and various other groups are experimenting with online channels whistleblowers can use to reveal 'secrets' to the world. Al Jazeera announced its Transparency Unit, the *Wall Street Journal* announced Safehouse, the *New York Times* envisioned something similar and the *Washington Post* considered opening an electronic drop box. The news media report they have seen other 'secret-revealing' internet channels: BalkanLeaks, IndoLeaks, BrusselsLeaks and OpenLeaks.

All of the 'leaks' sites aspire to protect the source's identity. That is probably impossible for three reasons. First, computer technical experts believe the websites and drop boxes are technically insecure. Second, governments – particularly the courts – have legal rights to subpoena information. Recently, the United Kingdom requested that the US Justice Department subpoena Boston College oral history interviews obtained from Irish Republican Army members on promise that their identities and what they disclosed would be held in confidence until they authorized disclosure or until they died. While one interviewer 'believed that there were no circumstances under which disclosure would be required',[3] US attorneys' position is that the impetus for collecting the oral history interviews was laudable but interviewers 'made promises they could not keep – that they would conceal evidence of murder and other crimes until the perpetrators were in their graves. … [T]he promise of absolute confidentiality was flawed'.[4] Third, and most powerfully, content analysis usually identifies the person(s) who had access to the particular information revealed. When WikiLeaks revealed thousands of classified US documents, investigation pointed toward a specific army private (still awaiting trial at the time of this writing) as the source.

Corporations do have 'police' issues with what employees post to the internet. An ambulance company fired an employee who criticized her boss on Facebook. But pay attention to 'the rest of the story': the National Labor Relations Board (NLRB) filed a lawsuit arguing her speech was protected by federal labor laws that allow workers to discuss wages, hours and working conditions with co-workers. The lawsuit was settled before trial: the ambulance company agreed to change its policy that prohibited employees from depicting the company in any way on the internet unless they had company permission. Lawyer and former NLRB member Chuck Cohen warned employees that there are boundaries to what people can say on social media sites. '[W]e just don't have a good sense yet of where the boundaries are.'[5] In any event, business ethics is not a 'police' function; it is a mentoring function.

Where we teach, college students see these Wikis as similar to a company's OpenLine and believe their strength is 'the tremendous potential the internet offers to create a community of informers and publishing outlets'. But they see weaknesses, too: lack of clarity about how to protect informants' identities, inability to verify information received by the Wiki[6] and the possibility that no one will do anything with information sent to a Wiki.

An OpenLine avoids those weaknesses. Within a company, callers' identities can remain unknown, competent managers and investigators can verify information they provide and the OpenLine process can guarantee diligent response to every call. So the ethics office role is important: provide a channel for questions and concerns inside the company, eliminating need for anyone to 'whistleblow' outside the company.

This strategy fits what we observe is the process people use in deciding to raise a question or express a concern. A qualitative study of OpenLine calls received by three companies over a two-year period suggested that people are inherently reluctant to call an OpenLine and must cross a psychological threshold before they will do so. That threshold has two components: cognitive (they must know the phone number or address)[7] and affective (they must feel a concern deeply enough to think about it repeatedly, to feel anxious about it, perhaps to feel worry or anger or lose sleep over it — to *ruminate*). To eliminate any cognitive block, companies widely advertise the OpenLine telephone number. To eliminate any affective block, companies train employees in corporate values,[8] frame the OpenLine as a helpful channel (an avenue for prosocial action), assure employees that their calls are wanted and will be acted upon fairly, and promise callers their identity will be protected to the extent possible if they so ask.

Callers cross the threshold at various values. Some indicate that the threshold for calling to complain of wrongdoing by a co-worker felt higher than the threshold for calling to ask how ethics policies apply to a decision they are about to make.

We observe that people follow an exclusionary process (Figure 7.1) before they reach the threshold to call the OpenLine.

- Decision 1 is whether the issue is an 'emergency' requiring their action. Most issues are not. Professors Bibb Latané and John Darley determined people use four steps to make this decision: (a) notice an event, (b) interpret it as an emergency, (c) accept responsibility, and (d) know an appropriate form of assistance.[9] Since the OpenLine is not a 9-1-1 line, people deciding an issue is an emergency are likely to call the police, fire department or security.
- If people decide an issue is not an emergency requiring their action, Decision 2 is whether it is an issue requiring 'whistleblowing' (which we define as an alert to 'authorities' *outside* the company[10]). Again, most issues are not. Building on the Latané and Darley's research, Marcia Miceli and Janet Near determined that people use four steps to make that decision: (a) recognize an issue; (b) assess it as serious; (c) accept responsibility; and (d) choose an action.[11] People deciding that an issue requires whistleblowing are likely to call law enforcement, journalists or lawyers to represent their issue in court.
- If people decide whistleblowing is not required (at the moment), Decision 3 is whether the issue requires an OpenLine call inside the company. Our review of the content of OpenLine calls suggests callers

use four steps to make that decision: (a) they ruminate about what is or could become a bad situation; (b) they create a mental frame explaining that the situation has been or would be created by someone violating a value (usually the value that people should be treated honestly, fairly and openly) and thus cause social damage (possibly hard to prove); (c) they feel a moral responsibility to somehow confront the issue; and (d) they expect an OpenLine call to result in the company solving the problem to benefit other people and themselves.

**Figure 7.1** Callers' exclusionary process (Observation indicates employees typically consider these decision-tree factors before calling the OpenLine)

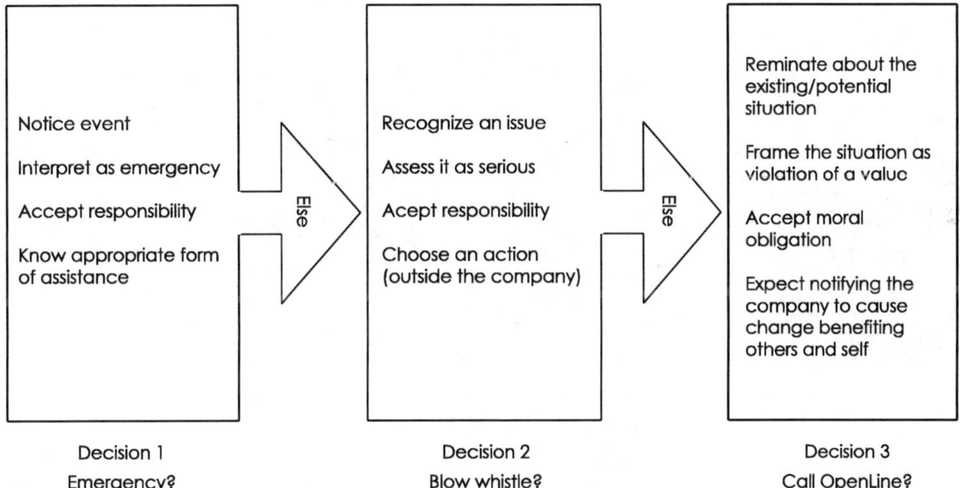


Overall, while an occasional employee will use the OpenLine process for a less-than-noble or even a mean-spirited purpose, employees generally call the OpenLine because they want to help their company, not hurt it. They want to help make their company a great place to work and sustain its reputation for high ethics.

## Make or buy?

An option frequently mentioned is outsourcing the OpenLine to one of a number of commercial firms that operate them. Which is better: an internal or an outsourced OpenLine? That is a make-or-buy decision each company needs to study. Table 7.1 highlights selected pros and cons.

Table 7.1 probably makes our 'considered judgment' clear: We prefer 'make'. We think an internal OpenLine creates substantial benefits for business ethics. Important strengths of this choice include (a) the capability an inside ethics officer has to immediately answer callers' questions and respond to their concerns based on company values and policies; (b) the closely-related opportunity an inside ethics officer has to coach callers on where to look for ethics policy themselves and how to recognize and apply it on their own in the future; (c) the potential for an inside ethics officer to obtain much higher quality information from callers than anyone outside the company, unfamiliar with its operations and current events, could get; (d) the climate sensing an inside ethics officer almost inevitably will develop over the course of handling many OpenLine calls;[12] and (e) the institutional trust symbolism that the company's senior management considers business ethics important enough to provide a company-operated ethics office and OpenLine. Also, in some circumstances, the internal ethics officer can personally meet with a caller if desired.

**Table 7.1** Selected OpenLine make-or-buy pros and cons

| Characteristic | Internal OpenLine | External OpenLine |
|---|---|---|
| Information quality | Pro: ethics officers *potentially* capture more complete information and can flexibly follow conversational leads. | Pro: intake officers complete a standardized checklist.<br>Con: intake officers *situationally* are less able to flexibly follow conversational leads. |
| Climate sensing | Pro: ethics officers hear the tone and perspective of the callers. | Con: intake reports provide incomplete climate sensing. |
| Process | Pro: ethics officers handle the complete process: intake, analysis, evaluation, inquiry, resolution, correction, feedback.<br>Pro: ethics officers are able to answer ethics questions based on company policy and experience.<br>Pro: ethics officers answering questions and discussing concerns have a teaching opportunity: They can coach callers to find the answer and to find future answers. | Con: outsource supplier handles only the intake. Company staff still must handle the rest of the process: analysis, evaluation, inquiry, resolution, correction, feedback.<br>Con: intake officers are unable to answer ethics questions based on company policy and experience; must refer to company.<br>Con: intake officers cannot teach callers to find ethics answers independently. |
| Institutional trust | Pro: visible symbol of tone-at-the-top message that business ethics is important. | Con: company leaders lack visible ownership of the ethics process. |
| Relational trust | Pro: callers can time call to reach either a person or a machine.<br>Con: callers may reach a person when they prefer not to or a machine when they would prefer a person. | Pro: phone staffed 24/7 so callers 'always' reach a person.<br>Con: some callers prefer to speak to a machine but cannot. |

| Characteristic | Internal OpenLine | External OpenLine |
|---|---|---|
| Calculative trust | Con: some callers might fear recognition or identity compromise by a company employee.<br>Pro: callers may use identity protection options: third party caller, anonymous mail, anonymous email | Pro: some callers might feel more anonymous and less vulnerable to identity compromise if speaking to a non-employee third party. |
| Professional development | Pro: focuses ethics staff on capturing 'calls' from all modes of communication, not just the telephone. | Con: tends to encourage ethics staff to only process calls documented by the outsource intake officer. |
| Schedule | Pro: can eliminate in-basket delays by processing calls as they are received. | Con: adds transmission and in-basket delays to the ethics process.<br>Con: some callers may incorrectly expect their call to a third party to cause faster response. |
| Cost | Pro: where ethics calls have low volume, ethics officer can be an additional duty. | Con: the perception of sharing costs with other clients is not likely to prove true; the outsource company must charge enough to cover the 'worst case' call volume. |

In addition, internal ethics officers who handle the many aspects of the entire OpenLine process – intake, analysis, evaluation, inquiry, resolution, correction and feedback – typically assume ownership responsibility for it. An external resource provides only intake service, which does not lead to feelings of ownership, and company employees must still handle the rest of the OpenLine process, which is the bulk of the work.

We have seen auditors recommend an outsourced OpenLine as a 'best practice', apparently swayed by the argument that the outsource firm is staffed to have a 'trained' person answer the phone 24/7 so callers never reach an answering machine. A related argument sometimes is that outsource firms are staffed by multi-lingual people, so callers can speak in their native language. We find neither argument persuasive. We concede that some might, but let us share with you why we feel that the OpenLine is not *just* a telephone reporting process:

- With respect to 24/7 staffing, one thing to keep in mind is that the OpenLine is not a 9-1-1 emergency line. If people face an emergency, they need to call the police or security. People can choose what time they call the OpenLine. We observe that some people choose to call during normal business hours when an ethics officer is present to answer the phone, and other people choose to call outside of normal business hours so they can leave a machine message. Some employees, for example, feel more comfortable because there is additional anonymity leaving a message on the answering machine during a time they know no human will answer, like the middle of the night. Another observation is that calls often arrive in bunches, so even at an outsource company the number of people available to answer calls at times will be insufficient and some calls must reach a busy signal or roll over to a machine. (An outsource company called one ethics officer on Sunday morning to say that so many calls were flooding the line that its staff was overwhelmed and disconnected the line – how responsible was that?)

- With respect to language, a company can choose to have its phone answered by a multi-lingual person. Many companies today have employees who speak one of a dozen or more languages as their native tongue, and no outsource company is staffed to routinely handle them all. A company can equally well identify linguists already available on its staff or contract with one of the professional interpretation firms that stand ready to provide instant service via telephone conference call.
- With respect to 'trained' staff, trained to do what? How likely is it that 'outsourced staff' are as aware as internal employees of the corporation's policies and procedures or can match internal employees' experience with the corporation's climate and culture?

Another argument in favor of outsourcing the OpenLine has been that some callers do not want to talk to a company employee, implying that they do not trust company employees, or they fear an employee will recognize them when they wish to remain anonymous, or they fear company channels will compromise their confidentiality and lead to adverse action against them. True, a few callers feel that way. A few even suspect that the company uses voice recognition devices or voice analysis to identify callers. It is also not unheard of for the occasional manager to ask the ethics office if the caller was male or female.

Perhaps it is useful to note that our auditors satisfied themselves that no one in the company – not in telephone services, or procurement, or accounts payable – had access to phone records that identified the originating phone number of calls coming in to the OpenLine. When they first looked, they discovered that was not true and the company asked the telephone company to omit that information on monthly reports, including billing records received on CDs. If the company offers someone anonymity and violates that in any way, the company loses trust.

Ethics officers must be firm that anonymity means what it says: revealing the identity, if known, and/or clues to help someone identify an anonymous caller would violate the company's commitment to its employees. Some callers creatively prevent voice recognition by having a third party call, by using anonymous mail, or by using anonymous email. But we have also received calls from people who make it clear they want to speak only with someone who works for the company.

We received such a call one day in which an anonymous caller said he/she was using a disguised voice and calling from a phone booth in the middle of 'the desert' where he/she could ensure no one was around for miles. The same person called from time to time over the next year, and the first few calls were from the phone booth. Later calls originated at more convenient phones as the caller felt more comfortable with the OpenLine process, more trusting of the ethics officers, and safer. Ultimately, anonymous volunteered her/his name but still requested confidentiality.

Some people extend the outsourcing argument to an expectation that the issue will be evaluated and investigated by the outsourced OpenLine provider or other independent third party, but in our experience no company subscribes to such service. Every company takes responsibility for its own evaluation and investigation of concerns. Since all call information from either an internal or outsourced OpenLine must be channeled to company staff for action anyway, a hallmark company policy understood and enforced by everyone must be that the company honors requests for anonymity and confidentiality without question or reservation, and makes no effort and takes no action to identify any anonymous caller.

Answering OpenLine calls internally opens a teaching opportunity at a 'teachable moment'. Internal ethics officers can lead the caller to company policy, guide review of that policy, and facilitate getting the caller to personally make the right decision. This has two benefits: research shows a person who makes a decision personally will willingly undertake to implement it and, in fact, will stick to that decision quite firmly. And a person who was able to find an answer to today's question in company policy is likely to find the answer to tomorrow's question as well. That is a desirable outcome: an employee now trained and able to independently perform the research needed to handle an ethics issue well.

## Operating an OpenLine

As a starting estimate for planning purposes, a company can expect a mature OpenLine to attract about 23 calls per thousand employees per year (some companies report either more or less). Maturity will depend on a number of factors, such as years of operation, a systematic approach, an acceptance by a majority of employees that it is a credible and potentially effective resource. Another starting estimate is that one ethics officer can easily process about 15 calls per week and can occasionally process about 30–45 per week.

All calls received at an OpenLine are important. The three types – question, issue, suspicion/allegation – usually have a ratio of 20:60:20 percent. Approximately 20 percent of the calls ask questions. The company responds, usually on the spot, by providing reliable information. Such calls represent the OpenLine working at its best by helping to prevent ethics violations from occurring in the first place. Approximately 60 percent express workplace concerns usually referred to the employee relations specialists in human resources. Approximately 20 percent allege fraud, waste, abuse or other compliance violations the company responds to by conducting simple investigative activity (such as checking attendance records) or, in the event of a severe infraction which has potential to do extensive harm, by launching a formal investigation coordinated with the law department.

Ethics officers answering the OpenLine use what trainers call 'active listening' skills to elicit maximum information and to build empathy with callers. Active listening skills can be developed and improved through formal training and practice.

## Confidentiality

A key principle is that the reputation your system has earned for honoring confidentiality affects the trust others have in you. There are two questions: can you keep *information* confidential and can you keep *identity* confidential. With respect to information, the ethics office exists to open channels to carry information, so the duty of the ethics officer is to make information available to company leaders and to not conceal it. 'Off the record' conversations with callers are not acceptable. Making information available to company leaders does not mean making it available to the public or generally available inside the company. Discretion is paramount.

With respect to identity, the ethics office exists to make it possible for people to ask questions or report situations confidentially or anonymously, so the duty of the ethics officer is to carefully conceal the identity of a caller when the caller asks for that and to be very conservative in protecting it even when the caller doesn't ask. Disclose information only to those who 'must know' to perform their part of the job or to respond to regulators or law enforcement in the event of a regulatory or criminal violation.

Three levels of identity protection — confidential, anonymous or open — are available for callers. Sometimes 'confidential' and 'anonymous' are considered the same. They are not. Inform callers of the difference between 'anonymity' and 'confidentiality' and make sure it is crystal clear. For 'confidentiality', ensure callers understand and agree that identity protection is not absolute, that identity sometimes must be released for legal reasons or to conduct investigation, but even then only on a 'must know' basis.

### *Confidential*

This means that the caller's identity is known to the ethics office but will not be disclosed unless required by law or by a demonstrated need to know for legal reasons, and then selectively and sparingly. Confidential is a default level. If a caller has not explicitly authorized disclosure of identity, then confidential protection should be provided. Even in the case where a caller has said, 'I don't care who knows', err on the side of protection rather than revelation. Avoid even disclosing whether the caller was female or male. In a small group, gender alone might allow a manager to think he or she knows the caller's identity.

It is important to advise the caller that identity disclosure may be required as a result of legal action or investigation. Ask permission to disclose caller's name selectively to people who have a 'need to know' to investigate and to determine appropriate action. Callers who express dissatisfaction with the rules for confidentiality should be advised that they can elect to make an anonymous report. They may call at any time to speak without disclosing their identity. If you do not know who is calling, then disclosure of identity becomes impossible.

A confidential caller's identity, to the extent known, should be documented in the ethics office file. One method for doing this is to record the caller's identification on a separate page marked 'Internal Data'. Using colored paper for that page helps to flag Internal Data as requiring special protection. In reports that do leave the ethics office, 'CONFIDENTIAL' can substitute where the caller's name, telephone number, or other identifying details otherwise would appear.

### *Anonymous*

'Anonymous' means the caller's identity is not known and therefore is impossible to disclose. Establish a time for anonymous callers to recontact you, and give them a memo identification number they can use instead of their name so you have an opportunity to ask them questions that may arise during inquiry and provide feedback on inquiry results. As a rule of thumb, aim for recontact to occur after two weeks. Any action to learn the identity of an anonymous caller is not only dishonest but can subject the entire ethics process to additional and maybe even fatal cynicism. We are talking about a very delicate relationship here. People's jobs and lives could be at stake.

### *Open*

This means the caller's identity is known and the caller has authorized disclosure of identity. In our experience, this is the norm. People often realize that the issue they are raising cannot be resolved unless the company examines their particular situation. Even so, disclose identity only selectively and sparingly to people who must know.

The long-term interests of the company are best served by absolutely honoring callers' requests for anonymity and confidentiality. Even one failure to do so will become the 'talk of the town' and have a chilling effect that discourages employees from trusting the company, trusting the ethics office or trusting the OpenLine, and they will not ask questions or report concerns in the future. The corporate culture will be closed, the reverse of the goal we are striving for: openness. The effectiveness of an OpenLine can be stillborn or aborted if any employee involved in it is viewed as a 'gossip', whether that is fair or not.

## Protect employees from retaliation

Published company policy must be clear: Company will not condone any act of retribution or retaliation against any individual who conscientiously seeks to follow and implement ethics policies. US statutes certainly forbid retaliation of any kind; some states and some other nations may have statutes forbidding retaliation as well.

For the most part, 'protecting' employees from retaliation really means 'preventing' retaliation. How can the ethics officer help? Here are several ways:

- Focus attention on resolving the issue raised rather than on trying to figure out who raised the issue.
- Encourage perception of the caller as a person motivated by good service to the company and by trust that if the truth is known then management will act to improve a situation, and as someone seeking this benefit to the company despite obvious personal risk of retaliation.
- In meetings with management, clearly stress the company policy against retaliation. Clarify that the policy applies to managers, supervisors and employees. Observe that the policy intends to also prevent retaliation by one group of employees against another, and caution that managers must prevent, detect and address adverse treatment of one employee by another employee. Counsel that anyone engaging in retaliation is subject to discipline. A special problem, where unions exist, is that one employee can be intimidated against using the OpenLine process if the offender is another union employee. Unions may also encourage members to use the OpenLine against a management or non-union employee, or to raise an issue that is already being, or can be, handled by the contractual grievance process. For example, a supervisor performing the work which the contract specifies for a union member is a grievance issue. The fact that the supervisor lied about it by falsifying time records would be an ethics and compliance matter.
- If necessary … if an ethics officer is sure a supervisor is apt to retaliate against an OpenLine caller, then the ethics officer should meet the supervisor and make the company's anti-retaliation policy absolutely clear.
- In post-investigation debriefings with the employee(s) who raised an issue, state the company's policy against retaliation and encourage the employee not to self-reveal one's role to others and to report any suspected retaliation that occurs.
- Warn persons found responsible for a violation against speculating about how the violation was discovered and that any retaliation will warrant further discipline.

The ethics officer also must guard the company against the occasional employee who seeks to invoke protection when the facts do not warrant it. For example, an employee who feels vulnerable to impending layoffs might (a) call the OpenLine then protest that the layoff notice must be retaliation by management; or (b) reveal information that the ethics office has kept private to supervisors and co-workers (who subsequently share the information 'confidentially' with third parties) and then blame the company for violating trust or claim retaliation occurred; or (c) call in adverse information – true or false – about a colleague in hopes it will get the colleague laid off instead of the caller.

What guards the company against such provocations? Investigation needs to focus on whether the company had, and objectively followed, fair policies and procedures for the circumstance.

### Provide feedback

Close the loop with callers by providing feedback. It is appropriate to indicate that inquiry has been completed and the issue was found to have merit, was disproved, or that best efforts failed to substantiate the allegation. Beyond that, it may be best to state that all appropriate actions, including discipline, have taken place to conclude the matter. Details of discipline are protected by privacy rules and are not to be disclosed to callers.

Closing the loop with callers on issues referred to a function with special expertise, like the human resources function and its employee relations specialists, properly should be done by a representative of that function. As a courtesy, when the caller remained confidential or anonymous, then the ethics officer may close the loop by reporting closure action to the caller.

## Challenge puzzle

In a 'perfect' world, callers contacting the ethics office would have their information organized:

- *For a question about what to do:* **Who** wonders what to do about **What**, which would affect **Whom**, **When**, **How** and **Why**? – the famous five Ws and one H.
- *For an existing situation:* **Who** did **What**, affecting **Whom**, **When**, **How**, and **Why**, plus the identity of witnesses and the location of physical evidence.

In the real world, callers tend to focus on just one or two of those questions. It is up to the ethics officer to extract from them as much of the rest of the information as possible, as accurately as possible. Sometimes that requires a long conversation, even a series of conversations.

The puzzle is: how much time to spend with one caller?

People who view the OpenLine as a 'call center' for 'intake' of issues may adopt call center metrics that expect a few ethics staffers to handle many calls – none longer than [arbitrarily] three minutes.

People who view the OpenLine as a 'coaching center' to help people learn to solve problems on their own may expect each ethics officer to invest whatever time it takes to reach 'resolution'.

The time-per-caller issue has staffing and therefore budget effects. If an ethics office receives 3,000 calls per year (250 per month, 58 per week, 11.5 per day), how many ethics officers are needed to receive the calls and complete all follow-up?

The answer lies in the company's goal: why does the company operate an ethics office and an OpenLine?

---

[1] Ethical Leadership Group, 1998, *Ethics Phone Lines Best Practices Report,* Wilmette, IL.

[2] Rhode, D 2006, 'How We Tackle the 'Woman Problem', *Stanford Report,* viewed 23 January 2012, http://news.stanford.edu/news/2006/may24/rhode-052406.html.

[3] 2011, 'Motion of Trustees of Boston College to Quash Subpoenas', in *In Re: Request from the United Kingdom Pursuant to the Treaty Between the Government of the United States of America and the Government of the United Kingdom on Mutual Assistance in Criminal Matters in the Matter of Dolours Price,* District Court, District of Massachusetts, US.

[4] 2011, 'Government's Opposition to Motion to Quash and Motion for an Order to Compel', in *In Re: Request from the United Kingdom Pursuant to the Treaty Between the Government of the United States of America and the Government of the United Kingdom on Mutual Assistance in Criminal Matters in the Matter of Dolours Price,* District Court, District of Massachusetts, US.

[5] Hananel, S 2011, 'Conn. Firm, U.S. Settle Case of Worker Fired After Criticism on Facebook', *Denver Post,* viewed 23 January 2012, www.denverpost.com/search/ci_17324449.

[6] Lee, A, Kennedy, A, Rice, M & Weber, Z 2011, 'Openleaks' Whistleblowing Model', in *Business Ethics Fortnight 2011: Intramural Qualifying Intercollegiate Business Ethics Case Competitions Team Executive Summaries,* Center for Ethics and Business, Loyola Marymount University, Los Angeles, CA.

[7] Miceli, MP, Roach, BL & Near, JP 1988, 'The motivations of anonymous whistle-blowers: the case of federal employees', *Public Personnel Management* 17(3): 281-296.

[8] Driscoll, DM & Hoffman, WM 2000, *Ethics Matters: How to Implement Values-Driven Management,* Center for Business Ethics, Waltham, MA.

[9] Latané, B & Darley, JM 1970, *The Unresponsive Bystander: Why Doesn't He Help?* Appleton-Century-Crofts, New York.

[10] People define 'whistleblowing' in varying ways. Some use a broad definition: revealing information to any 'authority' inside or outside an organization or company. Because we encourage internal reporting – revealing information to people inside the organization who can fix the problem – we choose a narrow definition of whistleblowing: external reporting only – revealing information to any 'authority' outside an organization or company.

---

11 Miceli, MP & Near, JP 1992, *Blowing the Whistle: The Organizational and Legal Implications for Companies and Employees,* Lexington, New York.

12 Treviño, LK & Nelson, KA 2004, *Managing Business Ethics: Straight Talk About How to Do It Right,* 3rd edn, Wiley, Hoboken, NJ.

# Chapter 8

# The test

## Program review and risk analysis

### LEARNING OBJECTIVES

By the end of this chapter you should:

- □ be able to assess company ethics, not the ethics program.
- □ understand program review.
- □ understand assessment surveys.
- □ be familiar with benefits of internal assessment.
- □ know the four faces of risk analysis.

### FALLACY 7:
### NO ONE CAN REALLY KNOW HOW ETHICAL COMPANIES AND THEIR PEOPLE ARE

Often, people feel that no one can really know how ethical companies and their people are. But program review and risk analysis are two processes, inextricably linked, to assess what a company needs to do for good ethics and how the company is succeeding in doing it. Emphasize the focus on *company,* not *ethics program* because, as some have learned the hard way, a company can have what looks like a terrific ethics program yet be ethically unsuccessful.

Managers want to assess performance, and although it seems perfectly logical to ask, 'How is the ethics program doing?' it would be far wiser to ask, 'How are the company's ethics doing?' The first question focuses on reviewing ethics program activities such as calls answered and training delivered. That channels attention too narrowly toward 'administrivia'. The second question focuses on the ethics mission: building the company culture toward ever-improving business ethics. A tougher question to answer, it channels attention toward critical outcomes. The difference in the two approaches is like on the one hand rearranging the *Titanic*'s deck chairs and on the other steering it safely through an iceberg zone.

## Program review

A program review should measure a selected set of the organization's ethical characteristics against expected norms. Like a routine physical examination at the doctor's office, a standardized assessment confirms presence of expected conditions or identifies deviations. A physician evaluates health deviations to diagnose whether a corrective intervention is warranted and, if so, to design a specific treatment plan. If a program review indicates an ethics deviation, then experience, judgment, and tailoring are required to diagnose whether a corrective intervention is needed and, if so, to design it.

### External assessments

Ethics assessments by authorities outside the corporation may give some degree of comfort and reassurance that a company's ethics are strong, especially to companies in an industry that faces aggressive regulatory agency demands for compliance. External assessments may provide visible evidence that a company cares enough to identify industry standards for ethics, undertakes to meet those standards and does what other companies also do. Organizations undertake such assessments to identify their ethics strengths and opportunities for improvement. Sometimes the impetus to conduct an assessment is that the company is in ethics hot water or under ethical scrutiny by regulators or other 'outsiders'. Sometimes the impetus is simply that the company wants to assess what outside stakeholders think the company needs to do for good ethics and how the company is succeeding in doing it.

A misunderstanding frequently encountered is the assumption that an assessment's purpose is to identify *changes* the organization needs to make. To automatically assume that change will be necessary would be a biased view. Objectively, assessments should indicate the organization's ethics are healthy more often than not because so many companies try hard to be ethical, particularly the companies likely to undertake an ethics assessment of themselves. Even the US Sentencing Guidelines for Organizations recognize that a company may have made an effective, good-faith effort and a violation that occurred was beyond its control, not preventable under any reasonable standard.

What if an assessment indicates no deviations from expected norms? Just as physical exams frequently indicate people are healthy and the physician provides advice on how to continue to build good health, an assessment indicating that company ethics are healthy should be the foundation for advice on how to continue to build good corporate ethics.

Two external program reviews available in recent years have been the *National Business Ethics Survey* (NBES) sponsored by the Ethics Resource Center and the *Corporate Ethics Audit* (CEA) sponsored by Human Synergistics/Center for Applied Research. When comparing such assessments, reasonable questions to ask are, 'What set of expected characteristics does the survey measure?' and 'How does it measure those characteristics?' Answering those questions in reverse order turns out to be most useful.

### *How to measure ethics characteristics*

Following a procedure known as grounded theory,[1] the NBES survey questions were generated from the real-life experiences of a panel of corporate ethics officers, ethics center directors, academics researching ethics, and professionals in fields related to business ethics, including people who worked in various organizations – government, for-profit and non-profit.[2] In contrast, following psychological theory, the CEA survey questions were generated using a model of human behavior, then were statistically tested in many organizations to examine their validity, reliability and appropriateness.[3]

Those two surveys constructed their norms of good business ethics differently:

- The NBES used a benchmark process comparing each individual organization to historical data for all participating organizations. NBES advisors' judgments defined the standards for good ethics.
- The CEA compared answers to two forms of the same survey. On one form, people's answers described the current organization 'as it really is'. On the second form, people's answers described the ideal organization, as they would like it to be. The CEA used the ideal characteristics as standards for good ethics, so the description of a company's current organization can be compared with both ideal values and to historical norms for all participating organizations.

Both surveys assumed corporate ethics should be built on agreement and consistency about what to do ethically and why. But both surveys also recognized that different subcultures may exist within the company and used demographic data to search for such subcultures. If a group is found that has 'different' ethics, additional analysis must diagnose whether a corrective intervention is needed and, if so, design the intervention. Subculture issues frequently arise during mergers and acquisitions. The trick is to remember that acquisitions are made because the acquired unit is perceived as having value, so it is important not to try to wipe out the acquired organization's culture but instead to integrate and adopt the best of it in a new synthesis.

### *What ethics characteristics to measure*

With respect to the set of expected characteristics the surveys measure, review of the question sets indicates that the NBES asked primarily about organizational climate (about 70 percent) and secondarily about organizational culture (about 30 percent). The CEA reversed the pattern, asking primarily about organizational culture (about 80 percent) and secondarily about organizational climate (about 20 percent).

'Climate' or 'culture' – what do we mean? Questions about organizational climate ask what the organization has or does (the organization's procedures). Does it have a written code of ethics? Does it have an OpenLine? Does it do ethics training? On the other hand, questions about organizational culture ask what people feel they are expected to do to fit in and be successful (the employees' behaviors). This is the realm of values, beliefs, norms and expectations: the informal rules that people feel guide their behavior. For example, does the culture expect employees to take risks or to play it safe? Does the culture expect employees to pay close attention to detail or to focus on big issues?

Culture also is the realm of corporate legends. Conceding that not all legends are positive, a company can foster those that are, such as the United Parcel Service (UPS) legend of being the only express service able to deliver packages on time when dense fog shut down all aircraft flights into Oregon. UPS managers would not say how its people solved the problem. They claimed their team was exceptionally brilliant and their method was proprietary, a trade secret. A 3M legend began when DuPont began marketing cellophane and a 3M employee thought of coating the cellophane with colorless adhesive – inventing Scotch tape. Another 3M legend honors an employee's idea to coat paper with a 'weak' adhesive – inventing Post-it notes. The trick is to focus broadly on reinforcing corporate values, not narrowly on individuals as 'heroes'. The focus on values builds teamwork and culture; a focus on individuals too often builds discouragement among other employees because their contributions were overlooked or underappreciated.[4]

The sponsors of the CEA argued that the difference between surveying climate and culture is important because a survey of climate may show that ethics codes and posters exist, just as they did at Enron, while a survey of culture may show the actual behavior of organization members is shaped by very different expectations, also just as it was at Enron. The general argument is that 'codes of ethics and values don't necessarily describe how people actually behave and make decisions', or, phrased differently, 'organizational culture trumps codes of ethics'.[5]

The sponsors of the NBES agreed that 'culture has a stronger impact on outcomes than formal program elements' and that ethical outcomes are best in organizations with strong ethical culture.[6] They valued their survey because they believed it comprehensively tested how well a company meets the public policy expectations defined by the US Sentencing Guidelines for Organizations, as revised in 2004,[7] but over the years they have deliberately adjusted it to reduce the focus on compliance (climate) that it had in 1994 and to increase its focus on values and culture.[8]

Of note, the authors of the CEA reversed that pattern. They began with questions strongly focused on values and culture, drawn from their long experience with their *Organizational Culture Inventory*, and adjusted by adding several questions that focused on organizational climate. In short, both surveys address climate and culture and no one survey is likely to tell a company all it wants to know about the health of company ethics.

## Internal assessments

A weakness of external assessments is that they must be broad enough to be relevant to all organizations. But companies have specific issues that not everyone shares. For example, take Gap, Inc. It is a clothing retailer, not a manufacturer. Gap encountered public concerns about how garment makers treat their employees, 'substandard' working conditions of people making garments that Gap sells. What Gap was selling was made in about 3,000 factories and 50 countries. Gap responded to the concerns by hiring about 90 full-time employees as 'vendor compliance officers' to visit all of the factories and determine if the way they actually treat their workers lives up to Gap, Inc.'s expected standards, published as the 'Code of Vendor Conduct'. Those standards prohibit child labor, forced labor, discrimination and require good environmental practices and good wages and working conditions (see www.gapinc.com). For Gap, Inc., assessing this aspect of its company ethics probably is important.

Interestingly, companies like Gap, Inc., face a nearly unsolvable oversight issue. Research by Paul Bundick at Fielding Graduate University determined that men and women in New Delhi, India, make their living as microentrepreneurs, subcontractors at the bottom layer of New Delhi's export garment industry. They obtain orders and outsource production to tailor shops and home-based workers, who usually are women paid for piecework not done in a factory setting. Bundick found inquiries about such workers often encountered consternation, suspicion and silence, so it would be difficult or impossible to assess their working conditions.[9]

An instructive exercise is to ask the members of any function to collectively brainstorm the laws and regulations that their function must comply with. A human resources department identified more than 100 in less than ten minutes. Examples include affirmative action, age discrimination, equal employment opportunity, HIV/AIDS in the workplace, violence prevention, privacy rights, safe harbor, sexual harassment, the *Americans with Disabilities Act* (ADA), child labor, the *Civil Rights Act* of 1964, the *Consolidated Omnibus Budget Reconciliation Act* (COBRA), the *Health Insurance Portability and Accountability Act* (HIPAA), the *Immigration and Naturalization Act* (INA), the *Employment Retirement Income Security Act* (ERISA), the *Fair Labor Standards Act* (FLSA), the *Family and Medical Leave Act* (FMLA), the *Occupational Safety and Health Administration Act* (OSHA).

The reality that all functions in corporations must, in aggregate, comply with thousands of laws and regulations leads to three conclusions. First, functions must take responsibility for compliance and the ethics office or other company compliance department should not attempt to replace them in that role. Second, the oversight task is so pervasive that it constitutes self-governance that corporate management should be organized to provide (as the *Sarbanes-Oxley Act* of 2002 addressed) and that internal auditors should routinely evaluate. Third, if the ethics office attempts any oversight of compliance it must choose a few key, high-priority topics and focus on over-the-shoulder checks to see that the functions are in fact fulfilling their responsibility. Risk assessments, specifically addressed later in this chapter, are what identify to the company which compliance topics would warrant such special oversight, why, and what priority they deserve.

A reality is that functions will recognize certain laws and rules that many employees need to know — all employees, or all managers, or all buyers, or all budget owners. Those are training needs the company must address. Some may be handled by the function itself, as when the safety organization teaches first aid. Some may be handled by a training function, as when technical trainers teach certification classes on welding. And some may be addressed by the ethics office, as when it publishes online or paper self-instruction on topics like proprietary information or conflict of interest. The ethics office also collaborates with and supports functional organizations' training, as for example when the manager of contracting or procurement undertakes to teach rules imposed by the *Truth in Negotiations Act* or the *Foreign Corrupt Practices Act*.

Large companies have internal auditors capable of performing over-the-shoulder testing of how functions are performing their compliance roles. Another approach to such checks is structured self-assessment. These have to be discounted because of the obvious self-interest, but not so much that they have no value. They could be coordinated by the company's ethics committee composed of senior function managers.

Some of the topics companies have chosen to identify as special compliance risks are kickbacks, antitrust, conflicts of interest, export control, foreign corrupt practices, gifts and gratuities, insider trading, intellectual property, political activity, privacy, procurement integrity, safety rules, sexual harassment and time charging.

Recently, several initiatives to enforce compliance have affected companies in the US and elsewhere. Specifically, the US government implemented a Mandatory Disclosure Rule requiring contractors to self-disclose credible evidence of fraud, conflict of interest, bribery, gratuities, overpayments and false claims. A second US government initiative has been to increase enforcement of the *Foreign Corrupt Practices Act* that outlaws bribery of foreign officials. A third initiative, which we have heard informally discussed but have not seen formally documented, is to use its experience prosecuting senior executives of Enron to undertake prosecution of senior executives of other companies that have compliance problems instead of saying such prosecutions are too difficult, as was past practice. A fourth initiative is the United Kingdom *Bribery Act*, which extends culpability to any organization that carries on business in the United Kingdom. And there are other initiatives. One company which had one vice-president for business ethics and conduct (including compliance) now has added a second, a vice-president focused solely on compliance. Why? '[T]he company felt it was important to have a Chief Compliance Officer due to the increased compliance activity in many core areas.'[10]

Basic compliance requirements cannot be ignored. An ethics office, in concert with other functions in a company, must be prudent in ensuring they are observed. This in no way suggests that our basic overall view as to the direction and emphasis of the ethics effort changes. Compliance remains a small part of business ethics, Stage 1 of the ethics dynamic. The compliance topics all are rule-based. Compliance oversight endeavors to mitigate risk to the business by ensuring that the company is achieving at least the minimum acceptable standards. This contrasts with the overall ethics program, based on values, that aims to help employees excel and properly resolve issues even in the gray areas where clear rules do not exist.

### Assessing vulnerabilities of the OpenLine

Figure 8.1 shows the OpenLine process and highlights defects to be alert for during a program review. The figure focuses on four major players: executives, employees, the OpenLine (ethics officers) and investigators (including experts in various functional departments). Arrows show major flows of information going between the players. Balloons identify six problems likely to arise and link them to the players likely to cause them. The toughest is Problem 6, investigators' failure to prove or disprove an issue. The other five problems are easy to remedy with a little initiative. But Problem 6 sometimes arises because even the best investigators sometimes cannot find key evidence or witnesses – they may not even exist. Some investigations simply go nowhere and no one can do anything about it.

## General model of a program review

The goal of a periodic program review is to improve the company's ethics performance and only incidentally to improve the ethics program. This expresses the perspective of the ethics program as a catalyst enabling people throughout the company to independently act ethically (rather than the perspective of the ethics program as a funnel through which the company processes all ethics matters).

**Figure 8.1** OpenLine process vulnerabilities: Six problems that may affect the quality of OpenLine operations

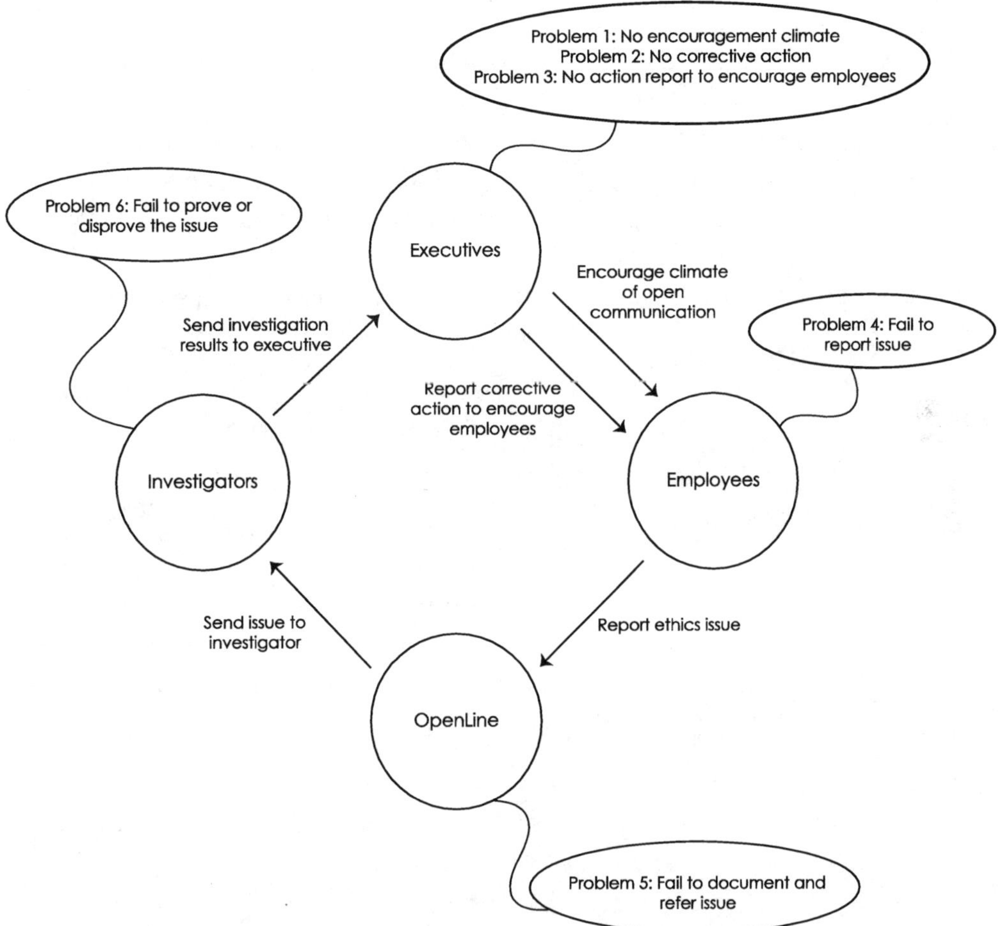


Writing in the *Wake Forest Law Review*, Frank Bowman criticized ethics and compliance programs for building Potemkin villages – facades that look good from a distance but lack substance and truth, ethics initiatives that show fine activity to passers-by but cause little, if any, improvement in people's actual behavior.[11] Therefore, a program review needs to deliberately look beyond each ethics initiative to see if substantive, related company ethics behaviors exist. Phase I calls for a two-column general model (Table 8.1). Representative of the program reviews some external ethics consultants undertake, and like the NBES, Phase I focuses principally on ethical climate – what the company does or has.

Phase II provides needed review of ethical culture. It aims to listen to employees' insights and candid comments about their experiences and perceptions at work. The CEA undertakes to do this using standardized survey questions. A company undertaking to do this itself likely will use interviews and focus groups built around its management development themes.

**Table 8.1** Review phase I — ethical climate

| | Ethics initiative | Company ethics behavior |
|---|---|---|
| 1. | Written risk assessment is current? | Company has real action plans to eliminate or reduce high priority risks? |
| 2. | Board of Directors 'oversees' ethics program? | Board of Directors reviews company action plans to eliminate or reduce high priority risks? |
| 3. | Management 'oversees' ethics program? | Management has an active, multi-function team ensuring the company properly responds to emerging ethics concerns? |
| 4. | Ethics program implementation personnel are trained, in place, and accessible to all employees? | All managers are trained to properly investigate and respond to ethics concerns, to recognize ethics dilemmas, to anticipate ethics implications arising from ordinary problems, and to engage the trust of employees? |
| 5. | Ethics awareness procedures are in place? | All new employees promptly receive orientation training on the company's values, ethics program and procedures? All employees receive frequent communication refreshing their knowledge and appreciation of those values, and the ethics program and procedures? |
| 6. | Compliance polices are published and accessible to all employees? | Employees are widely aware of and trained on compliance policies key to their particular job and take the initiative to look up or ask about compliance policies? |
| 7. | Compliance policies are enforced? | All managers document when and how their direct reports meet compliance policies? |
| 8. | Compliance is audited? | Management audits all functions to ensure they meet compliance policies and to detect and correct any violations? |
| 9. | Improper delegation of substantial discretionary authority is a concern? | Management uses published procedures to ensure substantial discretionary authority is not delegated improperly? |
| 10. | A system exists to receive ethics concerns, even anonymously or confidentially, and to report them to managers who can investigate and address them? | All managers ensure ethics concerns raised about their organization are objectively investigated and addressed? Managers appreciate the value of the OpenLine, support any employee's use of it, and ensure no user suffers any retaliation or retribution? |
| 11. | Violators of ethics and compliance policies are disciplined consistently? | Management uses published procedures to ensure discipline is consistent? |

| | Ethics initiative | Company ethics behavior |
|---|---|---|
| 12. | Incentives promote ethics and compliance? | Company culture gives a positive tone to ethics and compliance and documents rewards to people showing high ethics and penalties to people showing poor ethics? |
| 13. | Documentation adequately tracks ethics and compliance activities? | Company leaders analyze OpenLine calls and ethics events to identify trends, to reinforce good trends, and to intervene to correct bad trends? |
| 14. | Employee perceptions of the ethics program are systematically obtained? | The company systematically asks employees for their perceptions of company ethics and looks for issues and trends? |
| 15. | Non-employees, such as temporary employees, consultants and agents, are aware that while they are affiliated with the company their conduct must equal or exceed the company's code of conduct? | Non-employees, while they are affiliated with the company, are trained on the company's ethics culture, values, and procedures? |
| 16. | The ethics program fosters an overall culture of compliance? | Employees widely believe the company culture fosters a climate of compliance? |

Robert Cooke and Denise Rousseau[12] asked people in five diverse companies what they believe promotes good corporate culture, including both company effectiveness and employee satisfaction. Respondents chose achievement, self-actualization, affiliation and human encouragement. For example, people should feel rewarded for accomplishing tasks and goals (achievement). They should feel empowered and self-directing (self-actualization). They should feel that the company supports teamwork (affiliation). And, especially, they should feel respected and trusted (human encouragement). The respondents were not chosen at random. They were all attending employee and management development courses, which possibly introduced bias toward themes that leadership, management and employee development curricula have valued and promoted widely for years. That said, the themes might be valid for any organization that shares those same development values. An emergent concept might be that business ethics, which clearly should not be viewed as policing, has much more in common with management, organizational, and employee development.

Using the four themes – achievement, self-actualization, affiliation and human encouragement – sample discussion questions designed to draw out people's values, beliefs, norms, and expectations are listed in Table 8.2.

## Risk analysis

Where program review addresses what is true now, risk analysis looks toward the future. It identifies and prioritizes ethics risks *this specific company* faces. In the business ethics realm, risk assessment tends to be overwhelmingly compliance driven. Risk analysis in any domain is goal focused. It always tries to identify factors that may jeopardize success in achieving goals, then evaluates how likely that factor is to occur and the consequences if it does occur, and finally explores ways to systematically eliminate or minimize either the factor or its bad consequences. Risk analysis is widely used in engineering, general business and the insurance industry.

**Table 8.2** Review phase II — ethical culture

| | Management development theme | Question for discussion |
|---|---|---|
| 1. | Develop a team environment. (Affiliation) | What do you think, or what have you heard, would be some ideas for improving the way we work together in this company? |
| 2. | Promote a fair environment. (Human Encouragement) | What could people do to make sure everyone who works here is getting a fair deal? |
| 3. | Provide a supportive environment. (Human Encouragement) | What would help you and your colleagues do good work even better? |
| 4. | Encourage an orientation toward success. (Achievement) | What do you suppose you and your immediate co-workers could do more of, do less of, start doing or stop doing? |
| 5. | Provide opportunity for personal growth and development. (Self-Actualization) | What new opportunities do you think are open to people after they have worked here for a while? |
| 6. | Be open to creativity. (Self-Actualization) | If you want to make a change for the better in the way the company expects you to do your work, how do you go about getting permission to make the change? |
| 7 | Stimulate pride in quality work. (Achievement) | When do you find yourself expected to 'go the extra mile' to get your job done? |
| 8 | Foster enthusiasm for the job. (Achievement) | What do you like most about your job? |

## Four faces of risk analysis

In business ethics, risk analysis has four faces. The first three focus within the company: (a) ongoing assessment of every day's ethics events, (b) evaluation of all ethics investigations, including those conducted under attorney-client privilege (ACP), and (c) periodic review of patterns and trends. The fourth face attends to the environment: detection of outsiders' expectations that raise possible ethics vulnerabilities.

Face 1, ongoing assessment, focuses primarily on OpenLine issues each day. Senior management should be quickly alerted through the company's high-level person responsible for ethics – for convenience we will continue to call the position the corporate ethics director — and the law department to any issue which may have major impact on the company. This includes any information that indicates impending physical injury of any person, criminal charges against the company or anyone conducting company business, or widespread criticism and embarrassment of the company or anyone conducting company business.

In a company large enough to operate a decentralized ethics organization, where 'local' ethics officers usually are expected to operate independently, if not completely autonomously, a 'protective' procedure should be in place. As part of their daily risk assessment, front-line ethics officers should notify the corporate ethics director if an allegation involves any officer of the company or the senior manager of any site, or — due to the risk of actual or apparent conflicts of interest — if an allegation involves anyone the ethics officer reports to or that an investigator/subject matter expert currently working on an ethics inquiry reports to. Such notification helps to insulate the front-line ethics officer from any suspected or actual conflict of interest.

Face 2 of risk analysis focuses on investigations, including those conducted under ACP. That privilege should be selectively attached by the law department, not adopted as a blanket procedure for investigating all OpenLine allegations. Clearly, if a matter warrants treatment as an ACP it represents some high-risk issue that deserves special assessment. We prefer a check-and-balance consultation that tasks senior management to deliberately make a considered decision whether to attach ACP to an issue after receiving inputs from the ethics office, the law department, and any other stakeholder. A check-and-balance procedure protects managers from allegations of any suspected or actual conflict of interest, and may help regulators perceive the company's ethics program as being genuine and as effective as possible because the company has nothing to hide.

As an example of what can go wrong, in one instance where the law department unilaterally attached ACP, several OpenLine callers complained repeatedly for more than a year that the company was using an accounting procedure that violated US government regulations. Someone (never identified) in the law department stonewalled attempts by the ethics office to discover what the law department's investigation determined and what action had been taken. Ultimately, one caller used the procedure required by the *Sarbanes-Oxley Act* of 2002 to raise the issue with the audit committee of the board of directors. That forced the law department's hand and resulted in quick briefings to the OpenLine callers explaining that, months ago, both the company and the US government had reviewed the procedure in detail and reached agreement that it was authorized, legal, proper, ethical and in no way violated US government regulations.

When ACP is invoked, investigators then are obliged to act only at the direction of the responsible attorney, document investigation as directed by the attorney and not discuss the matter with any person except as directed by the attorney. Failure to follow this procedure will compromise and possibly void the privilege.

The third face of risk analysis commits the senior functional managers comprising the corporate ethics committee to schedule periodic reviews of patterns and trends in OpenLine calls. Where the committee discovers indicators of recurring trouble of a particular type or at a particular location, the committee should alert senior management to identify the root cause and correct it. This committee should take responsibility for oversight, ensuring that the company investigates every ethics allegation thoroughly and that other kinds of workplace issues have been properly addressed in a timely manner by the functions they were referred to for expert inquiry.

In its coordinating role, the committee should assess whether the company is meeting its obligations to be aware of and comply with laws, regulations and company policies, including compliance with prohibitions on retaliating against employees who call the OpenLine.

The fourth face of risk analysis requires everyone – ethics officers, ethics committee members, managers and employees – to attend to the broad social, ethical and legal environment the company operates in. The challenge is to recognize outsiders' expectations of the company and to detect potential ethics vulnerabilities in any and every company process so that checks and balances can be designed to prevent those ethics violations and to detect and minimize harm if they somehow occur despite the best prevention efforts.

For example, look again at Gap, Inc. To prevent garment maker mistreatment, Gap, Inc. created 90 vendor compliance inspectors. But the inspectors are a new vulnerability for Gap, Inc. because unscrupulous factory owners – the very kind likely to mistreat garment makers – might attempt to bribe inspectors to overlook bad conditions so they can get or keep large contracts. Forgiveness is one check and balance Gap, Inc. uses to prevent bribes. Perfection is *not* expected: 'few factories, if any, are in full compliance all of the time. Our goal is to work with factory managers to fix problems where we find them and prevent them from recurring. ... Our first choice is always to work with factory management to resolve issues, since this is in the best interest of the workers as well as our own business needs.'[13] The value of integrity is another check and balance Gap, Inc. has used: 'part of working with integrity is protecting ... our intangible assets, which includes our ... reputation'.[14]

For a second example, the Federal Acquisition Regulation (FAR) establishes procedures and controls affecting companies that do business with the US government – rules that companies must comply with. But more is involved. The government expects to see a cooperative working relationship with those companies. So, wise companies undertake not only to perform the minimum requirements set by the FAR but also to exceed those minimums to ensure all parties perceive the relationship as fully cooperative.[15]

For a third example, look at Cisco Systems' warning to its employees:

> *Gifts are banned to U.S. Congress and staff: The U.S. federal lobbying disclosure law (2007) bans, almost completely, giving gifts of any kind to Congressional officials, U.S. Senators and U.S. Representatives and their*

*staffs from Cisco or Cisco employees. The law forbids us from buying meals and event tickets and giving any sort of product discounts. Even courtesy gifts such as flowers, candy, or any small token that you might send to thank an official for help of some kind are banned. The law requires these restrictions because Cisco uses registered lobbyists to represent us before the Congress of the United States.*[16]

## General model of a business ethics risk assessment

When the US Sentencing Guidelines for Organizations were revised in 2004, they articulated as public policy the expectation that US public corporations should periodically prepare an assessment of business ethics, compliance and criminal conduct risks fine-tuned to their company. The guidelines did not provide a model for that risk assessment but did identify important elements:

- Assess the risk of criminal conduct.
- Take steps to achieve reasonable prevention and detection of criminal conduct.
- Evaluate the nature and seriousness of potential criminal conduct.
- Evaluate the likelihood that certain criminal conduct may occur because of the nature of the organization's business.
- Evaluate the prior history of the organization.
- The process must be ongoing.
- Organizations must periodically prioritize their compliance and ethics resources to target potential criminal activities that pose the greatest threat in light of the risks identified.

Various commercial suppliers offer proprietary formats for periodic risk assessments. Following is an eight-part experimental model for a written periodic assessment 'validated' by comparing it to recommendations made by ten speakers at two conferences on risk assessment sponsored by the Defense Industry Initiative (DII).

### 1. Purpose and standards

A statement of the purpose of the assessment and the external standards it is designed to meet.

*Example: As of (year) at (company), this is a periodic assessment of ethics, compliance, and criminal conduct risks as expected by the US Sentencing Guidelines for Organizations. The external standards considered include those Guidelines, as revised in 2004, and their Application Note 6, the Thompson Memo dated January 20, 2003, the* Sarbanes-Oxley Act *of 2002, and Security Exchange Commission and New York Stock Exchange rules. (Other guides may apply, such as the Compliance Program Guidance for*

*Hospitals,*[17] *Anti-Money Laundering Programs,*[18] *or the Compliance Programs of Investment Companies and Investment Advisers.*[19]*)*

## 2. Risk review

A review of business ethics issues historically facing the industry and the specific company. Evaluate the competence, experience and history of company personnel and the compliance areas known to be the current focus of regulators and law enforcement agencies.

*Example: A troubled relationship between the defense industry and the government in the 1980s led to development of the DII. Specific risk issues in the industry have been manufacturing defects, product substitution, foreign corrupt practices and time and labor mischarging. Regulators recently have spoken publicly about need for attention to 'revolving door' concerns. Specific responses have included conflict-of-interest certificates, ethics contact lines, statistical measures and incident assessments. Due to age demographics and mergers and acquisitions, about 20 percent of this company's population has 10-20 years of campaign model continuous training on compliance, values and ethics. About 80 percent of this company's heritage employees, new hires and transfers from other heritages have primarily experienced episodic compliance training and have accrued less than three years of campaign model continuous training on the values and ethics elements of the company's culture. Nonetheless, ethics incidents have been very low, involving only about 0.2 percent of all employees. A cautionary note: a low incident rate may be comforting to the company, but public perception disregards the low rate history if a serious incident occurs.*

## 3. Current priorities

A list of current priorities based on the last risk assessment and the associated actions designed to minimize those risks. Include a three-column table (Table 8.3):

- Column 1: Priority. #1, #2, #3 …
- Column 2: Risk. Name the risk.
- Column 3: Risk reduction actions. Describe the plan for reducing the risk.

**Table 8.3** Risk reduction analysis example

| Priority | Risk | Risk reduction actions |
|---|---|---|
| #1 | Defective manufacturing processes | OpenLine reports, communications and training on point, specific training on product substitution and the code of conduct. |

## 4. Assessment method

Description of the assessment method used: what company-specific data was examined to evaluate current risks? (OpenLine data and statistics? Employee surveys? Studies of special issues?) What external information was examined? (Industry surveys? Public reports of problems experienced at other companies? Briefings by regulators and law enforcement agency leaders? Best practices conference information?)

*Example: News reports during the past year alleged misconduct by interpreters supplied to the Department of Defense by another company. Our company also supplies interpreters, so potentially we might be vulnerable to similar misconduct allegations.*

## 5. Assessment findings

Tables, charts and text presenting results of the assessment described above. Compare patterns and trends over some period of years. This element could include description of the compliance areas identified by regulators and law enforcement as their current focus.

*Example: Based on the reports of Department of Defense concern about possible interpreter misconduct, all companies supplying interpreters on government contract, as our company sometimes does, need to recognize potential vulnerability to such risks and affirmatively prevent similar problems.*

## 6. Current risk assessment

Analysis of current risks based on the preceding sections. Include a four-column table (Table 8.4):

- Column 1: Risk. Name the risk.
- Column 2: Frequency. Estimate the likelihood (or probability) that the risk will occur in terms of low (unlikely to ever occur), medium (may have happened unpredictably at times in the past and seems likely to happen unpredictably again) and high (foreseeable; will happen at times).
- Column 3: Consequences. Estimate the damage likely if the risk does occur, again in terms of low, medium and high.
- Column 4: Reduction. Describe a plan for reducing the risk.

**Table 8.4** Current risk assessment example

| Risk | Frequency | Consequences | Reduction |
|---|---|---|---|
| False time reporting | Medium | Low | Prevent by training for awareness and applying time reporting process controls; detect discrepancies by floor audits of timecards and by reports called to the OpenLine. |

Columns two and three follow a standard method for estimating risk in two dimensions: frequency (or probability or likelihood the event will actually occur) and consequences (or impact expected) if the event does occur. Column four sets forth plans to reduce frequency, consequences or both.

### 7. Recommendations

Describe specific actions the company does use, or might use, to prevent and reduce risks. These might be categorized by type: some focused on assessing risks (e.g. quarterly statistical analysis to identify patterns and trends), some focused on detecting possible violations (e.g. calls to the OpenLine), and some focused on preventing violations (e.g. conflict of interest certificates).

### 8. Strategic direction

Consolidate the findings and recommendations into strategic goals for the company for the coming year, set ground rules for implementing them, and describe broad action plans to achieve the strategic goals. Include an update of the three-column table used in Part 3 above (Table 8.3).

In addition to risk assessment inputs prepared by the ethics office, other functions should produce their own risk assessment inputs. The law department may identify important legal compliance requirements that it must train corporate officers on. The finance department may identify process risks that need to be controlled to meet *Sarbanes-Oxley Act* requirements. Internal audit may list risks that auditors should attend to. Multiple, independent risk assessment inputs deserve encouragement to the extent that they do not create duplicative reporting requirements and to the extent that the outcomes are shared with the company's other risk assessment stakeholders, again suggesting the wisdom of charging the corporate ethics committee to coordinate a risk assessment by all corporate functions.

## Challenge puzzle

The critical question is: how will we know if our company is ethical — as ethical as it can be?

Analysis suggests that all business ethics ratings are based on subjective criteria. Methods used to rate companies' ethics include content analysis of their published documents, surveys by questionnaire or interviews, reputation and models based on one or more characteristics associated with ethics. Ratings typically are quantified — expressed as numbers that appear to rank one company better than another. Evaluations made by different persons using different measures yield different rankings. No unambiguous rating or rating scale exists today.

Another approach to 'assured business ethics' might be to focus on our company's employees as learners:[20]

1. What do we expect our employees to learn and know about compliance and ethics?
2. How will they learn it? What resources do we provide?
3. How will we know if they have learned it?
4. What will we do if they have not learned it?

Of those four questions, perhaps the most difficult to answer in a business setting is Question 3: how will we know if they – including board of directors' members, executives, managers, supervisors, employees, contract consultants, representatives and temporary employees – have learned it? – not just memorized it, but learned it sufficiently to apply it well in the normal course of business. That's a puzzle.

---

[1] Cresswell, JW 1998, *Qualitative Inquiry and Research Design: Choosing Among Five Traditions*, Sage, Thousand Oaks, CA.

[2] Joseph, J 2000, *Ethics Resource Center's 2000 National Business Ethics Survey, Vol. 1: How Employees Perceive Ethics at Work*, Ethics Resource Center, Washington, DC.

[3] Cooke, RA 1989, 'How to Use the Organizational Culture Inventory,' *Organizational Culture Inventory Leader's Guide*, Human Synergistics, Plymouth, MI: 1-10.

[4] Wilkins, AL, Perry, LT & Checketts, AG 1990, ''Please Don't Make Me a Hero': A Re-Examination of Corporate Heroes', *Human Resource Management* 29(3): 327-341.

[5] 2003, Corporate Ethics Audit Feedback Report: Sample, Human Synergistics, Plymouth, MI: 2.

[6] 2005, *National Business Ethics Survey: How Employees View Ethics in Their Organizations 1994-2005*, Ethics Resource Center, Washington, DC.

[7] 2005, National Business Ethics Survey.

[8] 2005, National Business Ethics Survey.

[9] Bundick, PL 2009, *Social Capital Strategies of Microentrepreneurs: An Inquiry Into the Business Use of Relational Models at the Base of New Delhi's Export Garment Industry*, PhD diss., Fielding Graduate University.

[10] [Redacted], Email, 2011.

[11] Bowman, FO III 2004, 'Drifting Down the Dnieper with Prince Potemkin: Some Skeptical Reflections About the Place of Compliance Programs in Federal Criminal Sentencing', *Wake Forest Law Review* 39(3): 671-690.

[12] Cooke, RA & Rousseau, DM 1988, 'Behavioral Norms and Expectations: A Quantitative Approach to the Assessment of Organizational Culture,' *Group and Organization Studies* 13(3): 245-273.

[13] 2006, What Is a Company's Role in Society? Gap Inc. 2005-2006 Social Responsibility Report, Gap, Inc., viewed 23 January 2012, www.gapinc.com/content/dam/csr/documents/2005-2006_Social_Responsibility_Report.pdf.

[14] 2009, *Our Code of Business Conduct*, Gap, Inc., San Francisco, CA, 19.

[15] 2011, *Public Accountability Report 2010*, Defense Industry Initiative, Washington, DC: 18.

[16] 2011, Cisco Code of Business Conduct: Connecting With Our Values, Cisco Systems, Inc., Milpitas, CA, 31-32, viewed 23 January 2012, http://investor.cisco.com/documentdisplay.cfm ?DocumentID=3263.

[17] Compliance Program Guidance for Hospitals, 63 Federal Register 8987, 1998.

[18] Anti-Money Laundering Programs, 31 C.F.R. 103.120, 2002.

[19] 2003, Compliance Programs of Investment Companies and Investment Advisers, 68 Federal Register 74714.

[20] 2007, Adapted from AACSB Assurance of Learning Standards: An Interpretation, Association to Advance Collegiate Schools of Business International (AACSB), Tampa, FL.

# Chapter 9

# The advantage

## Insights and opportunities

### LEARNING OBJECTIVES

By the end of this chapter you should:

- know that qualitative ethics evaluations develop important insights and opportunities to help employees achieve high ethics.
- be able to use ethics information to support mentoring, performance appraisal, inspirational storytelling, and to document ethics history.
- know the ethics vital records every company should have.

## FALLACY 8: 'WHINERS AND COMPLAINERS' SHOULD BE IGNORED

Should we not listen when opportunity knocks? Our experience is that people who raise ethics concerns most often have the best interests of the company at heart, should not be stereotyped as 'whiners and complainers', and should be listened to carefully.

Bob Lutz, leader of a Chrysler Corporation turnaround, warned that 'you ignore disruptive people at your peril' because, like irritating grains of sand, they can produce pearls — breakthroughs yielded by restudying what the company assumes and does. Lutz acknowledged — as do we — that careful listening and conscientious, due diligence follow-up tend to separate concerns into two categories: beneficial harbingers the company needs to act on, or negativity the company needs to understand so it does not become disruptive.[1]

Aphorisms say:

- Opportunity is often difficult to recognize.
- Learn to listen — opportunity could be knocking very softly.
- Opportunity is often missed because we are broadcasting when we should be tuning in.

At times, an OpenLine caller will seem to talk at endless length about one or more topics and then, at what appears to finally be the end of the conversation, will raise the true concern for the first time, often as an 'oh, by the way' that easily could be missed. Stay alert for such statements and be ready to start the interview process all over again. This reality carries an important message about giving callers priority, not allowing other events to cut short the time you have to listen to them, and generally giving callers the space to say all that is on their minds.

Almost every company we have seen uses only a small fraction of the information available from its ethics channels. They ignore opportunity to discover serious underlying problems. They do nothing with climate-sensing information that organizational consultants wish they could get. They throw away data that companies sometimes spend big bucks to try to acquire from surveys and focus groups. For example, connecting the dots in several people's concerns may reveal an unwanted pattern, such as systemic favoritism, bullying, retaliation, or behavior fueling a union organizing effort. All this can be done in a way that does not compromise confidentiality.

As CEO of Cummins, Inc., the diesel engine manufacturer, Tim Solso stands as an exception to the rule: he reads and learns the details of every substantive ethics investigation, and senior executives know that. 'If I do it, then they need to do it as well.' Solso does this to learn what is going on at the grassroots level and how the organization is responding. 'It's important that I know that.' The Cummins ethics organization actively looks for trends and spikes that indicate need for special management attention.[2]

## Collecting ethics program information

For many companies, ethics administration means tracking ethics incidents and doing quantitative analysis – compiling statistics describing how many issues and of what types were handled each month. Vendors sell computer software to collect incident reports in a database and generate statistics with a mouse click. This approach basically tells you only about ethics failures. Ethics administration should do more: it should aggressively develop opportunities and insights.

To date, the software designed for the business ethics community that we have seen focuses on collecting incident reports and generating statistics. It is designed to deliver quantitative analysis, specifically to deliver descriptive statistics. But this approach basically tells you only current counts. How many calls? How many complaints? Allegations? Questions? How many investigations closed? How many pending? How much time between incident report and closing memo? Electronic speed is a strength of computers. It is good for calculating statistics. It is good, if software has a good search engine, for locating key words in an electronic database.

A weakness is that relying on software raises issues of potential software obsolescence, extra costs for recurring software upgrades (if it is not 'plain vanilla' and customization to company specifications is always required), whether the data can be read by other software if necessary, and whether privacy protection really exists.

Commercial software to automate conflict-of-interest certifications has not been readily available because each company's certifications have been unique. But companies have created in-house software to capture certificates by computer and to retain them either as paper or electronic files. This can be as simple as creating a word processor form that people respond to and email back to the ethics office. A desirable control is electronic signature or other traceability process so authorized third parties can, at any time, link the document to the individual and verify the certificate's authenticity.

One thing missing from the software we have seen is capability for qualitative analysis. This weakness starts with a tendency for software databases to encourage cryptically brief entries. Cryptic entries may be suitable for a police blotter or ship's log, as a summary record indexing events, but they do not provide enough information to support qualitative analysis, well-reasoned judgments and sound decisions. 'Cryptic' runs counter to an historic principle in the investigations world: document everything. Be expansive in reporting. A detail that seems insignificant now may be critical and decisive later. The software we have seen also has lacked support for thematic analysis. Such software does exist to support academic research and intelligence analysis, but we have not seen it integrated into ethics databases.

Vendors' computer software is only designed to track and chart ethics incidents and investigations, to count ethics failures and ethics program inputs. This is fine as far as it goes, but it offers nothing to help companies to track and chart organizational culture development and to deliver qualitative evaluations that can develop important insights and opportunities to help employees achieve the high ethics they strive for.

At the time of this writing, adequate ethics programs require a mix of computer and paper systems. They need to sequentially log and document the *details* of all contacts that raise questions, concerns, or allegations whether received by phone, mail, email, or walk-in or other face-to-face meetings. One company unwisely allowed ethics officers to disregard 'trivial' calls. Aside from depending upon a subjective judgment, ignoring any call is unwise because conscientious inquiry often discovers unexpected merit and spin-off issues. Sometimes, too, the initial call is a 'feeler' to see how the company treats an OpenLine caller and, if the company passes that test, then the caller delivers the real question, concern, or allegation.

In pursuit of details, get written statements. Not every time. Frequently this will not be possible because the caller will feel limited by time, privacy or other factors. But generally it is good practice to hear what a caller has to say and then work with the caller to capture relevant information in a written statement. The process of talking through the information a second time and cooperatively writing it down often elicits new, important details and perspective.

Statements may be handwritten, hand-printed or typed by either the caller or the interviewer. Final decision on content or wording belongs to the caller so the writing explains the situation to the full satisfaction of the caller. Ask the caller to review the finished statement carefully with you and make any changes desired.

A 'telephone statement' is possible. If a statement is prepared during a telephone interview, explain at the bottom who wrote or typed the statement and that it was read back to the caller, who approved it. While the caller's signature would be nice, no signature is required.

The process of writing a statement explaining the caller's point of view usually impresses the caller favorably that someone is taking time to listen and to understand what the caller is trying to say. It also documents what the caller did say, so changes that come up later are clearly changes and not attributable to ambiguous misunderstandings during the initial interview.

If a caller does not prepare a statement, the interviewer should write the relevant results of an interview in as much detail as possible immediately after the meeting or phone call to ensure maximum accuracy and completeness. Make it clear the writing is the interviewer's detailed contemporaneous 'notes' of what the caller said. The term 'notes' is chosen carefully because notes can refresh memory about unwritten details but a 'report' may later be construed to be the complete record unalterable by other recollections. It should be clear that the interviewer has the time to commit to the process and is not pressured by management or other duties to do the minimum.

The ethics database should accommodate call logs, original statements, letters, memos, and interviewer's notes.

## Using ethics program information

Ethics and compliance administration tends to focus exclusively on compliance, and it should not. If organizational culture does indeed trump other aspects of an ethics program, ethics program administration should document the company's organizational culture outcomes.

To help employees achieve the high ethics they strive for, ethics administration should support mentoring and performance appraisal, enable inspirational storytelling and document the corporate ethics history — all of its challenges and successes. In addition, by doing qualitative analysis of the details and context of each issue, companies can detect systemic weaknesses and training needs.

### Mentoring

The mentoring that managers need is basically how to look at company ethics through the eyes and voices of their employees. If leaders personally and visibly own the company's ethics and do not delegate ethics to a silo ethics organization, then those leaders should mentor their employees, ask them to discuss ethics scenarios during regular staff meetings, and encourage them to discover potential ethics issues and to raise questions and concerns about possible ethics issues during the normal course of work. Managers should document those events for future use as positive comments in performance reviews. As mentors, leaders also should collect and document stories that demonstrate good ethics.

### Performance appraisals

Experienced managers say, 'What gets measured gets done.' Applying that to business ethics, companies often search for a way to measure their employees' demonstration of good ethics. Companies add an ethics category to the forms filled out for annual performance reviews ... and managers eventually decide the category is hard to evaluate in a meaningful way. Not that they do not want to rate ethics behavior properly: the problem is, what to look for? Do they rate people ethical for *not* having been convicted in the past year of fraud, conflict of interest, insider trading, or violation of the Byrd Amendment or the *Sherman Anti-Trust Act*? In contrast, if they have actively mentored their employees, then they have real-world data to assess ethical strengths and areas for further development.

Three ways a corporate ethics officer can help managers write effective performance appraisals:

- Performance management concepts teach managers to look forward, to help employees plan, and to coach employees to success in the coming year. So, provide managers with a list of ethics training and development topics and events to schedule for employees in the next 12 months.

- In keeping with the concept of catching employees in a success and rewarding it, at times we have been so favorably impressed by the ethical actions of specific employees that we asked their permission to share our observations with their supervisors at performance evaluation time — the employees readily agreed.
- Sometimes managers need inspiring examples, sample descriptions, not to copy into performance reviews but to borrow from and adapt. The ethics officer can draft some examples tailored to a company, or a department, or even a manager.

## Storytelling

Senior leaders, especially, need to set the storytelling tone by constantly collecting from their own direct reports positive stories about current ethics events, documenting those stories, and then sharing them with employees as inspiration.

Storytelling has been an effective leadership technique as long as leaders have existed. One of the best-known stories relevant to ethics was published by Mason Locke Weems (Parson Weems) in 1800, the year after George Washington died. Historians consider it possibly true or possibly apocryphal, but it unquestionably portrayed Washington as ethical:

> *[T]he following anecdote [was] related to me … by an aged lady, who was a distant relative, and, when a girl, spent much of her time in the family:*
>
> *'When George,' said she, 'was about six years old, he was made the wealthy master of a hatchet! of which, like most little boys, he was immoderately fond, and was constantly going about chopping everything that came in his way. One day, in the garden, where he often amused himself hacking his mother's pea-sticks, he unluckily tried the edge of his hatchet on the body of a beautiful young English cherry-tree, which he barked so terribly, that I don't believe the tree ever got the better of it. The next morning the old gentleman, finding out what had befallen his tree, which, by the by, was a great favourite, came into the house; and with much warmth asked for the mischievous author, declaring at the same time, that he would not have taken five guineas for his tree. Nobody could tell him anything about it. Presently George and his hatchet made their appearance. 'George,' said his father, 'do you know who killed that beautiful little cherry tree yonder in the garden?' This was a tough question; and George staggered under it for a moment; but quickly recovered himself: and looking at his father, with the sweet face of youth brightened with the inexpressible charm of all-conquering truth, he bravely cried out, 'I can't tell a lie, Pa; you know I can't tell a lie. I did cut it with my hatchet.' – 'Run to my arms, you dearest boy,' cried his father in transports [ecstasy], 'run to my arms; glad am I, George, that you killed my tree; for you have paid me for it a thousand fold. Such an act of heroism in my son is*

*more worth than a thousand trees, though blossomed with silver, and their fruits of purest gold.'*[3]

The ethical reputation of Abraham Lincoln was similarly bolstered by stories about his honesty. A story said that Lincoln, while working as a storekeeper, discovered one night that he had taken a few cents too much from a customer, so he closed the store and walked a long distance to pay the money back. Another story said Lincoln once discovered he had weighed out too little tea for the money paid. He took the extra tea to the customer, who was surprised because she had not known she had been shorted. As a lawyer traveling with the circuit court, Lincoln was nicknamed 'Honest Abe' – a lawyer never known to lie – and apparently lectured lawyers to always be honest, saying that if 'you cannot be an honest lawyer, resolve to be honest without being a lawyer. Choose some other occupation.'[4]

As vice-president of Armstrong International, David Armstrong had an epiphany that storytelling could make his company better - stories about goals, core values, visions and victories. In 1992, he published 75 stories he tells any time he wants to make a point without lecturing people. One reported a plant expansion decision. The most efficient location for a new building required demolishing the house retired employee Fred Kemp had called home from childhood to retirement. Armstrong's president chose to do the 'right thing,' refused to make Kemp move, and ordered the new building be constructed elsewhere.

Other Armstrong examples:

- *Honesty.* The company cafeteria has an open cash box. It has no cash register and no one watches the money. The honor system works fine.
- *Quality.* Employees self-inspect the parts they produce. One employee tagged a batch of 3,000 castings for close inspection because several clearly were bad.
- *Teaming.* A company that regularly supplied steel to Armstrong rejected another customer's offer to pay a premium price for high priority on a very large one-time order. The supplier instead honored its commitment to be on Armstrong's team and fulfill its promised shipments reliably and on time.
- *Service.* Despite a customer's written order that specified fittings should be cut at 41 degrees, when the customer complained the fittings should have been cut at 38 degrees Armstrong unquestioningly sent employees to the customer's plant to adjust the fittings.

Armstrong's advice is to look for 'heroic deeds'. This is a very relevant concept for business ethics and sometimes is expressed as 'going the extra mile'. Not just shows of extra input, like working extra hours, but people going beyond the call of duty to accomplish something really worthwhile. A similar biblical theme: if a man needs your shirt, give him your coat as well. It is more than 'compliance'; it is human heart and spirit. Armstrong says 'every company has a rich heritage of stories that can simplify, lead, inspire, motivate and solve ... but not every CEO searches them out … and retells them'. How Armstrong has done it: 'Last week as I was walking through the shop, I bumped into [a foreman]. I asked — as I always do — whether he had any stories ….'[5]

More recently, Stephen Denning built a career teaching leaders how to use storytelling. He discovered the power of stories while working for the World Bank, which he realized had great expertise and world-class experts, but no good system for sharing that knowledge with people who could use it to solve poverty problems. Denning credits storytelling with changing the bank's mission from just lending money to also sharing knowledge.[6] He has identified eight broad types of stories, each to achieve a different objective, e.g. sparking action, building reputation or transmitting values.[7]

Some of the best known storytelling has been about the early days of Southwest Airlines. Co-founder Herb Kelleher became a legend by winning a series of lawsuits, defeating existing airlines trying to block Southwest's first flight — its grand opening — a battle that ended when the US Supreme Court refused to hear the appeal filed by Braniff, Texas International, and Continental airlines. The legend of Southwest's culture began early. The airline started with four airliners but too little cash to make payroll. Its dilemma: lay off employees or sell one airplane. It sold the airplane, establishing itself as a company that cared for employees. Continuing that theme, Southwest often threw celebration parties and Kelleher ran an extra barbecue at the airport at 2 am so third-shift employees could be there. His legend continued: he expected executives to work field jobs at least once a quarter — reservations, baggage, dispatch — and himself worked 'on the lines' one day a month, sometimes 'slinging bags with the baggage handlers'.[8]

## Ethics history

In addition to collecting firsthand stories, another resource for effective storytelling is access to the company's ethics history. At an electronics plant near Baltimore, Maryland, ethics officer Donna Davis has one shelf in her office filled with binders containing ethics events that occurred each year, and every year, that she has led the ethics program. That is the model for an ethics history. The annual volume may be formalized to open with a description of the ethics program, staff, strategy, and communications plan at the beginning of each year, but the heart of it is a chronology: a copy of every ethics meeting agenda, every ethics publication, every ethics training course, every company newsletter about ethics, every executive speech that mentions ethics, every ethics item posted on the company's website, all ethics stories leaders collected throughout the year and every news story that mentions company ethics.

The history binder is evidence that the campaign model is working to bombard employees with ethics messages constantly throughout the year. What if you cannot find anything to put into the binder? That could be an important signal that the campaign model is not operating, that the company is not positively developing its organizational culture and that the ethics officer should help company leaders initiate some ethics interventions promptly to fix that problem.

Thus the history binder provides warning – perhaps even *early* warning – of an ethics culture problem. The set of history binders also is evidence that the company has a viable ethics program if unforeseen events make it necessary to prove so to outsiders – investigators, prosecutors, judges or juries.

## Ethics vital records

Three practical requirements drive the ethics vital records every company should have. The first requirement is company leaders' need to stay on top of *current events*, which is the role of OpenLine documentation. The second is the need to document the *incident and training record* for corporate management, both quantitatively and qualitatively – the numbers and the substance of incidents and training, which is the role of ethics analytical reports and training documentation. And the third is the need to *forecast* what the ethics and compliance program needs to do and will do, the role of ethics plans and budgets and ethics meetings.

### OpenLine documentation

*OpenLine log*

Some system is required to document each OpenLine call (received by phone, mail, email, fax or personal visit), to assign it a sequential identification number, record the date, whether it was Type 1, 2, or 3, and to whom it was sent for action.

*OpenLine memo files*

Operational memos document the details of incoming OpenLine calls and attach comments that more fully identify persons, organizations and events mentioned by the caller. Comments also can add perspective provided by related information already on file. For example, 'Over the past two weeks, the OpenLine has received six other calls, apparently from six different people, also reporting that buyer J Alpha apparently enjoyed a 2-week all-expenses-paid vacation in Paris they suspect was paid for by a real estate developer Alpha just awarded a $20 million contract to.'

*Case closure memos*

Each Type 3 issue requires formal documentation of results at the end of the investigation. Briefly summarize the investigation. State whether the situation was found to merit a corrective intervention or whether allegations were disproved or could not be substantiated. Summarize what corrective actions were taken, and report how closure with the original caller was completed.

### Ethics training documentation

*Training content*

Training content tends to evolve and change, if not improve, over the years. Some training is general and other training is specific to target a problem that is persistent, either everywhere or in a particular location, or is tailored to address vulnerabilities of specific employees, like marketing or procurement. Experience indicates that the stakeholder who most often and most urgently wants to know the content of a training course is an attorney preparing to represent the company's good practices in court. Therefore, it is good to consult the attorneys and mutually agree upon how long to keep a record copy of each version of a course.

### *Attendee rosters*

The names of employees who attended a particular course at a particular place, date, and time are useful in three ways. One is to support the attorney representing the company's good practices when that attorney needs to show that a particular person did or did not attend training. Another is to identify by exception people who should have attended training but did not so they can be rescheduled. The third is to assess and report to management who did complete ethics training — who got what ethics message.

### *Conflict-of-interest certificates*

Many companies ask employees to periodically answer a questionnaire and sign it as a certificate that they have disclosed to the company any potential conflict-of-interest situation they might be involved in. This process protects both the employees and the company by bringing potential issues to the surface so they can be addressed and prevented from becoming actual conflicts of interest that could carry penalties for the employee or the company. It also stands as periodic training and retraining to familiarize employees with various conflict of interest issues so they are sensitive to them and can recognize them should they arise in real life. This is especially important for, and protective of, the company's senior financial officers because the *Sarbanes-Oxley Act* of 2002 explicitly requires them to promote 'honest and ethical conduct, including the ethical handling of actual or apparent conflicts of interest between personal and professional relationships'.[9] The certificates may be filed with employment records, but they probably are easier to file and locate if they are kept as a single alphabetical file by the ethics office or human resources.

Certificates stating that no conflicts exist may be filed after the employee signs them. Certificates reporting an 'exception' or potential conflict should be routed to the employee's manager for review and signature (because the manager has responsibility for acting to safeguard both the company and the employee from a conflict situation) and then should be reviewed by the law department before being filed.

## Analytical reports

### *Weekly/monthly summary*

Call volume determines the appropriate period for this report. Experimentation in a *Fortune* 100 company showed that the minimum time period to establish useful patterns and trends was one week. If the volume of calls per week is less than a mean of about 10, then a longer time period should be used, perhaps a summary every two weeks or once a month.

The summary report can have two sections. One is a quantitative section composed of two charts. The first is a line chart marking the number of OpenLine calls (y-axis) each week during the year (x-axis). Using a different color for each year, the lines for this year and previous years can be presented for comparison. Expect the normal pattern to oscillate approximately in the pattern high, low, high, and so forth, and expect the pattern to look surprisingly similar each year.

This chart may show low numbers of calls just before pay raises are announced each year (when employees do not want to rock their boat), and high numbers just after annual performance reviews (if employees are disappointed by their ratings). The chart can provide 'early warning' of trouble by showing anomalies, perhaps sustained high numbers of calls for more than two weeks. Qualitative analysis of call content is required to identify the specific problem and location for further attention. Analysis also identifies subculture concerns: what is important to machinists may not be important to software programmers.

The second chart is a line chart showing the cumulative total number of OpenLine calls (y-axis) by week during the year (x-axis). As before, using a different color for each year allows this year to be compared to previous years. This shows whether the OpenLine workload is increasing or decreasing. Qualitative analysis would be required to explain the increases or decreases.

The second section of the weekly/monthly summary report is a qualitative analysis section. Call it 'highlights' and summarize significant OpenLine calls (and related investigative results if they are already available). 'Significant' may mean that the call fits what the company is watching as a high-risk category, or that it involves senior managers, or that the company may be exposed to a high-dollar loss, or that it indicates a growing trend – the possible criteria for including a call should be flexible.

*Quarterly statistics*

Every three months is a good interval to use for statistically summarizing OpenLine activity. The quarterly report is primarily data used as input for a wrap report totaling all activity for the year. The data to collect includes:

- Number of active ethics officers (full-time + part-time + additional duty = total).
- Number of OpenLine calls (Type 1 + Type 2 + Type 3 = total).
- Number of Type 3 Investigations opened during the quarter. (This can be subdivided by topic, if desired. For example, Time Charging, Financial and Accounting Irregularities, Misuse of Resources, Supplier Relations, etc.)
- Number of Type 3 Investigations closed during the quarter. (This can be subdivided by the same topics, if desired.)

  - Number of investigations closed with some merit found.
  - Number of investigations closed with all allegations disproved.
  - Number of investigations closed when investigation was unable to substantiate or disprove allegations. (Caution: because it is important to an accused employee who is innocent to have allegations fully disproved, do not settle for 'unable to substantiate' unless absolutely necessary.)
- Number of Type 3 Investigations still open at the end of the quarter.
  - Number of these investigations open longer than 60 days. (This can provide 'early warning' of case management difficulties. In an ideal world, no investigation would last as long as 60 days. Inquiry may uncover a correctable fault or it may determine a reasonable justification exists.)
- Corrective Actions from Type 3 Investigations (subdivided, e.g. employment terminations, employment suspensions, written warnings, verbal coaching, restitution, policy/procedure changes).

The quarterly statistical report also can capture communications and training numbers for the quarter by category, for example, classroom participants, video-only participants, computer-based training participants, articles published, speeches given, posters distributed, and so forth.

One useful analysis at this stage, prepared as a table but also potentially a pie chart, calculates the percentages of Type 1, Type 2 and Type 3 calls against the total number of OpenLine calls. For a mature OpenLine, these percentages often are roughly about 20 percent Type 1, 60 percent Type 2, and 20 percent Type 3.[10]

*Annual statistics*

The annual report has the same structure as the quarterly report and wraps up the quarterly statistics to a total for the year. It is the source document for reports comparing activity by year.

*Annual self-assessment and audit*

One of the time-tested principles adopted by the DII is that the company's ethics program should be audited every year to ensure it is working as intended. If, for some reason, disinterested auditors cannot visit a particular company element or site, then the ethics office should conduct a comparable self-assessment to assure itself and the company that the ethics program is in good order there.

The components of an audit or self-assessment include examination of the ethics climate: the effective presence of ethics communications, ethics policies and procedures, ethics training, OpenLine operation, ethics investigations, conflict of interest certifications, and special topics such as anti-retaliation efforts and procedures addressing receipt of gifts and gratuities.

The self-assessment also calls for examining the ethics culture: conducting focus groups or interviews to assess employees' familiarity with the company's values and code of conduct, their trust in the ethics system, and their assessment of the current ethical behavior of the company and its employees.

Where auditors visit, they should conduct a statistically valid survey of a representative sample of employees to assess whether they know how to contact an ethics officer and use the OpenLine, whether they know how to report anonymously or confidentially, whether they would feel safe from reprisal if they did call the OpenLine, whether they have received ethics training of some kind during the preceding 12 months, and whether they are familiar with the company's values and mission statement.

### *Periodic report to the audit committee of the board of directors*

The *Sarbanes-Oxley Act* of 2002 requires the audit committee to stay abreast of ethics activities related to the company's financial activities. Periodic – perhaps quarterly – inputs to the audit committee identify issues that have arisen through the OpenLine related to accounting irregularities and financial fraud. These reports can be prepared by flagging relevant OpenLine memos as they are prepared each day and reviewing the flagged memos once a quarter to compile the summary report.

### *Report to the board of directors*

This is a management review report, provided at least annually, that documents the ethics activities since the previous report for the OpenLine and for ethics communications and training and provides numerical comparisons to previous years to show patterns and trends. The report may also describe goals planned for the coming year. This report is prepared from two sources. First, it presents tables and charts showing the annual operational statistics. Second, it presents tables and charts showing results of the annual audit supplemented by results of self-assessments. Be prepared to answer a question that first acknowledges 'the hard work you have done' and then asks, 'How do you know it is working?'

### *Program review and periodic risk analysis*

See Chapter 8 for a full description of these reports.

### *Ethics plans and budgets*

On its face, this looks like it should be simple: identify goals for the coming year, break down those goals into tasks that need to be completed to achieve the goals, and prepare an annual operating budget by pricing those tasks. In practice, some people do this better and more easily than other people. Complications are introduced by financial managers who press for budget reductions even if that means abandoning 'low priority' tasks. The Periodic Risk Analysis is one source of data to support the annual plan and budget. The Annual Statistics reports, with their history of past years' activity, are another source that allows forecasting requirements for the next year.

The company should find ample justification for fully funding the ethics program in the explicit insistence in the US Sentencing Guidelines for Organizations that each company provide adequate resources: 'to carry out such operational responsibility, such individual(s) shall be given *adequate resources* [emphasis supplied].'[11]

## Ethics meetings

### *Ethics officer conferences*

For a small company operating at one location, the ethics staff may meet monthly. For a larger company, with more geographic dispersion, monthly meetings may require a telephone or video conference – if the quality of a video conference is poor (time delays or inability to always see and hear all participants), then a teleconference is preferred. Front-line ethics officers of a very large company (that has major facilities throughout the United States and in other countries as well) identified as a 'best practice' an annual two-day conference to discuss new directions for the company's ethics and compliance program. For a large, multi-site company, an advantage of gathering ethics officers from throughout the company to hold such a meeting at one of those sites is that participants have opportunity to personally see and experience a part of the company they otherwise would only know through hearsay. The agenda for each meeting, in telephone or in person, should be filed as a record of topics addressed. Detailed minutes may not be useful, although some process needs to identify and track to completion action items that emerge from the meetings.

### *Ethics committee meetings*

The ethics committee composed of senior functional managers needs to meet periodically, probably on a regular schedule, and the agenda should be filed for each meeting, as above, as a record of topics addressed. Again, detailed minutes may not be useful but a process needs to identify and track to completion action items that emerge from the meetings. An advantage an ethics committee gives to ethics officers is backing by a wider consensus as to what is beneficial and support if controversy arises – the ethics officers are not 'out there on their lonesome'.

## Records retention

Each company needs to set its own records retention policy. Good practice is to destroy records when they are no longer needed (always in consultation with the law department). As a general rule, retention for three years works well if that conforms to retention rules for other business documents. The exception would be to retain documents required longer by contract, legal proceedings, or audits, or by the possibility that the problem could develop over time into something more than it originally appeared to be.

## Challenge puzzle

Perhaps managers need to pay more attention to what kind of stories are shaping the corporate culture. Two examples:

- An agency with 2,000 investigators based worldwide divided each 'case' into research questions that were sent to multiple locations where investigators could obtain answers. Those answers were then collected at 'home base' as a completed investigative report. Clearly this agency depended on teamwork. But it tried to set up a Hall of Heroes featuring stories describing the exploits of individual investigators. A mismatch? Should not this agency feature stories describing exploits that could only be accomplished through exceptional teamwork?
- A corporation's human resources vice-president encouraged all managers to have an 'open door' and listen to employees. But one truth well known among employees, through stories of multiple incidents over the years, was that it was nearly impossible to contact the HR vice-president because you would have to somehow get past his secretary, who was nicknamed the Dragon Lady. When she was interviewed during a company-wide study, she described a major responsibility of her job as protecting the vice-president by blocking messages and visitors from getting to him. When the vice-president saw that study result, he was upset to say the least. 'That's not how I perceive her job,' he said, and he met with her to reorganize her priorities. But the Dragon Lady stories had shaped the corporate culture for years. Had the vice-president never heard them?

The stories that do (or can) shape a company's culture need to be collected, inventoried, and used, but, in addition, they need to be evaluated for what they do (or should) contribute to the culture. Figure 9.1 shows a relevant classification model looking at two dimensions: (a) Does the story speak to problem prevention or to fire-fighting after a problem surfaces? (b) Does the story speak to teamwork or to individual heroism? Possible cultural outcomes are described in the boxes composing the model's four quadrants.

Here is the puzzle: are stories that fit in one quadrant better than others? Should a company have stories to fit each quadrant? Should a company avoid and discourage stories that fit in a particular quadrant? What are the company's story needs? What should corporate stories promote?

**Figure 9.1** Model for assessing story contributions to corporate culture

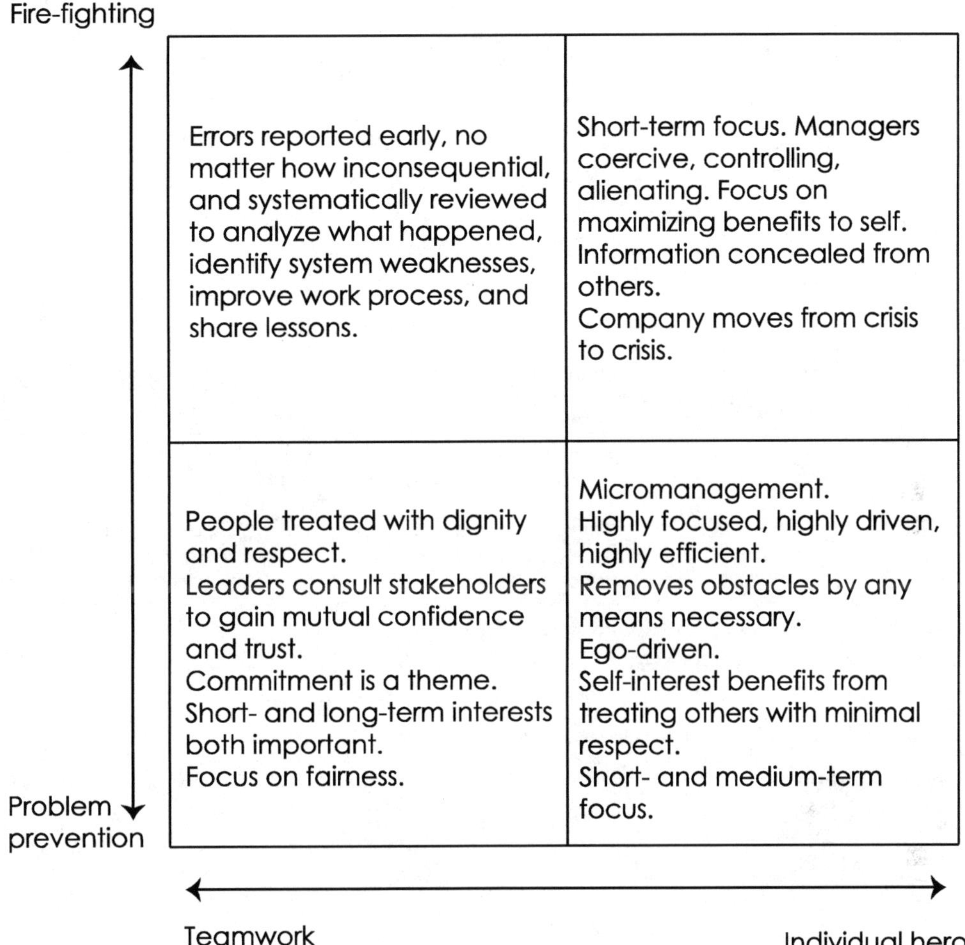

Fire-fighting
Errors reported early, no matter how inconsequential, and systematically reviewed to analyze what happened, identify system weaknesses, improve work process, and share lessons.
Short-term focus. Managers coercive, controlling, alienating. Focus on maximizing benefits to self. Information concealed from others.
Company moves from crisis to crisis.
People treated with dignity and respect.
Leaders consult stakeholders to gain mutual confidence and trust.
Commitment is a theme.
Short- and long-term interests both important.
Focus on fairness.
Micromanagement.
Highly focused, highly driven, highly efficient.
Removes obstacles by any means necessary.
Ego-driven.
Self-interest benefits from treating others with minimal respect.
Short- and medium-term focus.
Problem prevention
Teamwork
Individual hero

[1] Lutz, RA 2003, *Guts: 8 Laws of Business from One of the Most Innovative Business Leaders of Our Time* (rev. edn), Wiley, Hoboken, NJ.

[2] Singer, A 2010, 'Why Cummins Inc.'s CEO Reads His Firm's Ethics Investigation Reports – All 400 of Them', *Ethikos*, viewed 25 January 2012, www.ethikospublication.com/html/cummins.html.

[3] Weems, ML 1918 (1800), *A History of the Life and Death, Virtues and Exploits of General George Washington*, Lippincott, Philadelphia, PA, viewed 24 January 2012, http://xroads .virginia.edu/~CAP/gw /chap2.html .

[4] Lincoln, A quoted in Donald, DH 1995, *Lincoln*, Simon & Schuster, New York: 149.

[5] Armstrong, DM 1992, *Managing by Storying Around*, Doubleday Currency, New York.

[6] Denning, S 2007, *The Secret Language of Leadership: How Leaders Inspire Action Through Narrative*, Jossey-Bass, San Francisco.

[7] Denning, S 2005, *The Leader's Guide to Storytelling: Mastering the Art and Discipline of Business Narrative*, Jossey-Bass, San Francisco.

[8] Gibson, JW & Blackwell, CW 1999, 'Flying high with Herb Kelleher: a profile in charismatic leadership', *Journal of Leadership and Organizational Studies* 6(3-4): 120-137.

[9] *Sarbanes-Oxley Act* of 2002, §406.

[10] 2004, See Everything You Wanted to Know About Helpline Best Practices: Results of the 2004 Survey of Ethics Officer Association Sponsoring Partner Members, Ethical Leadership Group, Wilmette, IL.

[11] 2004, Guidelines Manual, United States Sentencing Commission, November, Washington, DC, §8B2.1 (b)(2)(C).

# Chapter 10

# The reputation

## Social responsibility

### LEARNING OBJECTIVES

By the end of this chapter you should:

- □ understand that corporate reputation is affected by benefits to stakeholders.
- □ know that laws and regulatory agencies enforce public policy that companies benefit stakeholders in addition to stockholders.
- □ know that business ethics is the bedrock foundation for corporate social responsibility.
- □ be able to recognize four approaches to corporate social responsibility.

## FALLACY 9:
## A COMPANY'S CHARITABLE CONTRIBUTIONS MAKE IT SOCIALLY RESPONSIBLE

Richard T De George is a notable business ethicist ('business ethics pioneer' actually may be more accurate) so when we see him write that 'business ethics' recently has merged into 'corporate social responsibility' (CSR) and is in danger of being co-opted by business,[1] we take his warning seriously. Fallacy 9 is the danger we think of. Business should not believe that simply spending money on charity equates to having good business ethics, showing good corporate social responsibility and being a good corporate citizen. It is not a good idea to put ethics, compliance, corporate social responsibility, conscious capitalism, philanthropy, stewardship and corporate citizenship in the same conceptual bucket. There are those who think that is the correct place for all of the above: however, the distinctions between them are important, and lumping them together does not enhance them individually. Quite the opposite, in fact. Richard De George is right. Business ethics and corporate social responsibility can be related, but they are not the same thing.

# Stockholder versus stakeholder debate

What is 'CSR'? We start our exploration of that question with the stockholder versus stakeholder debate.

In the historic, 'traditional' view of business called 'stockholder theory', the duty of any business was to earn profit for its owner or stockholders. Precursors for a different view can be found long before 1960, but it was the decade of the 1960s when significant discussion of a 'new' view of business called 'stakeholder theory' became visible. Its argument was that any business has significant social responsibilities beyond the company's interest in earning profits: duties to people other than owners and stockholders.

'Stakeholder' is broadly defined as everyone who has a voice in, or is affected by, the actions and decisions of a company. A criticism of stakeholder theory is that so many categories of people can be considered stakeholders that it is impractical to evaluate and adjust to all of their diverse interests. There is a continuum. At one extreme, the term stakeholder can be broadly defined to spread a wide net, and, at the other extreme, a narrow definition can limit stakeholders to people with contractual connections to the business – for example, stockholders, employees, creditors, suppliers. A 'practical' solution is to focus on 'major stakeholders', but the categories considered 'major' may vary from company to company.

As a generic solution, Sisodia, Wolfe and Sheth identify five major stakeholders of corporations today as 'SPICE' (Society, Partners, Investors, Customers, Employees). 'Society' includes local communities, the broader community, governments and societal institutions, including non-governmental organizations.

'Partners' include suppliers, team members, and retailers. 'Investors' and 'Customers' are self-explanatory. 'Employees' include present, past, and future employees and their families.[2] Others sometimes recognized as having interests so significant as to deserve inclusion as 'major stakeholders' are competitors and social activists.

On the internet, for everyone to study in detail, is a noteworthy debate between Mackey and Friedman. The question posed is which corporation adds more to society: (a) one focused on open and free competition to increase profits, or (b) one promoting desirable social ends – seriously taking on responsibility to provide employment, eliminate discrimination, avoid pollution, and donate time and money to charity?[3]

Opening the debate, businessman John Mackey's position was that wise corporations strive to benefit all of their stakeholders. Mackey's company, Whole Foods, measures success by benefits to six 'most important' stakeholders: customers, employees, investors, suppliers, communities, and the environment. For Mackey, the 'happiness' of those stakeholders is not merely means to an end; it 'is an end in itself'. Whole Foods' policy is to donate five percent of net profits to philanthropy because 'we care about [our communities] and feel a responsibility to help them flourish as well as possible'.[4] Mackey said he disagrees strongly with Friedman's position, which Mackey asserted is that a law-abiding business has only one social responsibility: to maximize profits.

Scholar Milton Friedman responded that businesses see most success when they put customer happiness first and support a certain amount of corporate philanthropy. But it is their core business that is – and should be – their 'contribution to society'. For Whole Foods, said Friedman that core business is 'to enhance the pleasure of shopping for food'.[5] With respect to philanthropy, Friedman asserted that corporations have no special competence in selecting charities.

*Corporate Responsibility Magazine* published a related debate. In this debate, Herman and Nair essentially argued that companies increase shareholder value by building and selling products and services that solve social and environmental problems and human needs. It is 'attractive to customers, inspiring to employees, and compelling for investors'.[6]

Karnani and Sullivan argued the opposite case, essentially by saying companies undertake socially desirable activities that are profitable. When they do, they may 'publicly trumpet their actions as CR (corporate responsibility). It is not surprising that CR initiatives in companies are often housed in the public relations department, and that public relations consulting firms are very active in the CR field.' They said companies will not *voluntarily* undertake socially desirable activities that are not profitable and do so only when law or regulation requires them to.[7]

Herman, Nair, Karnani, and Sullivan appear to define 'CR' the same as 'CSR', but as we will see later other people may sometimes define those terms differently.

Whether projects labeled CSR lead toward increased shareholder value, as Herman and Nair argued, or increasing shareholder value leads toward projects labeled corporate social responsibility, as Karnani and Sullivan argued, Sisodia, Wolfe, and Sheth expressed 'surprise' to discover that the publicly traded firms in a group of 28 'loved' by stakeholders [not necessarily for corporate social responsibility reasons] outperformed the S&P 500 over 3-, 5-, and 10-year periods. Investor returns were consistently and significantly higher: about double the S&P returns in three years, about ten times in five years, and about eight times in ten years.[8]

University of California professor David Vogel argued the opposite view, saying CSR doesn't pay. Essentially he said research can find companies with good CSR records that have done well financially (naming Patagonia and Seventh Generation, perhaps DuPont, Alcoa, IBM, and Toyota) and research can find 'at least as many' companies with good CSR records that have done poorly financially (naming Starbucks, Levi Strauss, Gap, Whole Foods, and Timberland). Likewise, research can find companies with poor CSR reputations that have done well financially (naming Exxon-Mobil) and companies with poor CSR reputations that have done poorly financially.[9]

Others have argued that CSR is important to civilization, so whether CSR is profitable or not is irrelevant. This view holds that CSR is not about giving away money, making money, or promoting 'our values'. It promotes CSR as simply caring for people, for humans, for mankind.

## Credibility issue

In addition to the stockholder versus stakeholder debate, scholars recognize that stakeholder theory has been used to drive a social improvement agenda. Management professor Sandra Waddock authored a book about 23 'difference makers', entrepreneurs working for social improvement.[10] Reviewing Waddock's book, noted business ethics professor William C Frederick was impressed by the way those social entrepreneurs operationalized 'ideals' by creating global standards, human rights principles and organizations to influence companies, governments, educators and the public, and thereby inspired creation of formal CR structures like Ceres, Caux Round Table, the UN Global Compact, and others.[11] Frederick reported that these entrepreneurs 'are not at all sure about the long-term outcome'. They feel they created a CR social movement, but it may not last.

One factor might be a public perception issue, because it affects a company's credibility and social responsibility reputation. If a company puts its corporate public relations office in charge of philanthropy and social responsibility, then even if the company's work in that domain is sincere and effective, even if the public relations staff does a superb job, a risk is that these corporate good works will be perceived as self-serving, not responsible, altruistic citizenship.

Another factor might be duplicity. In her book, *The Seven Signs of Ethical Collapse,* ethics professor Marianne Jennings accuses corporations of sometimes using philanthropic contributions as a smokescreen to hide reality: using goodness in some areas to atone for evil in others. As evidence supporting her allegation, she details behaviors of Enron, WorldCom, Tyco, Adelphia, HealthSouth, Lincoln Savings, Finova, Ford, Coca-Cola, and Fannie Mae.[12]

Jennings points to a bad mindset: 'As long as I am doing good … how could anything I possibly do in accounting or disclosure to achieve that good be wrong?' It affects for-profit corporations, and it 'particularly' affects non-profit organizations 'because they feel so noble in their work that a little embezzlement is justified'.[13] And some people would undertake charity just to generate more business, Jennings says. 'Tyco, WorldCom, Adelphia, Enron and HealthSouth all enjoyed the benefits of their name out there in the public because of those philanthropic activities … millions in free advertising.'[14]

Jennings argues a conflict of interest: managers, who have a fiduciary responsibility to investors, should not be allowed to disburse 'social responsibility' funds because the accolades they receive for doing so may combine with their ego and cause them to cross lines of good judgment. Even innocently, managers and employees may get so caught up in doing good for other organizations and causes that they neglect their own company's needs.[15]

The aforementioned debate between Friedman and Mackey is a bedrock in this discussion. Friedman said, 'Put the investors first.' Mackey said 'The investors are not the only people who matter. Corporations can exist for purposes other than simply maximizing profits.'[16] Famed business leader David Packard recalled getting into a discussion of the responsibility of management. In the face of an assertion that management's responsibility is only to the shareholders, Packard said, 'I think you're absolutely wrong. Management has a responsibility to its employees, it has a responsibility to its customers, it has a responsibility to the community at large.' Packard argued that people get together as a company 'to do something worthwhile – they make a contribution to society … The real reason for our existence is that we provide something which is unique.'[17] Sisodia, Wolfe and Sheth, at the conclusion of their book *Firms of Endearment,* say:

> *One of the things we thought we knew about doing business is that business should not concern itself with social benevolence. We now realize that companies can actually perform better when management is deeply concerned with the well being of society.*[18]

The 'crucial difference', they say, is for a business to serve *all* stakeholders: that is what gives a company competitive advantage over companies focused primarily on profits.[19]

## Models of CSR

Professor Archie Carroll created a pyramid model of CSR that showed it composed of four responsibilities layered one atop the other: economic (be profitable) at the base of the pyramid, with legal (obey the law) above it, ethical (do what is right) above that, and philanthropic (be a good corporate citizen –

contribute to community and quality of life) at the peak.[20] Some confusion arose because people interpreted the pyramid as setting priorities: first be profitable, then be legal, then be ethical, and then be philanthropic. Not what he meant at all, Carroll said. The four responsibilities are always equal; companies need to fulfill all four at all times.[21] Carroll's point was that corporate reputation is determined by how well a company fulfills the four responsibilities and benefits the company's broad range of stakeholders.

A strength of stakeholder theory is that it can cause managers to consider interests outside company profit and make decisions that help other people or at least avoid harming them. The manager can feel the reward of 'doing the right thing'. As previously mentioned, a weakness of stakeholder theory is that it is hard for managers to consider many categories of stakeholders, identify all of the interests and which interests compete, and then weigh and prioritize them to reach ethical decisions. The basis for decision-making may be muddled. What is the 'right thing' to do? Is it doing the greatest good for the greatest number? Or is it living up to a 'universal law'? Or is it honoring a societal, a company or a personal value?

Starting in the 1970s, the US began to use regulatory agencies to enforce public policies based on stakeholder theory. The US created the Environmental Protection Agency, the Equal Employment Opportunity Commission, the Occupational Safety and Health Administration, and the Consumer Product Safety Commission. These agencies enforce public policy expectations that businesses maximize benefits to stakeholders other than stockholders.

Professor Joseph DesJardins made the reality even clearer. Laws now impose legal duties on managers: legal obligations to employees, the disabled, the environment, consumers, and even competitors. '[A]s a matter of law, it is simply false to claim that management can ignore duties to everyone but stockholders.'[22]

A pillars model (Figure 10.1) offers a different perspective on Carroll's four elements of CSR. This model envisions CSR as a fragile, delicate outcome, a corporate image that can be true only if it is well supported by the company's fulfilment of three responsibilities: economic, legal, and social (philanthropic) — depicted as three pillars. The main point made by this model, however, is that those three pillars can successfully stand only if they are firmly anchored in the foundation of business ethics. If the company operates illegally, or if it fails to make a profit or is judged to reap excessive profit, or if public perception is that it is arrogant, uncaring, or otherwise not a good citizen in the community, then it cannot achieve a 'socially responsible' image.

The pillars model runs the risk of being too linear. It tends to focus thinking on silos — economic concerns *or* legal concerns *or* social/philanthropic concerns *or* ethics concerns. Reality is more complex; the four types of concern are more integrated. A process called 'stakeholder analysis' using the stakeholder/ responsibility matrix format suggested by Carroll[23] demonstrates the complexity. Table 10.1 is part of such a matrix prepared by students who chose to explore the ethics of testing cosmetics.

**Figure 10.1** A pillars model perspective of Carroll's four elements of CSR

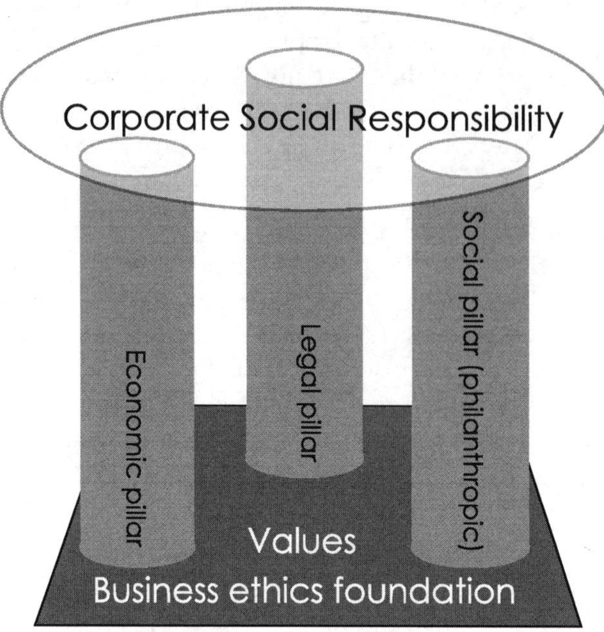


Stakeholder analysis is a technique to expand thinking, to guide people to discover and consider viewpoints other than their own. Following Carroll's general format, the analyst brainstorms to identify stakeholders relevant to the situation. These students chose to focus most strongly on five stakeholders: company owners, customers, animals (used for testing), social activists (in particular, PETA – People for the Ethical Treatment of Animals), and government agencies (FDA – Food and Drug Administration; APHIS – Animal and Plant Health Inspection Service).

**Table 10.1** Stakeholder/responsibility matrix for cosmetic testing

| Stakeholder | Legal | Economic | Ethical | Social |
|---|---|---|---|---|
| Owners | Strength: no current law violations<br>Strength: large legal staff<br>Weakness: current operations would violate new laws soon to take effect | Strength: researching alternatives to animal testing<br>Weakness: cost of animal testing and alternatives research | Strength: good intentions to protect consumers<br>Weakness: sacrifice animal lives | Strength: company can set exemplary standards<br>Weakness: may use others' standards that are less than exemplary |
| Customers | Strength: law protects from injury and liability<br>Weakness: may | Strength: can buy from competitors<br>Weakness: pay for products | Strength: good intentions<br>Weakness: complain about reactions to | Strength: awareness of testing issue may be increasing |

| Stakeholder | Legal | Economic | Ethical | Social |
|---|---|---|---|---|
| | be unaware of laws or regulations | tested inadequately Weakness: indirectly pay costs of testing | cosmetics | Weakness: many not fully aware of testing's harsh realities |
| Animals | Strength: protected by some laws Weakness: do not have a voice; not fully protected by law | Strength: none Weakness: none | Strength: none Weakness: death and injury during cosmetic testing | Strength: none Weakness: animals removed from natural habitat |
| Social activists | Strength: strong voice Strength: Past success in legal challenges to animal testing Weakness: Difficult to organize trial Weakness: Difficult to enact new laws | Strength: donations fund persistence Strength: publicity for specific issues increases donations Weakness: sometimes viewed as troublemakers | Strength: mission to protect animals Weakness: implementation is voluntary | Strength: campaigns reach millions of people Weakness: raising awareness can shock people and emotional impact may discourage involvement |
| Government agencies | Strength: legal power Strength: establish legislation Weakness: hard to enforce new laws quickly | Strength: can impose fines on violators Weakness: limited budget | Strength: authority to make regulations Strength: authority to enforce them Weakness: enforcement difficult; often easier to request than to mandate; companies may resist | Strength: support elimination of animal testing Weakness: many people do not have information these agencies have |

Having used the matrix to expand thinking, the analyst faces a complex array of ideas and now needs a technique to simplify thought, to organize and prioritize ideas, to escape silo thinking, to enable integrated, organic thinking, and to reach an informed decision – which indeed may be different than anyone's first impression of the problem and solution was. The technique to do that is to apply values: hopefully personal and corporate values will be congruent and both lead to the same answer.

An example from real life: in the late 1940s, plagued by blue smog so thick you could not see the house across the street, Los Angeles wanted the California legislature to enact a law authorizing smog control districts. Charles Jones, president of Richfield Oil Company, explained his first impression, saying all oil companies would oppose Assembly Bill 1. 'I am president of an oil company representing an investment of some $60,000,000. Do you think I am going to allow any smog administrator to tell me whether or not I can run my plant? Not on your life! You wouldn't either if you were in my place.' But he agreed to convene a meeting of executives representing all of the major oil companies in Southern California, including Standard, Union, Texaco, General Petroleum, Shell, and Richfield. At the meeting, top officers of those oil companies seriously discussed the situation and a breakthrough came when William Stewart, Jr., vice-president of Union Oil Company, expressed his values. Stewart said smog was an important community issue. It affected people's comfort, health, and the future prosperity of the entire community. The Union Oil Company, he declared, as a responsible citizen of Los Angeles would not oppose Assembly Bill 1. After Stewart declared support for the new law, said one observer, no other company's representative 'dared to stand up and say that he would oppose'. The major oil companies directed their lobbyist at the state Senate not to oppose the bill. The Senate voted for the new law, and it was signed by the governor on June 10, 1947.[24]

CSR is far more than 'charitable contributions'. Economic responsibilities may include consistently maximizing stockholders' earnings per share by being a strong competitor and operating efficiently. Legal responsibilities may include meeting government expectations as well as compliance with the law. Social (philanthropic) responsibilities – well, here is the heart of the Friedman-Mackey debate – may range from just interventions (e.g., bargain prices on items or services customers want) that generate business and increase profit to interventions that are – or appear to be – entirely altruistic (such as anonymous contributions to support artists and performers, educational institutions or charities), improve communities' quality of life, and meet other 'needs' of society. In practice, companies that make social interventions of any type usually want their name associated with it; truly anonymous corporate gifts probably are rare, but who could know for sure? The final CSR component, ethics responsibilities, certainly includes living up to society's moral norms and expectations.

## Measuring CSR

Much confusion about CSR can be traced to this truth: we lack agreement on the definition of what comprises corporate social responsibility.[25] For this book, we posit that if a company makes a good product or provides a good service and is responsive to its customers, if a company treats its employees well and honors diversity, if a company respects the communities and the environment in which it does business, then that company is practicing CSR.[26] Such a business is productive, and a valuable institution in society.

In an effort to identify empirically defensible benchmarks for CR, NYSE Euronext partnered with *Corporate Responsibility Magazine* for a survey that obtained responses from more than 650 companies around the world, a 'first attempt to document best practices'.[27] The principal outcome was a trend: for the companies responding to the survey, in 2006, only 1 percent of US companies had a formal CR officer; in 2010, 35 percent of US companies did, 47 percent of Canadian companies did and 65 percent of Western European companies did. More than 30 percent of the firms said they can demonstrate that CR has enhanced profitability.[28] But a question that remains unanswered is 'Are companies measuring the right things?' Are frequent practices necessarily 'best practices'? Is improved profitability the measure? Or is it improved trust? Or is it something else? What companies reportedly did measure were specific and 'publicly declared' goals in eight domains. One thing that is unclear is how this survey and its definition of CR relate to Carroll's four CSR responsibilities: the definition of CR here possibly differs from the definition of CSR. The survey's eight domains were:[29]

- environment, health, and safety;
- human resources, employee relations, and diversity;
- energy use, environmental impact, and climate change;
- corporate social responsibility and citizenship;
- governance, risk, and compliance;
- philanthropy and corporate foundation;
- supply chain management; and
- human rights.

## Visions of CSR

Noted scholars have described CSR as 'evolving', as having a different focus in each decade since 1950.[30] But we suspect it is more accurate to recognize four visions of CSR that co-exist at all times and that companies choose to adopt as they believe their situation warrants.

### Vision 1

One vision is company-centric, minding the company's own business, focusing on treating the company's customers, suppliers and employees right, producing a good product or service, and being a company of integrity – honest and ethical. Some would say this is the Friedman vision, although Friedman himself allowed companies a certain amount of philanthropy.

### Vision 2

A second vision is charity-focused, giving away goods, services, or company money to what appear to be good causes, without much examination of exactly how they use the gift.

## Vision 3

A third vision is stewardship-focused, giving away company money to verifiable good causes. Wisdom indicates that donations to some charities yield better outcomes. Channeling donations to the 'best', the most responsible, achieves 'stewardship'.

## Vision 4

A fourth vision is corporate citizenship, gifts invested to develop the infrastructure of society in beneficial directions.[31]

> *Give a man a fish and you feed him for a day. Teach a man to fish and you feed him for a lifetime.*
>
> – *Chinese Proverb*

College students who discover the differences in these visions in classroom exercises find the experience eye-opening.

To explore the charity-focused vision, five groups of about 30 college seniors were given these instructions: 'We work for a *Fortune* 500 corporation. Our CEO wants to present to the board of directors a corporate social responsibility plan. Prepare a list showing who the company should donate money to in the coming year and how much money the donation should be.'

The students perceived this as an easy task. Within an hour, they drafted plans. They all focused on giving away money — charity. The total amounts given away by the five groups were:

**Table 10.2** Charity

| Group 1 | Group 2 | Group 3 | Group 4 | Group 5 |
|---|---|---|---|---|
| $148 million | $41 million | $40 million | $82 million | $44 million |

Sample recipients were:

**Table 10.3** Charity recipient samples

| Recipient | Amount |
|---|---|
| Animal Shelter for Dogs | $3 million |
| Carolina Raptor Conservation | $20 million |
| Health | $4 million |
| HIV Testing in Developing Nations | $6 million |
| Inner-City Schools | $10 million |
| Komen Cancer Research | $5 million |
| Save the Music Foundation | $7 million |

CSR sometimes has this focus: charity.

In a second round of planning, the CEO of the students' imaginary corporation imposed a financial cap, allocating '$10 million to corporate social responsibility to start with. See what we can do with that.' The financial cap forced thrift and evoked more responsible philanthropy. The groups' corporate social responsibility vision became stewardship – careful, responsible management of funds the company allocated to donations. Without being told to switch from charity to stewardship, all five groups made the switch and discovered two insights. First, that employees would feel proud of their company if it supported charitable causes the employees themselves believed were most worthwhile. Second, that using corporate funds as seed money to match employees' personal donations could increase, perhaps double or triple, the impact of each corporate dollar, making the corporation look good from both ends of the stockholder-stakeholder debate scale. Stockholder proponents could appreciate that the corporation spent a minimum of dollars to achieve its social responsibility goals; stakeholder proponents could appreciate that the corporation's investment incentivized others' contributions to maximize impact on social responsibility goals. For $10 million of corporate money spent, the groups achieved the following impacts:

**Table 10.4** Impacts

| Group 1 | Group 2 | Group 3 | Group 4 | Group 5 |
|---|---|---|---|---|
| $19 million | $17 million | $13 million | $11 million | $20 million |

External consultants, watchdog groups, and companies themselves use measures like Triple Bottom Line and Balanced Scorecard to evaluate CSR. What they measure can vary, but they may tend to be biased against company-centrics and toward stewardship or citizenship. The CEO of the students' company arranged for 'impartial, third-party' evaluation of their second-round plans using both triple bottom line and balanced scorecard. For example, Group 1's measurement charts:

**Table 10.5** Triple bottom line

| Characteristic measured | Bad | Poor | OK | Good | Great |
|---|---|---|---|---|---|
| Economic | | | | | x |
| Social | | | | x | |
| Environmental | | | | x | |

**Table 10.6** Balanced scorecard

| Characteristic measured | Bad | Poor | OK | Good | Great |
|---|---|---|---|---|---|
| Financial | | | | | x |
| Internal operations | | | | x | |
| Customer | | | x | | |
| People/knowledge/learning | | | | | x |

These third-party reviews flagged general areas for possible improvement. The students' plan got rated good or great in most categories – they wanted 'great' in all categories. The students wanted to know the exact criteria and exactly how they were measured. The answer was frustrating: as recognized by NYSE Euronext and *Corporate Responsibility Magazine*, 'no roadmap exists'.[32] The criteria measured are fundamentally qualitative, subjective, and differ from one evaluator to another. So third-party evaluations may or may not direct attention to 'real weaknesses', but the students ultimately must develop improvements – just as a corporation's planners ultimately must develop improvements in a corporation's plan.

Perhaps demonstrating that what you measure is what you get, all five student groups switched from corporate stewardship to the corporate citizenship vision in their third round of planning to better address their 'blind spots' – usually perceived 'weaknesses' in the economic, social, environmental, and customer considerations. When they did this, their plans changed focus from giving away money to bolstering the infrastructure of society, contributing meaningfully to the development of society.

Third-round contributions now focused on developing the conservation infrastructure, developing the advanced medical care infrastructure, enabling a quick-reaction disaster response infrastructure, and building the local social infrastructure – a facility to foster community activities. Their plan looked like this (partial listing):

**Table 10.7** Impacts

| Employee gift matching 1:1 (up to $1,000/employee) | Corporate share | Total impact |
|---|---|---|
| Conservation (e.g. Carolina raptor, California Condor, snow leopard, dog shelters, World Wildlife Foundation, Surfrider Foundation) | Up to $1 million | Up to $2 million |
| Health Services and Research (e.g. Komen Cancer Research, St. Jude Medical Center, American Cancer Society) | Up to $2 million | Up to $4 million |
| **Corporate contributions** | | |
| Disaster relief (Rapid response) | $1 million | $1 million |
| **Community gift matching 1:2** | | |
| Community Center | Up to $1 million | Up to $3 million |

Through the lens of the Ethics Dynamic, CSR has roots in Stage 1 compliance with laws, and roots in Stage 2 values, but its real impact is in Stage 3: creating trust. The mechanism appears to be an implicit 'social contract' acknowledging that business and society need each other, that the company will undertake actions beyond just interests of the firm and requirements of law in order to improve society and that society will somehow reward the company.[33] This is the domain of Stage 3 of the ethics dynamic, trust. Sisodia, Wolfe, and Sheth[34] say a company is not in business to build trust and it is unproductive to focus on building trust as a primary business objective. What does work is to recognize that trust is an outcome realized by meeting or exceeding stakeholders' expectations, a way society rewards companies for working to improve society.

## Creating a good name

No rules prescribe exactly how to establish a 'good name'. No values mandate exactly what must be done. Trust is required. The governing policy is that initiatives should build trust.

> *Good name in man and woman … is the immediate jewel of their souls. Who steals my purse steals trash … but he that filches from me my good name … makes me poor indeed*
>
> – *William Shakespeare: Othello, Act 3, Scene 3*

Perhaps uncertain exactly what to do, business sometimes indicates it is aware it needs to do visibly better. Mattel is praised for giving more than $2 million to support more than 500 organizations serving children's needs around the world, including the children's hospital at UCLA, Save the Children, and Make-A-Wish Foundation, but critics have faulted Mattel for sometimes manufacturing toys with paint containing lead or design features like protruding knobs, things that may hurt a child. Mattel responded with corrections designed to prevent such faults in the future.

High school coaches praise Nike's support of their athletic programs, but critics have faulted Nike for sometimes selling products made in sweatshops. Nike responded with a supplier inspection system. Wal-Mart won praise for its delivery of much needed supplies to Hurricane Katrina victims, but critics have faulted Wal-Mart for a business model they say rewards employees with low pay and benefits, undercuts the prices of locally-owned stores and drives them out of business, and imports merchandise that used to be made in the US.

Gary Hirshberg's book, *Stirring It Up: How to Make Money and Save the World,* describes how he created a small yogurt business specifically guided by the goal of good environmental practices. 'For more than 25 years, I've been turning green ideas into greenbacks,' he says at the beginning of Chapter 1. The goal at Stonyfield Farms has been more than making money; 'we aim to be both sustainable and profitable'. Decisions consider which options move the company closer to environmental sustainability and profit. To ensure long-term access to high-quality milk, they pay more. They pay top dollar to produce the best yogurt, their gross margins are worse than competitors, but their net profits are better. Their strategy is to promise and deliver top-quality yogurt, not lowball the cost of goods and sell inferior product.[35]

## *Fortune 500* study

A study of ten *Fortune 500* companies selected by using a table of random numbers showed a difference between the largest six and the smallest four. The largest six had websites that stated how much their CSR contributions amounted to each year and described where that money went. The smallest four had websites that were silent about how much their contributions amounted to but did describe social concerns they donated money to.

The companies' reported investment in CSR ranged from $4.4 to $156 million. The largest company in the study spoke clearly about citizenship to build infrastructure, saying it funds non-profits improving the health of communities, managing chronic disease, and developing health interventions using mobile electronic devices such as cell phones and PDAs.

In contrast, the smallest company in the study focused on sending money, volunteers, and administrative support for Junior Achievement in six schools, participating in a fund raiser, and providing scholarship, stationery, and lab support for two schools.

Data was limited and showed citizenship, stewardship, and charity at all levels – that is all good – but tentatively indicated that large companies focused more often on citizenship initiatives, that medium companies focused more often on stewardship, and that smaller companies focused more often on charity. Why? Perhaps it's situational – larger companies might view the world more strategically and smaller companies might focus more on local opportunities. Or perhaps it's staffing – larger companies might employ specialists to organize CSR and smaller companies might have someone do it in addition to primary management tasks. Or perhaps it's fashion – on the internet, a company invited applications to work as CR Director and specified, as one qualification requirement, deep knowledge of current CR 'trends'.

Four companies made it clear they honor donation requests only from Section 501(c)(3) non-profit organizations. Two more restricted donations to only organizations identified by their staff (no unsolicited proposals). One said applicants must be non-profit, non-partisan, non-religious, non-political.

Corporations frequently self-impose restrictions like these on corporate donations:

**Table 10.8** Corporate self-imposed restrictions

| Do contribute to | Do not contribute to |
|---|---|
| 501(c)(3) organizations only | Individuals or 'walk-a-thons' |
| Communities where our employees live and work | Organizations that discriminate by race, creed, color, sex, age, or national origin |
| Organizations our employees serve as volunteers | Political activities or lobbying |
| Strengthen education | Partisan or terrorist entities or agents |
| Strengthen health and human services | Religious organizations for sectarian activities |

| Do contribute to | Do not contribute to |
|---|---|
| Strengthen diversity, equal opportunity, and advancement | Fraternal, social, or labor organizations serving mainly their own constituencies |
| Match contributions full-time employees make to schools and colleges | Capital campaigns |
| Strengthen the arts and diverse cultures | Endowment funds |
| | Conferences, workshops, or seminars unless directly related to this company's business interests |
| | Athletic teams, events (except Special Olympics) |
| | Trips, travel, or cultural exchanges |
| | Fundraising events |

Many companies operate PACs (Political Action Committees) to raise and distribute funds invested as political interventions, which are separate from CSR efforts, and some companies sponsor athletic teams and events. The self-imposed restrictions listed above are not 'standards' or necessarily widely adopted; they are just common examples of restrictions companies publicly adopt.

## Penney perspective

James C Penney, founder of the chain of JC Penney stores, demonstrated corporate social responsibility directed toward customers as stakeholders. As Penney told the story, he clerked at a store on Larimer Street as a young man in Denver in 1898. He noticed some items for sale at two different prices. In particular, men's socks were priced twenty-five cents a pair and identical socks were priced two pairs for a quarter. When Penney asked 'which price is the correct one?' the proprietor told Penney to mind his own business and sell at the prices marked. 'Sell the socks for twenty-five cents a pair if you can. If you can't, sell them two pairs for a quarter.' Penney felt 'there was no use in my continuing to work in a store that supported such a policy. I asked for my wages, got them, and left.'

Years later, according to Penney, one store in his chain reported unusually large profits. He suspected the manager was setting prices too high and had him confronted about it – 'This is not the way we do things in the Penney Company. We owe to our community the service of merchandise at a fair profit. We can't ever allow ourselves to make too much profit.'

Penney's way of setting prices became Principle 4 of the company's published code of ethics, the 'Penney Principles': 'to charge a fair profit for what we offer – and not all the traffic will bear'. Penney long advocated serving stakeholders: 'business never was and never will be anything more or less than people serving other people'. He aspired to see businesses serve society 'to brighten conditions and lighten burdens under which mankind gropes today'.[36]

## College perspective

Today's college students feel strongly about what CR should be and how important ethics is as the bedrock foundation. For example:

- Lauro: 'most of the values we hold highly as individuals also carry into the corporate world. If businesses remembered this, there wouldn't be any Enron-type scandals.'[37]
- Andrew: 'my father owns a construction company. Even though his corporation [has a small number of] employees, he recognizes that diversity is more present than ever. Thus he feels it is vital to the company to employ workers from South America, a few from Asia, one from Africa, and even a few from Central Europe. These varied employees have been working for my father for many years and do not plan on stopping soon.'[38]
- Chris: 'I think a company's values can be more important than tangible assets, such as money and factories. If you don't have a good set of values established within the company, you won't be able to use tangible assets correctly. A company run unethically could have all the money in the world but it doesn't matter because sooner or later, as we've seen, it will all come crashing down ... I think the most important part of corporate governance deals with ethics and integrity. Obviously it deals with stakeholders and shareholders as well, but when it boils down to it, if you run a company with integrity and focus on ethics a lot of those issues with shareholders and stakeholders will work themselves out.'[39]
- Francesca: the dream is to make business decisions that best benefit people's health and safety. 'We are all people and in the world of ethics there [should be] only a universal code for the correct moral ways a person should be treated. People should be treated at the highest standards because they are ultimately the force that will make or break a company. The customer is the means of the company; without them, a company will go bankrupt. Ethics and social responsibility go hand-in-hand and should be taken very seriously by companies, especially large conglomerates.'[40]

The major premise of the book written by Sisodia, Wolfe and Sheth, *Firms of Endearment*, is that companies should avoid the historic focus of going for a share of the customer's wallet and instead strive to gain a share of the customer's heart.[41] Leadership guru Warren Bennis supports that view, citing Timberland's Jeffrey Swartz as one example of a CEO who experienced an epiphany and began a campaign in his company to make the world a better place. When companies serve all of their primary stakeholders, said Bennis, stakeholders respond with 'uncommon trust' in the companies and their products and develop 'real affection for such companies'.[42]

## Challenge puzzle

The ethics dynamic model suggests that CSR initiatives – at least some of them – might build trust. In previous chapters, this book suggests how to measure trust. The puzzle is how to maximize corporate social responsibility initiatives' trust-building, and from a business viewpoint a maximum/minimum consideration: how to maximize the trust corporate social responsibility earns while minimizing corporate social responsibility costs.

In the three-stage classroom demonstration reported in this chapter, the students are somewhat handicapped because they are assigned to build a plan for a generic company. Inevitably, some ask 'What kind of a company?' 'What does the company make?' 'What does the company do?' Why? – because if they are a soup company, like Campbell's, they can attract customer participation by promising to donate ten cents to breast cancer research for each 'pink-label' can purchased. If they are a clothing retailer, they can attract customers by promising to inspect suppliers' garment factories to ensure sweatshop conditions do not exist. If they make computers, or cell phones, or other electronic hardware, they can attract customers by promising to properly recycle obsolete electronics to avoid poisoning the earth and its people. Companies' CSR efforts arguably are at their best when they relate directly to their core business.

So consider this example. A tsunami has caused serious damage in Japan. A company donates $10,000,000 to fund ten round-trip flights to deliver emergency supplies and evacuate victims who urgently need medical care. Should this earn more 'trust points' for an airline that uses its own aircraft and crews as the donation because that is its core business? Should a retail hamburger chain deserve fewer 'trust points' because nothing about those flights relates to its core business?

It's a puzzle. What counts, and how much? Does a company have a fiduciary – or a moral – responsibility to maximize CSR while minimizing its cost? Which of the following should your company do or avoid? And, for each, should the company invite publicity about it or simply make the decision and do the work quietly? Why?

A. $500,000 to sponsor the national Winter Olympics team.

B. $200 to purchase '100% recyclable' salt and pepper shakers for the company cafeteria.

C. $1,000,000 to appoint a corporate social responsibility vice-president with budget for two staff members, travel, supplies, and operating costs.

D. $500,000 to replace existing sinks in company restrooms with sinks made from recycled materials.

E. $100,000 to deliver diversity training sessions to all employees.

F. $1,000,000 to sponsor a yacht in the California to Hawaii yacht race.

G. $250,000 donation to the community's philharmonic orchestra.

H. At no cost, eliminate company use of all substances containing volatile organic compounds.

I. $10,000,000 to help a young movie director produce a motion picture, a feature film that employs actors to tell a fictional story.

J. $100,000 donation to a community non-profit dance studio that teaches choreographed dancing to intermediate school age students.

K. $250,000 donation to a community non-profit flight school that teaches children, age 12-18, to pilot light aircraft.

L. $10,000,000 donation to support a community theater; option to name the theater.

M. $5,000,000 donation to a charity that organizes activities for children who face adversity and need positive human contact to promote confidence and physical, academic, and personal success.

N. At no cost, and with a view toward offering the company's customers low prices, demand a supplier provide items at a deep discount or company will not order those items and other items from them.

O. $200,000 to install a biofuel boiler that will heat the company's main building by burning used cooking oil from the cafeteria and motor oil salvaged from vehicle maintenance.

P. $200,000 to replace fluorescent light bulbs with LED (light emitting diodes) that cut electricity use in half and reduce bulb replacement costs 95%.

Q. At no cost, use organically grown cotton and nontoxic inks in the company-branded T-shirts for sale in the company store.

---

[1] De George, RT 2010, '*BEQ* at Twenty', *Business Ethics Quarterly* 20(4): 722-723.

[2] Sisodia, RS, Wolfe, DB & Sheth, JN 2007, *Firms of Endearment: How World-Class Companies Profit from Passion and Purpose,* Wharton School Publishing, Upper Saddle River, NJ.

[3] 'Rethinking the Social Responsibility of Business: A *Reason* Debate Featuring Milton Friedman, Whole Foods' John Mackey, and Cypress Semiconductor's T. J. Rodgers', *Reason,* 2005, viewed 24 January 2012, http://reason.com/archives/2005/10/01/rethinking-the-social-responsi.

[4] 'Rethinking the Social Responsibility of Business'.

[5] 'Rethinking the Social Responsibility of Business'.

[6] Herman, RP & Nair, V 2011, 'Commit! Debate: The Shareholder Value of Sustainability: A Brief for Corporate Responsibility', *Corporate Responsibility Magazine* 2(5), viewed 24 January 2012, http://thecro.com/content/commit-debate-shareholder-value-sustainability.

[7] Karnani, A & Sullivan, G 2011, 'Commit! Debate: A Logical Trap: The Case Against Expending Resources on Corporate Responsibility', *Corporate Responsibility Magazine,* 2(5), viewed 24 January 2012, http://thecro.com/content/commit-debate-logical-trap.

[8] Sisodia, Wolfe, and Sheth, *Firms of Endearment.*

[9] Vogel, D 2012, 'CSR Doesn't Pay', *Forbes,* viewed 25 January 2012, www.forbes.com/2008/10/16/csr-doesnt-pay-lead-corprespons08-cx_dv_1016vogel.html.

[10] Waddock, S 2008, *The Difference Makers: How Social and Institutional Entrepreneurs Created the Corporate Responsibility Movement,* Greenleaf, Sheffield, UK.

[11] Frederick, WC 2008, 'Review of The Difference Makers: How Social and Institutional Entrepreneurs Created the Corporate Responsibility Movement, by Sandra Waddock', *Journal of Corporate Citizenship,* 32: 100-102.

[12] Jennings, MM 2006, *The Seven Signs of Ethical Collapse: How to Spot Moral Meltdowns in Companies . . . Before It's Too Late,* St. Martin's Press, New York.

[13] Jennings, *The Seven Signs of Ethical Collapse,* 237.

[14] Jennings, *The Seven Signs of Ethical Collapse,* 247.

[15] Jennings, *The Seven Signs of Ethical Collapse,* 252.

[16] 'Rethinking the Social Responsibility of Business'.

[17] Packard, D quoted in Jacobson, D 1998, 'Founding Fathers', *Stanford Magazine,* viewed 24 January 2012, www.stanfordalumni.org/news/magazine/1998/julaug /articles/founding_fathers/founding_fathers.html.

[18] Sisodia, Wolfe, and Sheth, *Firms of Endearment.*

[19] Sisodia, Wolfe, and Sheth, *Firms of Endearment.*

[20] Carroll, AB 1991, 'The Pyramid of Corporate Social Responsibility: Toward the Moral Management of Organizational Stakeholders', *Business Horizons* 34(4): 39-48.

[21] Carroll, AB 1999, 'Corporate Social Responsibility: Evolution of a Definitional Construct', *Business & Society* 38(3): 268-295.

[22] DesJardins, J 2009, *An Introduction to Business Ethics* (4th edn), McGraw-Hill, New York.

[23] Carroll, 'The Pyramid of Corporate Social Responsibility'.

[24] Royce, SW 1984, *A Life Remembered: The Memoirs Of Stephen W. Royce,* Royal Literary Publications, Laguna Niguel, CA: 95.

[25] Melo, T & Galan, JI 2011, 'Effects of Corporate Social Responsibility on Brand Value', *Journal of Brand Management* 18(6): 423-437.

[26] Melo, T & Galan, JI 2011, 'Effects of Corporate Social Responsibility'.

[27] Olin, D & Whitehead, J 2010, *CR: How Fast It's Growing, How Much It's Spending, and How Far It's Going* (CR Best Practices Study), viewed 24 January 2012, www .thecro.com/files/CRBestPractices.pdf.

[28] Olin & Whitehead, *CR: How Fast It's Growing.*

[29] *Corporate Responsibility Best Practices: Setting the Baseline, Corporate Responsibility Magazine* in association with NYSE Euronext and Corporate Responsibility Officer Association, April 2010, accessed January 24, 2012, http://www.croassociation.org/files/CR-Best-Practices-2010-Module-1.pdf.

[30] Frederick, WC 2011, 'Evolving Phases of Corporate Social Responsibility', in AT Lawrence & J Weber, *Business and Society: Stakeholders, Ethics, Public Policy,* 13th edn, McGraw-Hill Irwin, New York, 53.

[31] See generally Lawrence & Weber, *Business and Society.*

[32] Olin & Whitehead, *CR: How Fast It's Growing.*

[33] Melo & Galan, 'Effects of Corporate Social Responsibility'.

[34] Sisodia, Wolfe, & Sheth, *Firms of Endearment.*

[35] Hirshberg, G 2008, *Stirring It Up,* Hyperion, New York.

[36] All JC Penney information is from Penney, JC 1950, *Fifty Years With the Golden Rule,* Harper, New York, 37-40, 98-99, 103-104, 232.

[37] Lauro [Redacted], email to authors, 2008.

[38] Andrew [Redacted], email to authors, 2008.

[39] Chris [Redacted], emails to authors, 2008.

[40] Francesca [Redacted], email to authors, 2008.

[41] Sisodia, Wolfe, and Sheth, *Firms of Endearment.*

[42] Warren Bennis, 'Foreword', in Sisodia, Wolfe, and Sheth, *Firms of Endearment.*

# Appendix I

## Two years' experience in thirty minutes: Categorizing OpenLine calls

What can you expect to hear when you answer an incoming OpenLine call? It helps to start categorizing the content while the call is in progress.

### Macro analysis

One practical approach is to start with three broad categories:

- Type 1: Inquiries that the ethics office has the expertise to answer, usually on the spot.
- Type 2: Inquiries that the ethics office forwards to a function with the expertise to routinely handle.
- Type 3: Allegations that warrant a formal investigation.

## Test yourself: Call categories

Categorize each of the following calls as Type 1, 2 or 3:

**Table:** Call categories: Questions

| | Situation | Call type |
|---|---|---|
| 1 | What will the company do for me? Private medical tests show I have silicosis. An item used at work has been tested and found to contain materials known to cause silicosis. | |
| 2 | How can Employee Alpha get away with it? He consistently arrives at work about an hour late, leaves for home about an hour early, and gets paid for working a full 8-hour day. | |
| 3 | What is the deal? For the past week, Employee Bravo has worked on the factory floor without the required steel toes and hard hat. | |
| 4 | Can you make him stop? My supervisor keeps harassing me, trying to get me fired. | |
| 5 | This is the fifth time this year. My paycheck is short 32 hours. How can I get the money? | |
| 6 | The account representative of one of our major suppliers sent me a really nice picnic set as a holiday gift. Can I keep it? | |
| 7 | I know what my supervisor wants to prove to the boss. Should the data I give him respond more closely to his desire or to what my research actually shows? | |

| | Situation | Call type |
|---|---|---|
| 8 | A retired former co-worker emailed several jokes to me at work. I think they are funny but they might offend some people. Am I in trouble for getting them here? | |
| 9 | I sent two employees to work in another nation. They needed driver's licenses right away but the government licensing office said it would cost $75 each and take three months ... or they could pay a fee of $5,000 each and be licensed in three days. They each paid the $5,000 from company funds. OK? | |
| 10 | A manager is a close friend of a supplier. Should I report this relationship as a possible conflict of interest? | |

**Table:** Call categories: Answers

| | Call type | Detail |
|---|---|---|
| 1 | Type 2 | Refer to environmental health and safety function. |
| 2 | Type 3 | Working short hours for full pay is fraud. |
| 3 | Type 2 | Refer to the safety function. |
| 4 | Type 2 | Refer to the employee/labor relations function. |
| 5 | Type 2 | Refer to the payroll function. |
| 6 | Type 1 | Respond by guiding the employee to what company values, standards of conduct, and policies say about accepting gifts from suppliers. |
| 7 | Type 1 | Respond by guiding the employee to what company values, standards of conduct, and policies say about employees' obligation to provide current, accurate, and complete information. |
| 8 | Type 1 | Respond by guiding the employee to what company values, standards of conduct, and policies say about discouraging email not related to business and about not forwarding it to other employees. Receiving unsolicited email creates no culpability; sending unsolicited email not related to work could be a problem. |
| 9 | Type 3 | Paying a bribe violates the Foreign Corrupt Practices Act (FCPA). Notify the company's law department. Heavy fines and jail terms are possible. Attorney advice has been that $5 might be a 'facilitating payment', but $5,000 looks like a bribe. Either way, such payments even when determined to be legal can lead to FCPA prosecution if they were not recorded, or were improperly recorded, in the company's accounting system. |
| 10 | Type 3 | With disclosure, investigation can determine if the company needs to take steps to prevent a real conflict of interest or steps to prevent the appearance of a conflict of interest. That will protect the company, the manager, and the friend. |

# Perspective on the three types

## Combined types

Expect real life to be complex. Callers often raise issues that fit several types simultaneously. Judgment will guide you sometimes to report all issues in one memo and sometimes to separate issues into two or more memos. For combined issues, categorize the overall memo by the highest type its content calls for. For example, this question combines Types 1 and 3: 'Is it OK for me to accept a gift from a supplier's account executive this week? [Type 1] My boss usually gets it but he's out of town this month [Type 3].' Overall, the memo would be Type 3.

## Type 1

Type 1 also can be used to document calls that require merely an administrative response. 'I have a purchase order and I'm trying to contact the buyer or the accounts payable department.' Brush off the caller or try to help? For the good reputation of the OpenLine, try always to steer callers toward the right direction, and document what you've done. Give them a useful phone number. Refusing to take such a call, or refusing to help, can have a negative effect on the relevance of the OpenLine and the ethics process because the employee will feel that he/she got the brush-off.

## Type 2

Type 2 inquiries are inherently sensitive because other functions want the ethics office to properly refer to them issues they normally expect to handle. In a sense, Type 2 calls are 'wrong numbers' because the caller should have contacted the correct function directly, but either made an 'error' by calling the ethics office first or felt rejected by the correct function after calling it first. In the spirit of helping, the OpenLine accepts Type 2 calls as a courtesy and forwards them for the proper function to consider and respond to. If the caller requested anonymity or confidentiality, the function may respond to the caller through the OpenLine.

Referring a caller with a Type 2 issue directly to the right function can help the caller get an answer quickly. But care is required to avoid sending an employee into a bureaucratic maze. If a caller wants to call a function directly, the ethics office is well advised to say, 'If that doesn't work for some reason, please call me back and we'll look for another solution.' The ethics office often can 'grease the skids' by making contact with a specific person and facilitating conversation between that person and the caller.

Type 2 issues can create role confusion controversy. What if the right function fails to respond to a Type 2 issue or provides a response the employee perceives as inadequate? What would employees think of the OpenLine and the company then?

If the ethics office discovers Type 2 issues 'fell through the cracks' and remained unaddressed, try to work it out. Also, identify and prominently flag that failure as an ethics and compliance risk [see Risk Analysis] for management to address.

Another option, which some companies attempt, is to require the ethics office to actively track other functions' work on all Type 2 calls to ensure that resolution is properly achieved and results are communicated to the caller. Two downsides are that this expands the workload of the ethics office substantially and it places the ethics office in a policing, oversight role that may irritate functional managers.

The original concept of fraud, waste and abuse hotlines prompted the OpenLine to say 'Wrong number!' and reject Type 2 calls to force callers to contact other functions directly. That was judged unwisely restrictive and the practice was quickly and widely discarded as companies recognized that employees expect the OpenLine to listen to *all* of their concerns. The nature of ethics is that employees often broadly interpret it. A possibility would be to establish a council composed of the senior managers of each function expected to address Type 2 calls and charge that council with responsibility to actively oversee resolution and communication of results.

Whatever approach is chosen, the OpenLine has unique opportunity to cross intra-company boundaries. The ethics office can – and should – carry issues to any and every function that needs to address them, and to any and every level of management that needs to act on or be aware of them. Indeed, that is the specific role the US Sentencing Guidelines for Organizations intend by specifying that 'specific individual(s) shall have day-to-day operational responsibility for the compliance and ethics program, receive adequate resources and authority, report periodically to executives, and have direct access to the Board of Directors'.

## Type 3

Type 3 issues address violations of rules and laws *that govern company operations.* This includes violations of the company's code of conduct or company policies and procedures.

The interpretation of laws and procedures is full of gray areas. If the caller is reporting something that has not yet occurred, then the issue may be reported as a Type 1 issue. For example, if a caller wants to know, 'Would it be appropriate to give a US government customer tickets to a sports event?' If the caller is reporting something that has already occurred, then the issue is a Type 3. For example, if a caller wants to know, 'Was it all right for an employee to have taken an all-expenses-paid cruise provided by a supplier?'

# Appendix II

## Two years' experience in thirty minutes: Creating training scenarios

The scenarios below are samples for readers' general practice and orientation. They illustrate a successful training model based on a deck of scenario cards prepared by the corporate ethics director, tailored to situations company employees could possibly encounter, and standardized so a consistent message is delivered throughout the company.

**Figure:** Front and back of sample scenario card

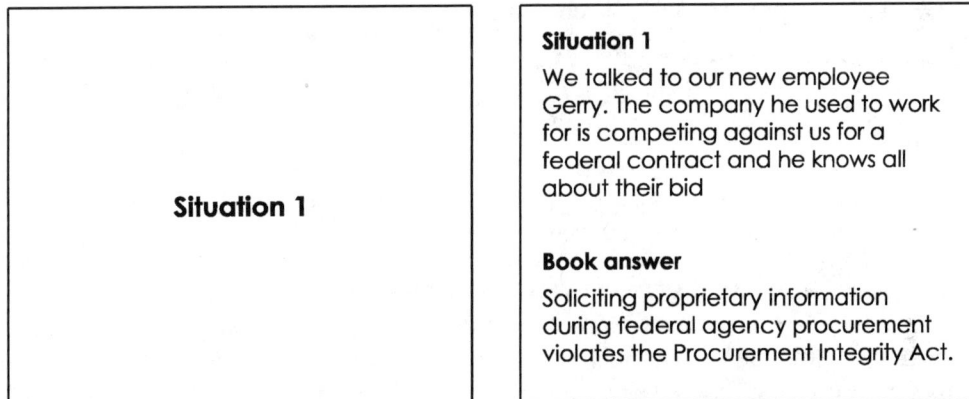

| Front | Back |
|---|---|
| **Situation 1** | **Situation 1**<br>We talked to our new employee Gerry. The company he used to work for is competing against us for a federal contract and he knows all about their bid<br><br>**Book answer**<br>Soliciting proprietary information during federal agency procurement violates the Procurement Integrity Act. |

Mechanically, the scenarios can be printed on 4×6 or 5×8 cards, or on half-sheets of standard paper (8½×5½) (see Figure above). Stock heavier than 20 lb is suggested so that opacity prevents any chance of seeing enough through a card to read some of the text printed on the back. One side of the card reads 'Situation X'. The other side presents the situation and, below it, the 'book answer'.

*Setting*: this exercise is designed for use by groups of four to eight people. The number of groups working simultaneously is limited only by room size and the number of situation card decks available. The exercise works best where people can sit facing each other on opposite sides of a table, but it can be adapted to other seating arrangements. This suits staff meetings, where we recommend practice on situation scenarios to open channels of communication on ethics topics between employees, and between employees and the manager leading the session.

When sponsoring such practice, encourage participants to: a) resolve the issue, and b) identify the company's relevant value(s). That helps elevate the practice session. We certainly want to provide people 'training' on information necessary to protect them and the company, but we also want to give people 'education', that is, the opportunity to develop what you might call ethical decision skills.

**Table:** Training scenario instructions

| | **Instructions** |
|---|---|
| 1 | Seat employees in teams of about two to four people that face each other, call them Team A and Team B. Use one set of cards for each pair of teams. Shuffle the cards so adjacent tables are working different situations. Place a set of situation cards between the two teams. |
| 2 | Team A draws the top card and reads the situation aloud to Team B. Team B discusses the situation, reaches an answer, and states its 'final answer' to Team A. |
| 3 | Team A uses the 'book answer' (deliberately not labeled the 'right answer') printed at the bottom of the situation card to score Team B 'right' or 'wrong'. Teams A and B can discuss whether they agree with the book answer, why or why not, and how the answer might change if facts were different or other facts were known. They might explore what else they would like to know, and how likely they are to know it, before judging the situation. |
| 4 | Team B draws the next card and reads the situation to Team A, and the process continues until the time allocated for the training has elapsed (suggested: 20-30 minutes). |
| 5 | If teams suspect a book answer may be wrong, they give that situation card to their manager so he or she can ask a company expert to fully explore the situation and the correct answer(s) with them later. |

This design focuses discussion on company-selected topics and provides company-selected guidance on correct answers. It does not require a professional instructor to run a session — any manager can conduct it. It does not require the manager to provide 'right answers' and it allows participants to proceed at any pace comfortable for them. It opens channels of communication on ethics topics between employees, and between employees and the manager leading the session. And it takes advantage of what research tells us: decisions made by small groups generally are wiser than decisions by any individual in the group. Participants almost universally enjoy the small group discussions, and peer pressure tends to pull any employees with deviant ethics perspectives toward the group norm.

# Test yourself: Values-based scenarios

Here are scenarios with answers primarily based on values. They would need to be tailored to your company's particular value set.

**Table:** Values-based scenarios

| | Situation | Answer |
|---|---|---|
| 1 | Ann got a written warning for losing a tool. When it disappeared, she was away at a training course and a supervisor had opened her toolbox so others could use her tools. | |
| 2 | To meet production targets, some employees are working mandatory 8-hour days 7 days a week. They are tired, sick, and making mistakes. The rework bins are full and inspectors are not catching all the defects. | |
| 3 | Pat moonlights as a realtor and handled the sale of one house and purchase of another for Dale, an employee Pat supervises at our company. | |
| 4 | A supplier is throwing a holiday party and has invited people from all of its customer companies. It will be a 5-hour barbeque. Food and beverages will be free. Attendees have the option to submit their names for drawings that award gifts. Can we attend? | |
| 5 | Dale has inspected subassemblies purchased from another company so long that over the past 12 years he has developed a personal friendship with the company's account representative. For an upcoming vacation, Dale and his wife want to join the account representative and his wife on the account representative's sailboat for a 2-week voyage. OK? | |
| 6 | Dale is on a 6-person team assigned to a customer's facility and is dating Pat, the customer's point of contact for the contract. Dale and Pat currently are on a 3-week vacation together at a resort. OK? | |
| 7 | Manager Dale opened a staff meeting with obscenities, wanting to know who is slowing down production today. Dale acted like a tyrant, used abusive language, and was condescending to everyone. | |
| 8 | Manager Pat promoted his son-in-law. Gale and Kelly got promoted because they buddied up to Pat. Other employees with better qualifications and more seniority were not considered. | |
| 9 | A woman who works for you confided that a male employee invited her to 'rub up against me if you want to'. She told him 'No, not now, not ever.' He laughed and now says, 'If you want to…' almost every time he encounters her. | |
| 10 | You have been approached by another company to moonlight doing for them exactly what you do for our company. The money they offer looks really good. OK to accept? | |

**Table:** Values-based scenarios answers

| | Answer |
|---|---|
| 1 | We value people and should not hold Ann accountable for a tool she had locked up when a supervisor allowed others to access her toolbox. |
| 2 | We value people, quality, and customers. We need to respect the balance people need in their lives, fix the processes so manufacturing defects do not occur, and deliver good products that will satisfy our customers. |
| 3 | We value integrity, honesty, fairness, openness, and trust. This situation creates a potential conflict of interest for Pat and Dale. The company needs to address it. |
| 4 | We value integrity. The party itself, with free food and beverages, is a gift from a supplier that creates a potential conflict of interest for our company's employees. Do not attend. |
| 5 | We value integrity. The voyage is a gift from a supplier that creates a potential conflict of interest for Dale. Do not make that trip. |
| 6 | We value integrity. The relationship and the joint vacation create at least the appearance of a possible conflict of interest. The company needs to address the issue. |
| 7 | We value people. We treat each other with respect. The company needs to address this issue. |
| 8 | We value people. We treat each other with respect. The company needs to address this issue by determining if Pat followed proper procedures in making the promotions. |
| 9 | We value people. We treat each other with respect. This is sexual harassment and the company is required by law to investigate this report she made to a supervisor, you. |
| 10 | We value integrity. Discuss this job with your manager before accepting. Avoid it if it will interfere with your responsibilities at our company. |

## Test yourself: Code-based scenarios

Here are scenarios with answers primarily based on a generic corporate code of conduct. They would need to be tailored to your company's particular code.

**Table:** Code-based scenarios

| | Situation | Answer |
|---|---|---|
| 1 | On personal time, Teddy uses the company's computer to manage the golf association's player handicaps and tournaments. | |
| 2 | Bill's wife sells real estate, so Bill gives her the name and address of every new hire who will need to relocate here. It is good for them, for the company, and for his wife! | |
| 3 | Dan wants to attend a computer conference sponsored by another company. The other company will pick up his airline and hotel tab. OK? | |

| | Situation | Answer |
|---|---|---|
| 4 | Alan is invited to join the board of directors of another company that supplies services to our company. | |
| 5 | Wendy is campaigning for election as mayor. She campaigns nights, weekends, and on vacation days. | |
| 6 | Wendy's boss proposes to use a small amount of company money to host a community picnic at the company's recreation park in support of her campaign to be elected mayor. | |
| 7 | Robert knew one of his employees had received golf lessons, then golf clubs, then a golf cart free from one of the company's suppliers, but he decided he should not poke his nose into what really was his employee's business. | |
| 8 | Ben works in manufacturing and his wife, who does not report to him, inspects the quality of his work. | |
| 9 | Gregory received the new insurance forms late and asked all his employees to backdate them to 60 days ago. | |
| 10 | According to hearsay, Evan drinks vodka throughout the day from a bottle kept in his desk. | |

**Table:** Code-based scenarios answers

| | Answer |
|---|---|
| 1 | Investigate. Company equipment should be used for authorized business purposes only. Exceptions require written approval from a company officer. |
| 2 | Investigate. Employees may not use any of the company's business information for personal gain unless that information is available to the general public. |
| 3 | Dan may attend but must not allow the other company to pay his airline and hotel tab. The company will reimburse employees for reasonable expenses justified by their work. |
| 4 | Before serving as a director of a supplier, obtain our company management's written approval. |
| 5 | The company respects the right of employees to be involved in political activity on their own time and using their own resources. |
| 6 | The company does not contribute money or other resources to political candidates. |
| 7 | Investigate. The employee may have a conflict, and Robert may be culpable to the extent that he provided inadequate supervision or lack of diligence. |
| 8 | Refer to employee relations. Avoiding the appearance of a conflict of interest can be as important as avoiding an actual conflict. |
| 9 | Refer to benefits. Providing misleading information on company documents is strictly prohibited. |
| 10 | Refer to employee relations. Company rules prohibit liquor on the premises and this situation may require a fitness-for-duty medical examination. |

# Test yourself: Compliance-based scenarios

Here are scenarios with answers primarily based on compliance requirements set forth in well-known federal laws. They would need to be tailored to your company's particular compliance requirements.

**Table:** Compliance-based scenarios

| | Situation | Answer |
|---|---|---|
| 1 | We talked to our new employee, Ben. The company he used to work for is competing against us for this federal contract and he knows all about their bid. | |
| 2 | We gave Ellen's daughter a job. Ellen heads the federal procurement office, her daughter needed work, so this will be a big help to her. | |
| 3 | We used a lobbyist to encourage a Congressman to approve funding the next phase of our federal contract. We included the lobbyist's fees as part of management costs charged to the contract. | |
| 4 | We knew the government was about to award us a $25 billion contract, so we invested heavily in our own company's stock. | |
| 5 | I made a deal with the competition. Half the time they will bid high and half the time we will. That way we will split the business and not have to cut prices. | |
| 6 | What the government did not know when it signed the contract was that we put pad into part of our cost estimate to make doubly sure we earn some profit from this work. | |
| 7 | We ran out of the J22 condensers required by the federal contract so we substituted J54 condensers. They are the same thing but higher quality. We paid the extra cost. The government should be glad to get them. | |
| 8 | The contract required us to use a damping fluid that would perform down to -65 degrees Fahrenheit. What we used will freeze if you hold it at -65 F long enough, but the product will never get that cold that long so it is OK. | |
| 9 | The contract required a vibration test applying 19 gravities of force. It turned out that our equipment was incapable of testing at that high a force, but our test engineer was able to adjust the potentiometer so it looked like it was applying 19 gravities of force when actually the force was much less. | |
| 10 | Some European countries are interested in our new radar. We are not licensed to take it overseas, so we had their people come here to our US development center to see it. | |

**Table:** Compliance-based scenarios answers

| | Answer |
|---|---|
| 1 | Investigate. Soliciting proprietary information during federal agency procurement violates the *Procurement Integrity Act*. |
| 2 | Investigate. Providing anything of value, even indirectly, to improperly obtain or reward favorable treatment on a federal contract violates the *Anti-Kickback Act*. |
| 3 | Investigate. Using federally appropriated money to pay anyone to influence federal officials about federal contracts violates the Byrd Amendment. |
| 4 | Investigate. Persons who know material, non-public information may not conduct insider trading. |
| 5 | Investigate. Agreements with a competitor to fix prices violate the *Sherman Anti-Trust Act*. |
| 6 | Investigate. In federal procurements, all cost and pricing statements must be complete, current, accurate, and truthful or they violate the *Truth in Negotiations Act*. |
| 7 | Investigate. In federal contracts, all products must be exactly as specified by the customer. |
| 8 | Investigate. The specification said -65 degrees Fahrenheit, and by contract we are required to meet that. |
| 9 | Investigate. We must live up to the letter of the contract. If that does not make sense, you have to meet with the customer and, if you both agree, modify the contract. |
| 10 | Investigate. Disclosing technical information to representatives of other nations, even if done in the United States, is an export that requires a license from the US government. |

# Bibliography

*AACSB Assurance of Learning Standards: An Interpretation,* 2007, Association to Advance Collegiate Schools of Business International (AACSB), Tampa, FL.

Angier, N 2011, 'Thirst for Fairness May Have Helped Us Survive', *New York Times,* viewed 21 Jan 2012, www.nytimes.com/2011/07/05/science/05angier .html.

Anti-Money Laundering Programs, 2002, 31 C.F.R. 103.

Armstrong, DM 1992, *Managing by Storying Around,* Doubleday Currency, New York.

Bamberger, M & Yaeger, D 1997, 'Over the Edge', *Sports Illustrated,* 86(15).

Bandura, A 1997, *Self-Efficacy: The Exercise of Control,* W. H. Freeman, New York.

Benedict, XVI 2012, 'Encyclical Letter 2009: Caritas In Veritate', viewed 20 January 2012, www .lifeissues.net/writers/doc/civ/civ_caritas.in.veritate5.html.

Bennis, W 2007, in RS Sisodia, DB Wolfe & JN Sheth, *Firms of Endearment,* Wharton School Publishing, Upper Saddle River, NJ.

Bersoff, DM 1999, 'Why Good People Sometimes Do Bad Things: Motivated Reasoning and Unethical Behavior', *Personality and Social Psychology Bulletin,* 25(1): 28–39.

Bowman, FO 2004, 'Drifting Down the Dnieper with Prince Potemkin: Some Skeptical Reflections About the Place of Compliance Programs in Federal Criminal Sentencing', *Wake Forest Law Review,* 39(3): 671–690.

Brodsky, R 2010, 'Defense Scales Back Organizational Conflict-of-Interest Rule', *Government Executive,* viewed 22 January 2012, www.govexec.com/story_page.cfm?articleid=46798.

Brown, KG 2001, 'Using Computers to Deliver Training: Which Employees Learn and Why?' *Personnel Psychology,* 54(2): 271–296.

Brzezinski, M 2010, 'Obama's Foreign Bribery Crackdown', *Washington Post,* A23.

Bundick, PL 2009, *Social Capital Strategies of Microentrepreneurs: An Inquiry Into the Business Use of Relational Models at the Base of New Delhi's Export Garment Industry,* PhD diss., Fielding Graduate University.

Burke, J quoted in Finney, DP 2002, 'Tylenol Hero Tells CEOs to Develop, Follow Ethical Code', *McClatchy-Tribune Business News.*

Bush, GW 2001, *President Speaks at Pittsburgh Steelworkers Picnic,* viewed 20 January 2012, http://georgewbush-whitehouse.archives.gov/news/releases /2001/08/20010826.html.

2003, *Business Conduct Officer Handbook,* 4th edn, Northrop Grumman Corporation, Los Angeles, CA.

Carroll, AB 1999, 'Corporate Social Responsibility: Evolution of a Definitional Construct', *Business & Society* 38(3): 268–295.

Carroll, AB 1991, 'The Pyramid of Corporate Social Responsibility: Toward the Moral Management of Organizational Stakeholders', *Business Horizons,* 34(4): 39–48.

Caux Round Table, *Principles for Responsible Business*, 2009, viewed 22 January 2012, www.cauxroundtable.org/view_file.cfm?fileid=143.

2011, *Cisco Code of Business Conduct: Connecting With Our Values,* Cisco Systems, Inc., Milpitas, CA, viewed 23 January 2012, http://investor.cisco.com/documentdisplay.cfm ?DocumentID=3263.

1999, *Coca-Cola 'Regrets' Contamination*, viewed 21 January 2012, http://news.bbc .co.uk /2/hi/europe/371300.stm.

Cohen, R 2011, 'Doing What the Company Wants', *New York Times*, MM-18.

2006, *Communicators Divided Over Role as Ethics Counsel to Management: New ABC Study*, PRWeb, viewed 22 Jan 2012, www.prweb.com/pdfdownload/38419.pdf.

Compliance Program Guidance for Hospitals. 63 Federal Register 8987, 1998.

Compliance Programs of Investment Companies and Investment Advisers, 68 Federal Register 74714, 2003.

Conaboy, RP 1995, 'Welcome and Conference Overview', in *Corporate Crime in America: Strengthening the "Good Citizen" Corporation, Proceedings of the Second Symposium on Crime and Punishment in the United States,* United States Sentencing Commission, Washington, DC.

'Conflict of Interest', *Wikipedia,* 2011, viewed 16 October 2011, http://en .wikipedia.org/wiki/Conflict_of_interest.

Connor, JM & Mazanov, J 2009, 'Would You Dope? A General Population Test of the Goldman Dilemma', *British Journal of Sports Medicine,* 43(11): 871–872.

Cooke, RA 1989, 'How to Use the Organization Culture Inventory', *Organizational Culture Inventory Leader's Guide,* Human Synergistics, Plymouth, MI, 1–10.

Cooke, RA, & Rousseau, DM 1988, 'Behavioral Norms and Expectations: A Quantitative Approach to the Assessment of Organizational Culture', *Group and Organization Studies,* 13(3): 245–273.

Cooperrider, DL & Sekerka, LE 2003, Toward a theory of positive organizational change, in KS Cameron, JE Dutton & RE Quinn (Eds.), *Positive Organizational Scholarship: Foundations of a New Discipline*, Berrett-Koehler, San Francisco, 225.

1995, *Corporate Crime in America: Strengthening the "Good Citizen" Corporation, Proceedings of the Second Symposium on Crime and Punishment in the United States,* United States Sentencing Commission, Washington, DC.

2003, *Corporate Ethics Audit Feedback Report: Sample,* Human Synergistics, Plymouth, MI.

2004, 'Corporate Governance Rules', *NYSE Listed Company Manual,* New York Stock Exchange, New York.

*Corporate Responsibility Best Practices: Setting the Baseline*. *Corporate Responsibility Magazine* in association with NYSE Euronext and Corporate Responsibility Officer Association, 2010, viewed 24 January 2012, www.croassociation.org/files /CR-Best-Practices-2010-Module-1.pdf.

Cragg, W 2010, 'The State and Future Directions of Business Ethics Research and Practice', *Business Ethics Quarterly,* 20(4): 720–721.

Cresswell, JW 1998, *Qualitative Inquiry and Research Design: Choosing Among Five Traditions,* Sage, Thousand Oaks, CA.

Cruver, B 2002, *Anatomy of Greed: The Unshredded Truth from an Enron Insider,* Carroll & Graf, New York.

Cummings, TG, & Worley, CG 1993, *Organization Development and Change,* 5th edn, West, St. Paul, MN.

Daly, FJ 2002, 'Commonwealth North Forum Proceedings'.

Daly, FJ 1998, 'Rules and Values Are Ethical Allies', *Center for Business Ethics News,* 6(2): 3, 7.

Daly, FJ 'The Ethics Dynamic', *Business and Society Review,* 102/103(1): 37–42.

Daniel, CA 2009, 'How Two National Reports Ruined Business Schools', *Chronicle of Higher Education.*

Dardick, H 2010, 'Cook County Employees to Get Online Ethics Training', *Chicago Tribune.*

De George, RT 2010, '*BEQ* at Twenty', *Business Ethics Quarterly,* 20(4): 722–723.

DeLia, R 2006, 'Privileged Communication' [email to Kevin Hunsaker, February 7, 2006], in *Hewlett-Packard's Pretexting Scandal, Hearing Before the Subcommittee on Oversight and Investigations of the House Committee on Energy and Commerce,* 109th Cong. 375, serial no. 109–146.

Denning, S 2005, *The Leader's Guide to Storytelling: Mastering the Art and Discipline of Business Narrative,* Jossey-Bass, San Francisco.

Denning, S 2007, *The Secret Language of Leadership: How Leaders Inspire Action Through Narrative,* Jossey-Bass, San Francisco.

DesJardins, J 2009, *An Introduction to Business Ethics,* 4th edn, McGraw-Hill, New York.

Devine, T & Maasarani, TF 2011, *Whistleblower's Survival Guide,* Berrett-Koehler, San Francisco.

'The DII Principles', Defense Industry Initiative on Business Ethics and Conduct, 2010, viewed 22 January 2012, www.dii.org/files/DII-Principles.pdf.

Donald, DH 1995, *Lincoln,* Simon & Schuster, New York.

Doney, PM, Cannon, JP & Mullen, MR 1998, 'Understanding the Influence of National Culture on the Development of Trust', *Academy of Management Review,* 23(3): 601–620.

Driscoll, DM 2003, 'Sarbanes-Oxley: Pardon Me If I'm Underwhelmed', *Ethics Matter Magazine.*

Driscoll, DM & Hoffman, WM 2000, *Ethics Matters: How to Implement Values-Driven Management,* Center for Business Ethics, Waltham, MA.

Dunn, P 2006, 'My Role in the Hewlett-Packard Leak Investigation', in *Hewlett-Packard's Pretexting Scandal, Hearing Before the Subcommittee on Oversight and Investigations of the House Committee on Energy and Commerce,* 109th Cong. 44-76 (September 28, 2006), serial no. 109-146.

Earle, B 1996, 'The United States' Foreign Corrupt Practices Act and the OECD Anti-Bribery Recommendation: When Moral Suasion Won't Work, Try the Money Argument', *Dickinson Journal of International Law,* 14: 207–242.

Ethical Leadership Group. 1998, *Ethics Phone Lines Best Practices Report.* Wilmette, IL.

Ethics Officer Association 2002, 'Letter to James L. Cochrane, New York Stock Exchange', in *New York Stock Exchange Corporate Accountability and Listing*

*Standards Committee Report*, viewed 21 January 2012, www.iasplus.com /resource/nysegovf.pdf.

2004, *Everything You Wanted to Know About Helpline Best Practices: Results of the 2004 Survey of Ethics Officer Association Sponsoring Partner Members*, Ethical Leadership Group, Wilmette, IL.

Fehr, E, Bernhard, H & Rockenbach, B 'Egalitarianism in Young Children', *Nature*, 454(7208): 1079–1084.

Fehr, E, Rützler, D & Sutter, M 2011, 'The Development of Egalitarianism, Altruism, Spite and Parochialism in Childhood and Adolescence' Discussion Paper No. 5530, Institute for the Study of Labor website, viewed 21 January 2012, http://ftp.iza.org/dp5530.pdf.

Frederick, WC 2011, 'Evolving Phases of Corporate Social Responsibility', in AT Lawrence & J Weber, *Business and Society: Stakeholders, Ethics, Public Policy*, 13th edn, McGraw-Hill Irwin, New York.

Frederick, WC 2009, 'Review of Business Ethics and Ethical Business by R. Audi', *Journal of Business Ethics Education*, 6: 201–202.

Frederick, WC 2008, 'Review of The Difference Makers: How Social and Institutional Entrepreneurs Created the Corporate Responsibility Movement', *Journal of Corporate Citizenship*, 32: 100–102.

Fukuyama, F 1995, *Trust: The Social Virtues and the Creation of Prosperity*, Free Press, New York.

Gawande, A 2002, *Complications: A Surgeon's Notes on an Imperfect Science*, Picador, New York.

Gentilucci, AR 2006, 'Re: Phone Records' [email to Kevin Hunsaker, January 30, 2006], in *Hewlett-Packard's Pretexting Scandal, Hearing Before the Subcommittee on Oversight and Investigations of the House Committee on Energy and Commerce*, 109th Cong. 306, 28 September 2006, serial no. 109–146.

'Germany: Phase 3', Directorate for Financial and Enterprise Affairs, OECD, 2011, viewed 22 January 2012, www.oecd.org/dataoecd/6/46/47413672.pdf.

Gibson, JW & Blackwell, CW 'Flying High With Herb Kelleher: A Profile in Charismatic Leadership', *Journal of Leadership and Organizational Studies*, 6(3–4): 120–137.

Gioia, DA 1992, 'Pinto Fires and Personal Ethics: A Script Analysis of Missed Opportunities', *Journal of Business Ethics*, 11(5, 6): 379–389.

'The Global Sullivan Principles of Social Responsibility', n.d., Leon H. Sullivan Foundation, viewed 22 January 2012, www.thesullivanfoundation.org/about/ global _sullivan_principles.

Goldman, B, Bush, P & Klatz, R 1984, *Death In the Locker Room: Steroids and Sports*, Icarus Press, South Bend, IN.

Gordon, DI 2005, 'Organizational Conflicts of Interest: A Growing Integrity Challenge' (Public Law and Legal Theory Working Paper No. 127), George Washington University Law School, Washington, DC, viewed 22 January 2012, http://papers.ssrn .com/so13/papers.cfm?abstract_id=665274.

2009, 'Government Update on Mandatory Disclosure Program', *Federal Ethics Report*, 16(11): 7–8.

2011, 'Government's Opposition to Motion to Quash and Motion for an Order to Compel', in *In Re: Request from the United Kingdom Pursuant to the Treaty Between the Government of the United States of America and the Government of the United Kingdom on Mutual Assistance in Criminal Matters in the Matter of Dolours Price*, District Court, District of Massachusetts, US.

1991, *Guidelines Manual*, United States Sentencing Commission, Washington, DC.

2004, *Guidelines Manual*, United States Sentencing Commission, Washington, DC.

1999, 'The Gurus Speak: Complexity and Organizations', *Emergence*, 1(1): 73–91.

Hananel, S 2011, 'Conn. Firm, U.S. Settle Case of Worker Fired After Criticism on Facebook', *Denver Post*, viewed 23 January 2012, www.denverpost.com/search/ci_17324449.

Herman, RP & Nair, V 'Commit! Debate: The Shareholder Value of Sustainability: A Brief for Corporate Responsibility', *Corporate Responsibility Magazine*, 2(5), viewed 24 January 2012, http://thecro.com/content /commit-debate-shareholder-value-sustainability.

Hersey, P & Blanchard, KH 1982, *Management of Organizational Behavior: Utilizing Human Resources*, 4th edn, Prentice-Hall, Englewood Cliffs, NJ.

*Hewlett-Packard's Pretexting Scandal, Hearing Before the Subcommittee on Oversight and Investigations of the Committee on Energy and Commerce, House of Representatives*, 109th Cong. 2, 28 September 2006, serial no. 109–146.

*Hewlett-Packard's Pretexting Scandal, Hearing Before the Subcommittee on Oversight and Investigations of the House Committee on Energy and Commerce*, 109th Cong. 113, 28 September 2006, serial no. 109–146 (testimony of Fred Adler).

Hirshberg, G 2008, *Stirring It Up*, Hyperion, New York.

Holland, JH 1998, *Emergence: From Chaos to Order*, Perseus, Cambridge, MA.

Hosseini, K 2007, *The Kite Runner*, illustrated edn, Riverhead, New York.

Huskins, PC 2008, 'FCPA Prosecutions: Liability Trend to Watch', *Stanford Law Review*, 60(5): 1447–1457.

Ivester, D 1999, quoted in 'Coca-Cola 'Regrets' Contamination', viewed 21 January 2012, http://news.bbc .co.uk /2/hi/europe/371300.stm.

Jacobson, D 1998, 'Founding Fathers', *Stanford Magazine*, viewed 24 January 2012, www.stanfordalumni.org/news/magazine/1998/julaug/articles/founding_fathers /founding_fathers.html.

Jennings, MM 2006, *The Seven Signs of Ethical Collapse: How to Spot Moral Meltdowns in Companies . . . Before It's Too Late*, St. Martin's Press, New York.

Joseph, J 2000, *Ethics Resource Center's 2000 National Business Ethics Survey, Vol. 1: How Employees Perceive Ethics at Work*, Ethics Resource Center, Washington, DC.

Karnani, A & Sullivan, G 2011, 'Commit! Debate: A Logical Trap: The Case Against Expending Resources on Corporate Responsibility', *Corporate Responsibility Magazine*, 2(5), viewed 24 January 2012, http://thecro.com/content /commit-debate-logical-trap.

Kidder, RM 1996, *How Good People Make Tough Choices: Resolving the Dilemmas of Ethical Living*, Fireside, New York.

Kotler, P & Roberto, EL 1989, *Social Marketing: Strategies for Changing Public Behavior,* Free Press, New York.

Kouzes, JM & Posner, BZ 2003, *Credibility: How Leaders Gain and Lose It, Why People Demand It,* Jossey-Bass, San Francisco.

Krell, E 2006, 'Compliance Watch: The Walking, Talking Compliance Risk', *Business Finance.*

Lagace, M 2002, 'Paul O'Neill: Values Into Action', *Working Knowledge for Business Leaders,* Harvard Business School, Cambridge, MA, viewed 21 January 2012, http://hbswk.hbs.edu/archive/3159.html.

Latané, B & Darley, JM 1970, *The Unresponsive Bystander: Why Doesn't He Help?* Appleton-Century-Crofts, New York.

Lawrence, AT & Weber, J 2011, *Business and Society: Stakeholders, Ethics, Public Policy,* 13th edn, McGraw-Hill Irwin, New York.

Lee, A, Kennedy, A, Rice, M & Weber, Z 2011, 'Openleaks' Whistleblowing Model', in *Business Ethics Fortnight 2011: Intramural Qualifying Intercollegiate Business Ethics Case Competitions Team Executive Summaries,* Center for Ethics and Business, Loyola Marymount University, Los Angeles, CA.

Leith, S 2002, 'Coke's European Challenge: 3 Years After Recall, Sales in Belgium at Their Best', *Atlanta Journal-Constitution,* 1A.

Light On Productions, producer. 'In Search of the Good Corporate Citizen: Hitting the Numbers' [transcript], 2009, viewed 20 January 2012, www.lightonpro.com/transcripts/InSearch_Hitting.pdf.

Los Angeles County Superior Court. 'In Camera Hearing on Furman Tapes, Disqualifying Ito' [transcript], 1995, viewed 22 January 2012, www.lectlaw.com/files /cas48.htm.

'Lucent Technologies World Services Inc', GAO Decision B-295462, 2005.

Lutz, RA 2003, *Guts: 8 Laws of Business from One of the Most Innovative Business Leaders of Our Time,* Revised and updated edn, Wiley, Hoboken, NJ.

'Maslow's Hierarchy of Needs', 2011, viewed 21 January 2012, www.abraham-maslow.com/m_motivation/Hierarchy_of_Needs.asp.

McGraw, BA 1998, *Business Ethics Fellowship Study*, Unpublished manuscript.

Melo, T & Galan, JI 2011, 'Effects of Corporate Social Responsibility on Brand Value', *Journal of Brand Management,* 18(6): 423–437.

'Members of New York State Senate Will Get Ethics Training', Fox23 News, 2011.

2001, 'A Message from the Chairman and Chief Executive Officer', *Standards of Business Conduct,* Northrop Grumman Corporation, Century City, CA.

Meyers, L 2006, 'Still Wearing the 'Kick Me' Sign', *Monitor on Psychology,* 37(7): 68–70.

Meyerson, D, Weick, KE & Kramer, RM 1996, 'Swift Trust and Temporary Groups', in RM Kramer & TR Tyler (eds), *Trust in Organizations: Frontiers of Theory and Research,* Sage, Thousand Oaks, CA, 166–195.

Miceli, MP & Near, JP 1992, *Blowing the Whistle: The Organizational and Legal Implications for Companies and Employees,* Lexington, New York.

Miceli, MP, Roach, BL & Near, JP 1988, 'The motivations of anonymous whistle-blowers: The case of federal employees', *Public Personnel Management,* 17(3): 281–296.

Milgram, S 1963, 'Behavioral Study of Obedience', *Journal of Abnormal and Social Psychology,* 67(4): 371–378.

Milgram, S 1974, *Obedience to Authority,* Harper & Row, New York.

Morris, T 1997, *If Aristotle Ran General Motors: The New Soul of Business,* Henry Holt, New York.

2011, 'Motion of Trustees of Boston College to Quash Subpoenas', in *In Re: Request from the United Kingdom Pursuant to the Treaty Between the Government of the United States of America and the Government of the United Kingdom on Mutual Assistance in Criminal Matters in the Matter of Dolours Price,* District Court, District of Massachusetts, US.

2005, *National Business Ethics Survey: How Employees View Ethics in Their Organizations 1994–2005,* Ethics Resource Center, Washington, DC.

Nye, V 2006, 'Cell Phone Information (Call Data)' [email to Ted Crawford, March 17, 2006], in *Hewlett-Packard's Pretexting Scandal, Hearing Before the Subcommittee on Oversight and Investigations of the House Committee on Energy and Commerce,* 109th Cong. 464, September 28, 2006, serial no. 109–146.

Nye, V 2006, 'Re: Privileged Communication' [email to Anthony R Gentilucci, February 7, 2006], in *Hewlett-Packard's Pretexting Scandal, Hearing Before the Subcommittee on Oversight and Investigations of the House Committee on Energy and Commerce,* 109th Cong. 362, September 28, 2006, serial no. 109–146.

2011, *OECD Guidelines for Multinational Enterprises,* Organisation for Economic Cooperation and Development, Paris, France.

'The OECD Guidelines for Multinational Enterprises: Summary of the Guidelines', viewed 22 January 2012, http://actrav.itcilo.org/actrav-english/telearn/global/ilo/guide/oecd.htm.

Olin, D & Whitehead, J 2010, *CR: How Fast It's Growing, How Much It's Spending, and How Far It's Going* (CR Best Practices Study), viewed 24 January 2012, www.thecro.com/files/CRBestPractices.pdf.

Oliver, CR 1985, 'A Psychological Approach to Preventing Computer Abuse--A Case History', *Computer Security Journal,* 3(2): 51–56.

Oliver, CR 2004, 'Looking For a HERO? Four Public Policy Initiatives on Business Ethics', unpublished manuscript.

O'Neill, PH quoted in Lagace, M 2002, 'Paul O'Neill: Values Into Action', *Working Knowledge For Business Leaders,* Harvard Business School, Cambridge, MA, viewed 21 January 2012, http://hbswk.hbs.edu/archive/3159.html.

O'Reilly, CA III & Pfeffer, J 2000, *Hidden Value: How Great Companies Achieve Extraordinary Results with Ordinary People,* Harvard Business School Press, Boston.

'OSHA Identifies 13,000 Workplaces with Highest Injury and Illness Rates', *OSHA Workplace Injury Statistics and News,* 2011, viewed 21 January 2012, www.ehso.com/OSHA_Injuries.htm.

2009, *Our Code of Business Conduct,* Gap, Inc, San Francisco, CA.

Packard, D quoted in Jacobson, D 1998, 'Founding Fathers', *Stanford Magazine,* viewed 24 January 2012, www.stanfordalumni.org/news/magazine/1998/julaug/articles/founding_fathers /founding_fathers.html.

Packard, D 1995, *The HP Way,* Harper Business, New York.

Paine, LS 1997, *Cases in Leadership, Ethics, and Organizational Integrity: A Strategic Perspective,* Irwin/McGraw-Hill, New York.

Patsuris, P 2002, 'Accounting: The Corporate Scandal Sheet', *Forbes,* last modified, viewed 20 January 2012, www.forbes.com/2002/07/25/accountingtracker_print.html.

Penney, JC 1950, *Fifty Years With the Golden Rule,* Harper, New York.

Pirson, M & Malhotra, D 2008, 'Unconventional Insights for Managing Stakeholder Trust', *MIT Sloan Management Review,* 49(4): 43–50.

Pisano, GP, Bhmer, RMJ & Edmondson, AC 'Organizational Differences in Rates of Learning: Evidence from the Adoption of Minimally Invasive Cardiac Surgery', *Management Science,* 47(6): 752–768.

President's Blue Ribbon Commission on Defense Management, 1986, *Conduct and Accountability: A Report to the President,* Washington, DC.

*Public Accountability Report, 2010,* Defense Industry Initiative on Business Ethics and Conduct, Washington, DC, 2011.

'PURVIS Systems, Inc', GAO Decision B-293807.3; B-293807.4, 2004.

Raiborn, CA & Payne, D 1990, 'Corporate Codes of Conduct: A Collective Conscience and Continuum', *Journal of Business Ethics,* 9(11): 879–889.

Reidbord, S 2010, 'Would You Trade Years of Life for Happiness?' *Psychology Today,* viewed 20 January 2012, www.psychologytoday.com/node/37681.

'Rethinking the Social Responsibility of Business: A *Reason* Debate Featuring Milton Friedman, Whole Foods' John Mackey, and Cypress Semiconductor's T. J. Rodgers', *Reason,* 2005, viewed 24 January 2012, http://reason.com/archives/2005/10/01 /rethinking-the-social-responsi.

Rhode, D 2006, 'How We Tackle the 'Woman Problem'', *Stanford Report,* viewed 23 January 2012, http://news.stanford.edu/news/2006/may24/rhode-052406.html.

Robin, D, Giallourakis, M, David, FR & Moritz, TE 1989, 'A Different Look at Codes of Ethics', *Business Horizons,* 32(1): 66–73.

Rothschild, J & Miethe, TD 1999, 'Whistle-Blower Disclosures and Management Retaliation: The Battle to Control Information about Organization Corruption', *Work and Occupations,* 26(1): 107–128.

Rousseau, DM, Sitkin, SB, Burt, RS & Camerer, C 1998, 'Not So Different After All: A Cross-Discipline View of Trust', *Academy of Management Review,* 23(3): 393–404.

Royce, SW 1984, *A Life Remembered: The Memoirs Of Stephen W. Royce,* Royal Literary Publications, Laguna Niguel, CA.

Rubin, NM 1998, 'A Convergence of 1996 and 1997 Global Efforts to Curb Corruption and Bribery in International Business Transactions: The Legal Implications of the OECD Recommendations and Convention for the United States, Germany, and Switzerland', *American University International Law Review,* 14(1): 257–320.

Rudman, WB, Parker, RP, Elliott, RS, Olson, JH, Futch, AM & Vorwig, PA 2003, *A Report to the Chairman and Board of Directors of The Boeing Company Concerning the Company's Ethics Program and Its Rules and Procedures for the Treatment of Competitors' Proprietary Information*, Boeing, Chicago, IL, viewed 22 January 2012, www.boeing.com/news/releases/2003/q4 /rudman.pdf.

Sarbanes-Oxley Act of 2002.

Schein, EH 1992, *Organizational Culture and Leadership,* 2nd edn, Jossey-Bass, San Francisco.

'Selected Agencies' Efforts to Identify Organizational Conflicts of Interest', GAO Report to Congressional Committees GAO/GGD-96-15, 1995.

Seyedin-Noor, B & Lain, T 2006, 'Interviews of Kevin Hunsaker' [draft memorandum, August 21, 2006], in *Hewlett-Packard's Pretexting Scandal, Hearing Before the Subcommittee on Oversight and Investigations of the House Committee on Energy and Commerce,* 109th Cong. 661, September 28, 2006, serial no. 109–146.

Singer, A 2010, 'Why Cummins Inc.'s CEO Reads His Firm's Ethics Investigation Reports--All 400 of Them', *Ethikos,* viewed 25 January 2012, www .ethikospublication.com/html/cummins.html.

Sisodia, R, Wolfe, DB & Sheth, JN 2007, *Firms of Endearment: How World-Class Companies Profit from Passion and Purpose,* Wharton School Publishing, Upper Saddle River, NJ.

Spade, AC 2001, *The Beginning of a Journey: Posttraumatic Change in Women Who Take a Stand,* PhD diss., Fielding Graduate University.

Stambor, Z 2006, 'Bullying Stems from Fear, Apathy', *Monitor on Psychology,* 37(7): 72–73.

'State Employees Fail Ethics Test by Going Too Fast', *Associated Press,* 2007, viewed 27 January 2012, www.pantagraph.com/news/state-employees-fail-ethics-test-by-going-too-fast/article_6d96ea47-d64b-5a48-b443-e0ca2ba15770.html.

Stevens, B 1994, 'An Analysis of Corporate Ethical Code Studies: 'Where Do We Go from Here?'' *Journal of Business Ethics,* 13(1): 63–69.

Sugar, RD 2003, *Business Conduct Officer Handbook,* 4th edn, Northrop Grumman Corporation, Los Angeles, CA.

'Sullivan Principles', Wikipedia, 2011, viewed 22 January 2012, http://en.wikipedia.org/wiki/Sullivan_Principles.

Swenson, W 1995, 'The Organizational Guidelines' 'Carrot And Stick' Philosophy, and Their Focus on 'Effective' Compliance', in *Corporate Crime in America: Strengthening the "Good Citizen" Corporation, Proceedings of the Second Symposium on Crime and Punishment in the United States,* United States Sentencing Commission, Washington, DC, 28–29.

Sykes, GM & Matza, D 'Techniques of Neutralization: A Theory of Delinquency', *American Sociological Review,* 22(6): 664–670.

Szumal, JL 2003, *Organizational Culture Inventory Interpretation and Development Guide,* Human Synergistics, Plymouth, MI.

'The Ten Principles', U.N. Global Compact, n.d., viewed 22 January 2012, www .unglobalcompact.org/AboutTheGC/TheTenPrinciples/index.html.

Thomas, T, Schermerhorn, JR Jr & Dienhart, JW 'Strategic Leadership of Ethical Behavior in Business', *Academy of Management Executive,* 18(2): 56–66.

Thompson, LD 2003, *Principles of Federal Prosecution of Business Organizations,* Department of Justice Memorandum, US.

Toffler, BL & Reingold, J 2003, *Final Accounting: Ambition, Greed, and the Fall of Arthur Andersen,* Doubleday, New York.

Trace International. 'Global Enforcement Report', 2011, viewed 22 January 2012, www.traceinternational.org.

Treviño, L 2006, 'The Honorable Student', *BizEd,* 5(6): 26.

Treviño, LK & Brown, ME 2004, 'Managing to Be Ethical: Debunking Five Business Ethics Myths', *Academy of Management Executive,* 18(2): 69–81.

Treviño, LK & Nelson, KA 2004, *Managing Business Ethics: Straight Talk About How to Do It Right,* 3rd edn, Wiley, Hoboken, NJ.

2011, 'California Mid-Winter Fair and Fiesta Last Chance Ethics Training', *Holtville Tribune.*

Tyler, TR & Degoey, P 1996, 'Trust in Organizational Authorities: The Influence of Motive Attributions on Willingness to Accept Decisions', in RM Kramer & TR Tyler (eds), *Trust in Organizations: Frontiers of Theory and Research,* Sage, Thousand Oaks, CA, 331–356.

UNODC [United Nations Office on Drugs and Crime] in Cooperation with PricewaterhouseCoopers Austria. 'Anti-Corruption Policies and Measures of the *Fortune* Global 500', vol. 1, section 1.1, 2011, viewed 22 January 2012, www.unodc.org/documents/corruption/PWC_report/Report_Volume_1.pdf.

Vogel, D 2012, 'CSR Doesn't Pay', *Forbes,* viewed 25 January 2012, www.forbes.com/2008/10/16/csr-doesnt-pay-lead-corprespons08-cx_dv_1016vogel.html.

Waddock, S 2008, *The Difference Makers: How Social and Institutional Entrepreneurs Created the Corporate Responsibility Movement,* Greenleaf, Sheffield, UK.

Waldrop, MM 1992, *Complexity: The Emerging Science at the Edge of Order and Chaos,* Simon and Schuster, New York.

Weaver, GR, Treviño, LK & Cochran, PL 1999, 'Corporate Ethics Practices in the Mid-1990's: An Empirical Study of the *Fortune* 1000', *Journal of Business Ethics,* 18(3): 283-294.

Weems, ML 1918, *A History of the Life and Death, Virtues and Exploits of General George Washington,* Lippincott, Philadelphia, PA, viewed 24 January 2012, http://xroads.virginia.edu/~CAP/gw/chap2.html. Original work published 1800.

Weick, KE 1993, 'The Collapse of Sensemaking in Organizations: The Mann Gulch Disaster', *Administrative Science Quarterly,* 38(4): 628–652.

Weick, KE & Sutcliffe, KM 2001, *Managing the Unexpected: Assuring High Performance in an Age of Complexity,* Jossey-Bass, San Francisco.

*What Is a Company's Role in Society? Gap Inc. 2005–2006 Social Responsibility Report,* Gap, Inc., 2006, viewed 23 January 2012, www.gapinc.com/content/dam/csr/documents/2005-2006_Social_Responsibility_Report.pdf.

Wheatley, MJ 2006, *Leadership and the New Science: Discovering Order in a Chaotic World,* 3rd edn, Berrett-Koehler, San Francisco.

White, TI 2012, *Extending Carter Daniels: Substantive and Methodological Reflections on Business Ethics' Ongoing Slide Into Irrelevance*, College of Business Administration, Loyola Marymount University.

White, TI 2012, 'Jan 31 Research Seminar', *College of Business Administration*, Loyola Marymount University.

Whitener, EM, Brodt, SE, Korsgaard MA & Werner, JM 1998, 'Managers as Initiators of Trust: An Exchange Relationship Framework for Understanding Managerial Trustworthy Behavior', *Academy of Management Review,* 23(3): 513–530.

Wilkins, AL, Perry, LT & Checketts, AG 1990, ''Please Don't Make Me a Hero': A Re-Examination of Corporate Heroes', *Human Resource Management,* 29(3): 327–341.

Wilson, JQ 1993, *The Moral Sense,* Free Press, New York.

2006, *Zero Tolerance Policies Are Not as Effective as Thought in Reducing Violence and Promoting Learning in School, Says APA Task Force [press release]*, American Psychological Association, Washington, DC.

Zimbardo, PG 2007, *The Lucifer Effect: Understanding How Good People Turn Evil,* Random House, New York.

# Index

## F



## G



## H



## I



## J



## L



## M



## N



## O



## P



## R